MULTICULTURAL FOUNDATIC
PSYCHOLOGY AND COUNSELING

Series Editors: Allen E. Ivey and Derald Wing Sue

Clinical Practice
with People of Color

A GUIDE TO
BECOMING CULTURALLY COMPETENT

Edited by

MADONNA G. CONSTANTINE

TEACHERS
COLLEGE
PRESS

Teachers College, Columbia University
New York and London

Published by Teachers College Press, 1234 Amsterdam Avenue, New York, NY
10027

Library of Congress Cataloging-in-Publication Data

Clinical practice with people of color : a guide to becoming culturally competent /
    edited by Madonna G. Constantine.
    p. cm. – (Multicultural foundations of psychology and counseling)
    Includes bibliographical references and index.
    ISBN-13: 978-0-8077-4753-7 (pbk. : alk. paper)
        1. Cultural psychiatry. 2. Ethnopsychology. 3. Cross-cultural counseling.
    4. Minorities–Counseling of.   I. Constantine, Madonna G.
        [DNLM: 1. Psychotherapy–methods. 2. Counseling–methods. 3. Ethnic
    Groups–psychology. 4. Minority Groups–psychology. WM 420 C64169 2007]
    RC455.4.E8C585   2007
    616.89'0089–dc22   2006025553

ISBN-13: 978-0-8077-4753-7 (paper)

Printed on acid-free paper
Manufactured in the United States of America

14 13 12 11 10 09 08 07   8 7 6 5 4 3 2 1

Contents

Part I:
Applying the Multicultural Guidelines to Specific Populations

Part II:
Considerations in Applying the Guidelines to People of Color

Preface

Many view the American Psychological Association's "Guidelines on Multicultural Education, Training, Research, Practice, and Organizational Change for Psychologists" (APA, 2002) as a living document to be expanded and further probed by mental health professionals who work in a variety of contexts. As such, there is an ongoing conversation among mental health professionals about how to ethically and competently incorporate these "multicultural competencies" into education, training, research, and practice. Students, trainers, educators, and practitioners have faced the challenging task of translating these competencies into concrete and practical skills. Although the Guidelines categorize people of color as a single entity, the varied sociopolitical and historical contexts of different populations of color require the development of knowledge and skills that are particular to the population of interest. The intersections of race and ethnicity with other identities (e.g., gender and sexual orientation) characterize additional distinct groups of people of color with unique needs and experiences. This edited book enthusiastically contributes to the present discourse about expanding the Multicultural Guidelines by applying these competencies to work with specific populations of color. Thus, this book was developed in recognition of the idea that there is no "one size fits all" approach to gaining multicultural competence.

The increasing racial and ethnic diversity of U.S. society is reflected in those who seek mental health services, and mental health professionals are increasingly challenged to meet the unique and diverse needs of populations of color. This book presents concrete and specific examples of ways to operationalize each of the Multicultural Guidelines for effective multiculturally centered clinical work with specific populations of color. I believe that this book will be of interest not only to trainees in psychology and other mental health professions, but also to newer and seasoned psychologists and mental health personnel who are counseling culturally diverse individuals. Through use of critical incidents and case vignettes, chapters in this book provide concrete strategies to help mental health professionals increase their multicultural competence in working with specific populations of color. The authors include well-known scholars, practitioners, and researchers in the area of multicultural counseling who are employed in a variety of work settings.

Work on this book would not have been possible without the valuable assistance of Christina Capodilupo and Rebecca Redington. I thank them immensely for their untiring efforts in pulling everything together for this book. I also am indebted to the contributors for the knowledge and insights they bring via their excellent writings in this text.

This book is dedicated to the clients of color over the centuries that have suffered irreparable harm at the hands of mental health professionals who were incompetent in addressing their needs in a culturally sensitive manner. I apologize for the pain and distress caused by members of our field, many of whom just did not know better at the time. I hope this book, along with the plethora of contemporary writings in the multicultural counseling and psychology areas, can begin to heal the wrongs enacted and perpetuated by our predecessors. To the readers of this book, I hope you enjoy the journey!

–Madonna G. Constantine

REFERENCE

American Psychological Association. (2002). *Ethical principles of psychologists and code of conduct.* Retrieved May 12, 2005, from http://www.apa.org/ethics/code2002. html#general

The APA Multicultural Guidelines on Education, Training, Research, Practice, and Organizational Change: A Brief Overview

Madonna G. Constantine,
Christina M. Capodilupo,
and Mai M. Kindaichi

In August 2002, the American Psychological Association's (APA) Council of Representatives endorsed the "Guidelines on Multicultural Education, Training, Research, Practice, and Organizational Change for Psychologists," herein referred to as the Guidelines (APA, 2003). They consist of six central pronouncements for psychologists with respect to their work with culturally diverse populations. These Guidelines were developed to reflect the mental health needs of a changing U.S. society, to advance the study of psychology, and to address the differing mental health care needs of populations of color that historically have been marginalized or disenfranchised within and by psychology based on racial, ethnic, or social group membership.

The first two Guidelines underscore the need for psychologists to be aware of (1) their own cultural worldview and how conscious and unconscious biases influence interactions with those who are ethnically and racially dissimilar from themselves, and (2) the cultural worldviews of ethnically and racially dissimilar individuals and how these worldviews shape the attitudes, perceptions, and beliefs of those with whom they work. The third Guideline addresses the application of multiculturalism in education, specifically the inclusion of multiculturalism and culture as areas of study. The fourth Guideline refers specifically to research, and the significance of conducting culture-centered and ethical psychological research among populations of color. The fifth Guideline focuses on the area of psychological practice, and the importance of applying culturally appropriate skills in clinical and applied settings. The final Guideline addresses the area of organizational change and policy development, recognizing that psychologists should promote organizational change to support culturally informed policy and practice.

The purpose of this chapter is to familiarize readers with the Multicultural Guidelines by unpacking the major components of this vast document. First, readers are introduced to the principles upon which the Guidelines are founded. Next, each Guideline is examined through a discussion of the related empirical and theoretical literature.

FOUNDATIONAL PRINCIPLES OF THE MULTICULTURAL GUIDELINES

The Guidelines were created to assist psychologists in seeking and using culturally appropriate education, training, research, practice, and organizational change. Several ethical principles created for psychologists by the APA for the foundation of the Guidelines: to be competent to work with a variety of populations (Principle D), to respect others' rights and dignity (Principle E), and to be concerned not to harm others (Principle A) (APA, 2002). The philosophical underpinning of the Guidelines is that race and ethnicity are dynamic constructs that impact all aspects of psychological practice and interactions. Thus, "psychologists are in a position to provide leadership as agents of prosocial change, advocacy, and social justice, thereby promoting societal understanding, affirmation, and appreciation of multiculturalism against the damaging effects of individual, institutional, and societal racism, prejudice, and all forms of oppression based on stereotyping and discrimination" (APA, 2003, p. 382). Based on the ethical principles for psychologists (APA, 2002) and the salience of race, ethnicity, and multiculturalism in all aspects of psychology, six central principles were created upon which the Guidelines are founded.

> **Principle 1:** Ethical conduct of psychologists is enhanced by knowledge of differences in beliefs and practices that emerge from socialization through racial and ethnic group affiliation and membership and how those beliefs and practices will necessarily affect the education, training, research, and practice of psychology.

As mandated by the APA ethical code, psychologists must respect the rights of others (Principle E) (APA, 2002) by gaining insight and knowledge about their potential biases and beliefs that may, if left unchecked, cause harm to those who are racially and ethnically dissimilar from themselves (Principle A) (APA, 2002). The historical notions of the tabula rasa, objective researcher, unbiased teacher, and neutral leader have reflected beliefs within and by the profession that psychologists are immune to the socialization process in the U.S., which creates and maintains beliefs about race and ethnicity. Yet, these beliefs and biases inevitably affect the education, training, research, and practice of psychology. This principle rejects these historical notions and calls upon psychologists to examine their own beliefs and practices, even as they have asked their clients, students, and research participants to do.

> **Principle 2:** Understanding and recognizing the interface between individuals' socialization experiences based on ethnic and racial heritage can enhance the quality of education, training, practice, and research in the field of psychology.

The second principle urges psychologists to consider and explore the social contextual aspects of an individual's experiences, with emphasis on the role of ethnic and racial heritage in these experiences. In the United States individuals are socialized with beliefs and biases about racial and ethnic groups, and including this socialization process as a salient dimension in understanding an individual transcends traditional psychological notions of the "internal world" and enhances the quality of psychological education, training, practice and research.

> **Principle 3:** Recognition of the ways in which the intersection of racial and ethnic group membership with other dimensions of identity (e.g., gender, age, sexual orientation, disability, religion/spiritual orientation, education attainment/experiences, and socioeconomic status) enhances the understanding and treatment of all people.

The third principle underscores the idea that multiple identities intersect to influence individuals' knowledge of self and others. Thus, an individual should not be understood solely by a single entity, but, instead, should be conceptualized and understood as having concurrent membership in multiple cultural groups (Constantine, 2002). By considering identity intersections instead of maintaining a narrow focus on single membership identities, understanding and treatment of all people are enhanced.

Principle 4: Knowledge of historically derived approaches that have viewed cultural differences as deficits and have not valued certain social identities helps psychologists to understand the underrepresentation of ethnic minorities in the profession and affirms and values the role of ethnicity and race in developing personal identity.

Principle 4 emphasizes the need for psychologists to critically examine the history of the profession with regard to racial and ethnic difference, and to acknowledge that those who have differed from the dominant White European American culture have been portrayed historically as deficient and/or abnormal. Recognizing that the underrepresentation of people of color in the profession stems from their historical marginalization underscores the roles of ethnicity and race in developing personal identity. Further, ignoring and/or dismissing social identities such as race and ethnicity inevitably leads to a narrow understanding of human development. In psychology this view has reflected ethnocentric monoculturalism, or consideration of identity development from a dominant European American perspective, while maintaining a valence of color blindness as if this lens were universal and therefore applicable to all people.

Principle 5: Psychologists are uniquely able to promote racial equity and social justice. This is aided by their awareness of their impact on others and the influence of their personal and professional roles in society.

Psychologists can serve as agents of social change. Thus, it behooves them to be aware of the power and influence inherent in their role and to use their influence to promote social justice and racial equality. For example, psychologists are considered to be experts of human psychological conditions and often are called upon in varied societal settings and through myriad mediums to educate the public about interpersonal dynamics and individual development. Principle 5 calls upon psychologists to disseminate their multicultural knowledge and skills in ways that further racial equality and promote social justice in the United States.

Principle 6: Psychologists' knowledge about the roles of organizations, including employers and professional psychological associations, is a potential source of behavioral practices that encourage discourse, education and training, institutional change, and research and policy development that reflect, rather than neglect, cultural differences. Psychologists recognize that organizations can be gatekeepers or agents of the status quo, rather than leaders of a changing society, with respect to multiculturalism.

The sixth and final principle highlights the idea that psychologists are uniquely positioned to either maintain the status quo or change it. For example, armed with an awareness that cultural differences have long been ignored by society at large and the psychology profession specifically, psychologists have the option to reject this traditional stance and bring conversations of multiculturalism and diversity to their educational institutions, professional organizations, and workplaces.

THE MULTICULTURAL GUIDELINES

The aforementioned six principles serve as the foundation for the Multicultural Guidelines. The Guidelines address five specific domains: (1) commitment to cultural awareness and knowledge of self and others, (2) education, (3) research, (4) practice, and (5) organizational change and policy development. The first two Guidelines fall under the umbrella of commitment to cultural awareness and knowledge of self and others.

> **Guideline 1:** Psychologists are encouraged to recognize that, as cultural beings, they may hold attitudes and beliefs that can detrimentally influence their perceptions of and interactions with individuals who are ethnically and racially different from themselves (APA, 2003, p. 382).

Since individuals represent a variety of intersecting sociocultural groups, all interactions between people are considered to be cross-cultural in nature (Constantine, 2002). The worldview of White European Americans often has been mislabeled as the "norm" or the "human" perspective in the United States, which consequentially has led to the overvaluation of this worldview over worldviews that are racially and ethnically different. For example, rugged individualism and competition are two values equated with the White European American worldview, whereas interdependence and harmony toward others are associated with the values of many people of color in the United States (Sue & Sue, 2003). Research has shown that worldviews that differ from one's own can be negatively judged automatically (Greenwald & Banaji, 1995) and that it is common to have automatic biases and unconscious stereotypic attitudes toward those in devalued cultural groups (Fiske, 1998). These unconscious biases and stereotypes prove to be powerful as disconfirming information does not serve to alter their presence (Kunda & Thagard, 1996). These automatic biases influence interpretations of behavior and people's judgment about that behavior, and can lead to cultural miscommunication (Fiske, 1998; Kunda & Thagard, 1996). For example, if an Asian American employee who values harmony toward others participates in group meetings by observing turn taking in speaking, this behavior could be labeled as "passive" or "submissive" by European Americans who do not recognize that they value assertiveness and competition as necessary ingredients for achieving success.

Not recognizing inherent cultural beliefs and biases is common among the dominant group, and research has suggested that immunity from negative beliefs about and stereotypes of populations of color is impossible (Dovidio & Gaertner, 1998). In fact, studies have found that those who adamantly deny that they are racist and/or prejudiced (Dovidio & Gaertner, 1998) and those who consciously hold egalitarian beliefs (Greenwald & Banaji, 1995) do, in fact, endorse unconscious negative beliefs about and stereotypes of populations of color. Deriving from this very framework of immunity from unconscious bias is an emergent discourse of "color blindness" that asserts that removing cultural difference as a focus will improve relations among different groups. In reality, this approach minimizes cultural differences, while presuming to take a "universal" approach to understanding human behavior (Constantine, Myers, Kindaichi, & Moore, 2004). This approach is "color-blind" only if White is not a color, because often a "universal" or "human" approach is actually a reflection of the dominant White European American experience (Sue & Sue, 2003), and suppresses the experience of people of color. Research has shown that the color-blind approach does not fulfill its intended purpose in leading to equitable treatment across groups (Brewer & Brown, 1998). Self-awareness and self-exploration have been shown repeatedly to be crucial methods for becoming aware of unconscious beliefs and bias and reducing stereotypic attitudes (Devine, Plant, & Buswell, 2000; Gaertner & Dovidio, 2000). Awareness and knowledge of others' racial and cultural background are not sufficient without psychologists' knowledge of their own worldview and how this worldview affects interactions, interventions, and practice.

Guideline 2: Psychologists are encouraged to recognize the importance of multicultural sensitivity/responsiveness to, knowledge of, and understanding about ethnically and racially different individuals (APA, 2003, p. 385).

Research has shown that prejudice and stereotyping are reduced and intercultural communication is enhanced with greater knowledge of and contact with other groups (Gaertner & Dovidio, 2000). Developing a greater understanding of the worldview and perspective of those who are culturally dissimilar from themselves is necessary for psychologists who intend to work with diverse groups. Various identity models such as racial identity (Atkinson, Morten, & Sue, 1998; Cross, 1971; Helms, 1984), ethnic identity (Phinney, 1992) and spiritual identity (Myers et al., 1991) are helpful for psychologists to gain knowledge about the worldviews and perspectives of those who are dissimilar from themselves. Similarly, it is important for psychologists to understand the experiences of racism, prejudice, and discrimination faced on a daily basis by those in culturally devalued groups (Constantine & Sue, 2006), as well as how psychologists may be viewed by other people (Sue & Sue, 2003). This is pertinent in the clinical realm in particular. Research has shown that the notable underutilization of mental health services by people of color is due largely to cultural misunderstandings and miscommunication between therapists and clients (APA, 2003). Finally, psychologists have a responsibility to gain knowledge about the historical and sociopolitical experiences of distinct populations of color in the United States (e.g., Japanese American internment camps and the American Indian holocaust), as well as historical and current federal legislation, all of which influence worldview and experience.

Guideline 3: As educators, psychologists are encouraged to employ the constructs of multiculturalism and diversity in psychological education (APA, 2003, p. 386).

Psychologists may resist the incorporation of multicultural issues in psychology education and training because of their discomfort with topics of race and ethnicity, fear of being perceived as prejudiced or racist, or belief that culture is not a valid area of study (Constantine & Sue, 2006). Despite this resistance, psychology programs at the graduate level increasingly have included multicultural curriculum (Constantine, Ladany, Inman, & Ponterotto, 1996), and there is sufficient empirical support that multicultural education and training are positively associated with the development of multicultural competence (Smith, Constantine, Dunn, Dinehart, & Montoya, 2006), as well as promoting student self-awareness (Brown, Parham, & Yonker, 1996). Further, multicultural education can lead to awareness of and counteraction against unconscious negative and stereotypic attitudes about populations of color (Abreu, 2001). Psychology educators are urged to infuse their curriculum with multicultural theory and practice, as opposed to teaching a single course on multicultural issues or practice, which is not uncommon (Mio & Awakuni, 2000).

There is an abundance of literature available on empirically based approaches for promoting multicultural competence, including topics such as adapting existing curricula to create safe learning environments for what has proven to be emotional coursework (Arredondo et al., 1996). Because research on the development of multicultural competence has shown that experiential learning techniques can be more effective than traditional didactic learning (Arthur & Achenbach, 2002), psychology educators are encouraged to employ multiple teaching modalities to accommodate multiple learning styles. In keeping with the APA ethical code, psychologists are urged to stay informed about the most recent research and empirical findings with regard to developing multicultural competence, as this area of study is relatively new. Lastly, psychology educators also are encouraged to actively participate in the recruitment and attainment of prospective students and faculty of color.

> **Guideline 4:** Culturally sensitive psychological researchers are encouraged to recognize the importance of conducting culture-centered and ethical psychological research among persons from ethnic, linguistic, and racial minority backgrounds (APA, 2003, p. 388).

Psychological research should reflect the rapidly changing racial demographics of the United States. However, past psychological research has had several cultural limitations, such as viewing culture as a variable to be controlled and statistically manipulated (as opposed to central or explanatory), underrepresentation of people of color in research samples, and omission of the consideration of within-group differences (Quintana, Troyano, & Taylor, 2001). Culture-centered researchers are encouraged to address these limitations by being aware of cultural assumptions that shape their research questions; choosing culturally appropriate theories and models; utilizing assessment techniques and standardized instruments whose validity, reliability, and measurement equivalence have been investigated across culturally diverse sample groups; analyzing and interpreting data by examining moderator effects; and considering cultural hypothesis as potential explanations for their findings (Egharevba, 2001; Quintana et al., 2001). Lastly, culture-centered researchers are urged to report the exact demographics of their research sample and be clear about the generalizability of their findings.

> **Guideline 5:** Psychologists strive to apply culturally-appropriate skills in clinical and other applied psychological practices (APA, 2003, p. 390).

The changing racial and ethnic demographics of U.S. society underscore the idea that psychologists increasingly will interface with multiculturally pluralistic populations across a variety of professional contexts (APA, 2003; Constantine, 2002). The underutilization of mental health services by populations of color has been attributed to a lack of cultural sensitivity of therapists, distrust of services by clients of color, and the belief that therapists may misuse their power to mistreat clients (Sue & Sue, 2003). Psychologists are strongly urged to develop multicultural competence (awareness, knowledge, and skills) in order to be effective, competent, and ethically responsible practitioners. To develop multicultural competence and culturally appropriate skills, practitioners should focus on the client within his/her cultural context (e.g., understand how experiences of racism and oppression are associated with the client's presenting concerns or how acculturation and immigration experiences are related to stress levels) (Arredondo, 2002; Fuertes & Gretchen, 2001; Ruiz, 1990). Practitioners also should make an effort to recognize the cultural limitations of assessment practices in intake interviews and their subsequent case conceptualizations (Constantine & Ladany, 2000) and should utilize culturally appropriate assessment tools in their practice. Moreover, a culturally sensitive practitioner should employ a variety of interventions that take into account the worldview and cultural background of clients and should recognize that culture-specific therapy may require the use of nontraditional interventions, such as including indigenous healers, herbalists, or meditation.

> **Guideline 6:** Psychologists are encouraged to use organizational change processes to support culturally informed organizational (policy) development and practice (APA, 2003, p. 392).

The changing racial and ethnic demographics in the United States are affecting the composition of the nation's schools, work force and communities. This phenomenon is resulting in psychologists being called upon to forge new policies and guidelines that promote social justice and human development (APA, 2003; Constantine & Sue, 2006). Psychologists are urged to "scan the environment and anticipate trends and changes allowing for a systemic proactive, rather than reactive, response" (APA, 2003, p. 393). In order to embark upon the multiple roles psychologists will face within a changing society, they are encouraged to learn the methods, frameworks, and models for multicultural organizational development (Garcia-Caban, 2001), to review examples of multicultural organizational change, and to promote multicultural organizational change and policy development by familiarizing themselves with effective practices.

CONCLUSION

The development, publication, and recognition of the Guidelines mark an historic landmark within APA specifically and the field of psychology as a whole. These Guidelines can assist psychologists as they seek to increase their awareness, knowledge, and skills in multicultural education, research, training, practice, and organizational change. However, the creators of the Guidelines have underscored that the Guidelines are a living document that is meant to be further probed and expanded.

This book was created to aid psychologists and other mental health professionals in incorporating the Guidelines into their existing repertoire of skills, regardless of professional setting and context. Readers might note that the authors in this edited volume sometimes have interpreted the Guidelines in different ways. These differing interpretations reflect the diverse ways in which practitioners understand and apply the Guidelines in their work; their representation in this volume brings a richness to the exploration of how the Guidelines can be applied in clinical practice situations.

Further, the purpose of this book is to begin to address the unique needs and experiences of people of color in relation to the Guidelines. The underrepresentation of people of color in psychology is evident in the dearth of available material about specific populations of color; the Guidelines represent a beginning in filling this void. However, the Guidelines categorize people of color as a single entity without discussion of the diversity of worldview, attitudes, and beliefs that exist within and among groups of color. As one way to begin to differentiate among those manifold, unique needs and experiences, this book is divided into two parts: Applying the Multicultural Guidelines to Specific Populations (Part I) and Considerations in Applying the Multicultural Guidelines (Part II). Although chapters in both sections incorporate illustrations to demonstrate the usefulness of the Guidelines in a variety of contexts, the chapters in Part I specifically explore race, ethnicity, and/or intersecting cultural identities. The chapters in Part II examine broader considerations in applying these Guidelines, in addition to salient social justice issues.

In an effort to be ethical, competent, and proactive, psychologists and other mental health professionals will be well served by incorporating an expanded understanding of the Guidelines in their work. The work represented in these pages is at the forefront of efforts in the field to put such an understanding to good clinical use.

REFERENCES

Abreu, J. M. (2001). Theory and research on stereotypes and perceptual bias: A resource guide for multicultural counseling trainers. *Counseling Psychologist, 29*, 487–512.

American Psychological Association. (2002). *Ethical principles of psychologists and code of conduct.* Retrieved May 12, 2005, from http://www.apa.org/ethics/code2002.html#general

American Psychological Association. (2003). Guidelines on multicultural education, training, research, practice, and organizational change for psychologists. *American Psychologist, 58*, 377–402.

Arredondo, P. (2002). Counseling individuals from specialized, marginalized and underserved groups. In P. B. Pedersen, J. G. Draguns, W. J. Lonner, & J. E. Trimble (Eds.), *Counseling across cultures* (5th ed., pp. 241–250). Thousand Oaks, CA: Sage.

Arredondo, P., Toporek, R., Brown, S. P., Jones, J., Locke, D. C., Sanchez, J., & Stadler, H. (1996). Operationalization of the multicultural counseling competencies. *Journal of Multicultural Counseling and Development, 24,* 42–78.

Arthur, N., & Achenbach, K. (2002). Developing multicultural counseling competencies through experiential learning. *Counselor Education & Supervision, 42,* 2–14.

Atkinson, D. R., Morten, G., & Sue, D. W. (Eds.). (1998). *Counseling American minorities* (5th ed.). Boston: McGraw-Hill.

Brewer, M. B., & Brown, R. J. (1998). Intergroup relations. In D. T. Gilbert & S. T. Fiske (Eds.), *The handbook of social psychology* (4th ed, Vol. 2, pp. 554–594). Boston: McGraw-Hill.

Brown, S. P., Parham, T. A., & Yonker, R. (1996). Influence of a cross-cultural training on racial identity attitudes of White women and men. *Journal of Counseling and Development, 74,* 510–516.

Constantine, M. G. (2002). The intersection of race, ethnicity, gender, and social class in counseling: Examining selves in cultural contexts. *Journal of Multicultural Counseling and Development, 30,* 210–215.

Constantine, M. G., & Ladany, N. (2000). Self-report multicultural counseling competence scales: Their relation to social desirability attitudes and multicultural case conceptualization ability. *Journal of Counseling Psychology, 47,* 155–164.

Constantine, M. G., Ladany, N., Inman, A. G., & Ponterotto, J. G. (1996). Students' perceptions of multicultural training in counseling psychology programs. *Journal of Multicultural Counseling and Development, 24,* 241–253.

Constantine, M. G., Myers, L. J., Kindaichi, M., & Moore, J. L. (2004). Exploring indigenous mental health practices: The roles of healers and helpers in promoting well-being in people of color. *Counseling and Values, 48,* 110–125.

Constantine, M. G., & Sue, D. W. (Eds.). (2006). *Addressing racism: Facilitating cultural competence in mental health and educational settings.* Hoboken, NJ: Wiley.

Cross, W. E. (1971). The Negro-to-Black conversion experience: Toward a psychology of Black liberation. *Black World, 20,* 13–27.

Devine, P. G., Plant, A. E., & Buswell, B. N. (2000). Breaking the prejudice habit: Progress and obstacles. In S. Oskamp (Ed.), *Reducing prejudice and discrimination* (pp. 185–208). Mahwah, NJ: Erlbaum.

Dovidio, J. F., & Gaertner, S. L. (1998). On the nature of contemporary prejudice: The causes, consequences, and challenges of aversive racism. In J. L. Eberhardt & S. T. Fiske (Eds.), *Confronting racism: The problem and the response* (pp. 3–32). Thousand Oaks, CA: Sage.

Egharevba, I. (2001). Researching an "other" minority ethnic community: Reflections of a Black female researcher on the intersections of race, gender, and other power positions in the research process. *International Journal of Social Research Methodology: Theory and Practice, 4,* 225–241.

Fiske, S. T. (1998). Stereotyping, prejudice and discrimination. In D. T. Gilbert & S. T. Fiske (Eds.), *The handbook of social psychology* (4th ed., Vol. 2, pp. 357–411). Boston: McGraw-Hill.

Fuertes, J. N., & Gretchen, D. (2001). Emerging theories of multicultural counseling. In J. G. Ponterotto, J. M. Casas, L. A. Suzuki, & C. M. Alexander (Eds.), *Handbook of multicultural counseling* (2nd ed., pp. 509–541). Thousand Oaks, CA: Sage.

Gaertner, S. L., & Dovidio, J. F. (2000). *Reducing intergroup bias: The common ingroup identity model.* Philadelphia: Brunner/Mazel.

Garcia-Caban, I. (2001). *Improving systems of care for racial and ethnic minority consumers:*

Measuring cultural competence in Massachusetts acute care hospital settings. Unpublished doctoral dissertation, Brandeis University, Waltham, MA.

Greenwald, A. G., & Banaji, M. R. (1995). Implicit social cognition: Attitudes, self-esteem,
and stereotypes. *Psychological Review, 102,* 4–27.

Helms, J. E. (1984). Toward a theoretical explanation of the effect of race on counseling: A
Black and White model. *The Counseling Psychologist, 12,* 153–165.

Kunda, Z., & Thagard, P. (1996). Forming impressions from stereotypes, traits, and behaviors: A parallel-constraint-satisfaction theory. *Psychological Review, 103,* 284–308.

Mio, J. S., & Awakuni, G. I. (2000). *Resistance to multiculturalism: Issues and interventions.*
Philadelphia: Brunner/Mazel.

Myers, L. J., Speight, S. L., Highlen, P. S., Cox, C. I., Reynolds, A. L., Adams, E. M., &
Hanley, C. P. (1991). Identity development and worldview: Toward an optimal conceptualization. *Journal of Counseling and Development, 70,* 54–63.

Phinney, J. S. (1992). The Multigroup Ethnic Identity Measure: A new scale for use with
diverse groups. *Journal of Adolescent Research, 7,* 156–176.

Quintana, S. M., Troyano, N., & Taylor, G. (2001). Cultural validity and inherent challenges in quantitative methods for multicultural research. In J. G. Ponterotto, J. M.
Casas, L. A. Suzuki, & C. M. Alexander (Eds.), *Handbook of multicultural counseling* (2nd
ed., pp. 604–630). Thousand Oaks, CA: Sage.

Ruiz, A. S. (1990). Ethnic identity: Crisis and resolution. *Journal of Multicultural Counseling
& Development, 18,* 29–40.

Smith, T. B., Constantine, M. G., Dunn, T. W., Dinehart, J. M., & Montoya, J. A. (2006).
Multicultural education in the mental health professions: A meta-analytic review. *Journal of Counseling Psychology, 53,* 132–145.

Sue, D. W., & Sue, D. (2003). *Counseling the culturally diverse: Theory and practice* (4th ed.).
New York: Wiley.

Part I

APPLYING THE MULTICULTURAL GUIDELINES TO SPECIFIC POPULATIONS

Part I of this book includes nine chapters that focus on how the Multicultural Guidelines can be applied to specific populations of color. Several chapters explore aspects of identity related to race and ethnicity. Several other chapters examine additional identities (e.g., gender, gay, lesbian, and bisexual) that intersect with race and ethnicity. Kim (Chapter 2) opens this part with a discussion of Asian Americans and the within-group cultural variations among this population. This chapter also outlines cultural characteristics specific to Asian Americans and uses the Multicultural Guidelines to illustrate culturally appropriate practice with this population. In Chapter 3, Martin expounds upon the Guidelines within an historical context to promote the development of cultural competence when working with African American populations. Moreover, she explores relevant and timely issues, such as racial identity and spirituality, as they pertain to African Americans in the context of the Guidelines.

Through discussion of significant issues such as immigration, language, and cultural beliefs, de las Fuentes focuses on mental health practice with Latina/o Americans in Chapter 4. The cultural genogram, a specific strategy used in teaching and/or clinical practice with Latina/os, is described in depth and specific examples of its applicability are provided. Next, in Chapter 5, mindful of the variations in language, spirituality, and acculturation among Native American and Alaskan native tribes, Peregoy and Gloria provide a primer for addressing concerns within the Native American/Alaskan Native population. The chapter explores current theories of Indian/Native identity development and highlights pertinent mental health issues among this population, such as post traumatic stress disorder and academic dropout. In Chapter 6, Nassar-McMillan discusses the sociopolitical context and history of Arab Americans, along with ethnic discrimination in a post-9/11 U.S. culture. She also examines the role of collectivistic values, particularly in the areas of religion, gender, and family, and explores how these values may affect the counseling process.

In Chapter 7, Gillem, Lincoln, and English present salient information regarding biracial populations. They encourage mental health practitioners to acknowledge the various unique ways biracial people may conceptualize their identities beyond understandings offered through monoracial identity models. Ecological frameworks for understanding biracial identity are provided, and various mental health implications of identity conflict also are discussed. In Chapter 8, Chung and Bemak explain key components of multicultural practice with immigrant and refugee clients by distinguishing between immigrant and refugee migration status, and discussing psychological adaptation and adjustment challenges faced by this population after their migration to the United States. Mental health practitioners are urged to develop a fuller understanding of their immigrant and refugee clients by considering not only premigration experiences, but also adaptation, adjustment, and acculturation to a new country.

In recognition of the multiple oppressions faced by gay, lesbian, and bisexual people of color, Chapter 9 fuses the guidelines created specifically for psychotherapy with lesbian, gay, and bisexual clients with the Multicultural Guidelines. In this chapter, Chung highlights current understandings of the intersection of racial and sexual identities for various racial/ethnic groups and provides a theoretical model of Asian American gay men to demonstrate this relationship. Olkin provides a framework for applying the Multicultural Guidelines to persons with disabilities in Chapter 10 by reviewing 13 elements of disability culture. Empirical and conceptual literature related to disability and ethnicity is examined, and relevant issues such as conflicts between cultural values and traditional rehabilitation services are explored.

2

Asian American Populations

Bryan S. K. Kim

In recognition of the increasing racial and ethnic diversification of the United States, the American Psychological Association (APA) published the "Guidelines on Multicultural Education, Training, Research, Practice, and Organizational Change for Psychologists" (2003). As explained in Chapter 1, the Guidelines describe the ways in which psychologists can become multiculturally relevant, sensitive, and competent in meeting the challenges posed by this demographic diversification. One of these challenges involves meeting the unique mental health needs of Asian Americans, the group of focus for this chapter. Among the Guidelines, three are critically relevant to engaging in multiculturally centered clinical work by psychologists and other mental health professionals—specifically a commitment to cultural awareness and to knowledge of self and others, and the application of culturally appropriate skills in practice.

Although the suggestions in the Guidelines are helpful, one of the shortcomings is that they do not adequately offer concrete ideas, recommendations, and explanations for implementation within the day-to-day clinical activities of psychologists and other mental health professionals. Hence, the purpose of this chapter is to describe ways in which APA Guidelines 1, 2, and 5 can be operationalized to meet the mental health needs of a sizable racial/ethnic group in the United States, namely, Asian Americans. To help illustrate the information throughout the chapter, we will use case vignettes involving the following Asian Americans, Michael and Phuong.

> Michael is a 20-year-old, fifth-generation Filipino American who is attending a local college. He has serious concerns about completing his major in pre-med because he does not like his classes and is not doing well in them. However, he knows that going into medicine is prestigious and eventually will lead him to a well-paying job. He is afraid to speak to his parents about this dilemma because they are both in medical professions (his father is a

doctor, and his mother is a nurse). Plus, they have repeatedly told him that he should pursue becoming a physician and they expect no less. Lately, Michael has had a lot of trouble sleeping and eating. He also has had thoughts of "ending it all."

Phuong is a 50-year-old, first-generation Cambodian American who works as a salesclerk in a gift store at a local mall. She entered the United States just 5 years ago after marrying a Cambodian American man. She divorced this person a year ago because of his abusive attitudes toward her, and she currently is living alone. Recently, Phuong has noticed that little things get her upset. She doesn't enjoy going to work and feels lonely without having co-workers who are of the same ethnicity. Phuong has been to a doctor's office because of recurring stomach pains, but the doctor can't find anything physically wrong with her.

GUIDELINES 1 AND 2: CULTURAL AWARENESS AND KNOWLEDGE

APA Guidelines 1 and 2 suggest that a multiculturally competent psychologist is committed to becoming culturally aware of and knowledgeable about people from diverse racial/ethnic backgrounds. Thus, the goal of this section is to help psychologists and other mental health professionals to become more informed about the characteristics and experiences of Asian Americans. The section will begin with a brief overview of demographic characteristics of Asian Americans. This will be followed by descriptions of important cultural characteristics of Asian Americans and social factors affecting their mental health.

Demographic Characteristics

The Asian American population has been one of the fastest growing groups in the United States during the past 3 decades. As of 2000, the number of Asian Americans stood at nearly 11.9 million, or 4.2% of the total U.S. population (Barnes & Bennett, 2002). These numbers represent an increase of more than 70% since the previous census in 1990. It is estimated that by 2050, one out of 10 people living in the United States will be able to trace their ancestry in part or full to Asian countries (U.S. Bureau of the Census, 2004). This dramatic increase in the number of Asian Americans is largely a result of the huge influx of immigrants from Asia; nearly 7 of 10 Asian Americans were born in Asia. Coinciding with its large size, the Asian American population also represents a very heterogeneous group comprising many ethnic backgrounds that have distinct cultural norms. Although Asian Americans have been classified as a single group because of their common geographical origins on the Asian continent, the group encompasses no fewer than 25 ethnic groups, including Cambodians, Chinese, Filipinos, Hmong, Indonesians, Japanese, Laotians, and Vietnamese. These ethnic groups also vary significantly in their language, traditions, customs, societal norms, and immigration history. For example, Asian Americans represent both descendants of Asians who arrived during the Gold Rush (in California) and sugar plantation (in Hawaii) eras in the mid-1800s, like Michael, and recent immigrants who entered the United States just yesterday, like Phuong. Given this wide range of time in the United States, an important cultural characteristic that psychologists and other mental health professionals must be aware of and knowledgeable about is the vast within-group variations in terms of adherence to U.S. cultural norms and retention of Asian cultural norms.

Within-Group Cultural Variations

To better understand the experiences of Asian Americans, psychologists must become familiar with the within-group cultural variations among them. To this end, the theory of acculturation and enculturation can be helpful. Acculturation first was defined by Redfield, Linton, and Herskovits (1936): "Acculturation comprehends those phenomena which result when groups of individuals sharing different cultures come into continuous first-hand contact, with subsequent changes in the original culture patterns of either or both groups" (p. 149, cited in Kim & Abreu, 2001). Embedded in the concept of acculturation is the concept of enculturation. Herskovits (1948) defined enculturation as the process of socialization to the norms of one's indigenous culture. Kim and Abreu (2001) explained that the adaptation process among culturally different individuals includes both adapting to the norms of the dominant culture and retaining the norms of the indigenous culture. They proposed that the term *acculturation* be used to describe the former process and the term *enculturation* be used to describe the latter process. Current theory of acculturation and enculturation suggests that Asian Americans who are farther removed from immigration, like Michael, will adhere to mainstream U.S. cultural norms more strongly than Asian Americans who are recent immigrants (Kim, Atkinson, & Umemoto, 2001). On the other hand, Asian Americans who are closer to immigration, like Phuong, will adhere to Asian cultural norms more strongly than their counterparts who are many generations removed from immigration.

The literature on acculturation and enculturation suggests that adherence to Asian and European American values is related to Asian Americans' psychological functioning. In particular, John Berry and his colleagues (e.g., Berry, Kim, Power, Young, & Bajaki, 1989) theorized that individuals experience a process of adaptation that can be categorized into four acculturative statuses that are expressed in terms of the combined level of acculturation and enculturation: *Integration, Assimilation, Separation,* and *Marginalization.* Integration occurs when an individual becomes proficient in the culture of the dominant group (high acculturation), while retaining proficiency in the indigenous culture (high enculturation); this status also is known as biculturalism. Assimilation occurs when an individual absorbs the culture of the dominant group (high acculturation), while rejecting the indigenous culture (low enculturation). Separation occurs when an individual is not interested in learning the culture of the dominant group (low acculturation) and wants only to maintain and perpetuate the culture of origin (high enculturation). Finally, marginalization represents the attitude of an individual with no interest in maintaining or acquiring proficiency in any culture, dominant or indigenous (low acculturation and enculturation). Marginalization is perhaps the most problematic of the four statuses because marginalized Asian Americans will adhere to neither value system and tend to reject both cultural norms. Given these descriptions of various adaptation statuses, it would be helpful to understand which categories apply to Michael and Phuong.

The theory of racial and ethnic identity development is another useful tool for examining the cultural variability that exists within the Asian American group. Among the various models of this theory, Atkinson, Morten, and Sue's (1998) Minority Identity Development (MID) model "defines five stages of development that oppressed people may experience as they struggle to understand themselves in terms of their own minority culture and the oppressive relationship between the [minority and majority] cultures" (p. 34). The five stages are as follows: Conformity, Dissonance, Resistance and Immersion, Introspection, and Synergistic Articulation and Awareness.

According to the MID model, Asian Americans who are in the Conformity stage give preference to mainstream U.S. cultural values over Asian values. They have self- and group-depreciating attitudes, while viewing the European American group with positive attitudes. Because they reject their status as members of a minority group, these Asian Americans have discriminatory attitudes toward other minority groups.

Asian Americans who are in the Dissonance stage may have reached this stage gradually or as a result of a monumental event. For instance, a critical event for a Japanese American might be learning about how over 100,000 Japanese Americans were unjustly placed in internment camps during World War II, while many of these "prisoners" joined the 442nd Regimental Combat Team that fought courageously for the United States in Europe (Chan, 1991). Asian Americans in this stage are faced with information that brings positive light to their Asian American group as well as negative light to the European American group. As a result, these individuals are forced to re-evaluate their attitudes toward the Asian and European American groups and to reconcile these dissonant pieces of information. Hence, Asian Americans in this stage are in a state of conflict between self- and group-depreciating attitudes. Similarly, they are in a state of conflict over their positive and negative attitudes toward the European American and other minority groups.

Asian Americans in the Dissonance stage eventually may move to the Resistance and Immersion stage, which is characterized by a complete endorsement of Asian cultural values and a complete rejection of mainstream U.S. values. Hence, Asian Americans have an appreciating attitude about Asian American groups, and negative attitudes toward the European American group. In addition, Asian Americans in this stage experience feelings of empathy and a growing sense of camaraderie with members of other minority groups.

In the Introspection stage, Asian Americans experience feelings of discontent and discomfort with the views held in the Resistance and Immersion stage. They may begin to have concerns about their overwhelmingly positive view about Asian American groups and the ethnocentric basis for judging others. They also may begin to recognize the utility of many mainstream U.S. cultural elements but be uncertain about whether to incorporate such elements into their own cultural norms.

Finally, Asian Americans in the Synergistic stage experience a sense of self-fulfillment with regard to their own identity. According to Atkinson and colleagues (1998), the conflict and discomfort that were experienced during the Introspection stage have been reconciled, allowing for greater individual control and flexibility. Given these ideas, it would be helpful to explore Michael's and Phuong's identity development.

An important similarity between the theory of acculturation and enculturation and the MID model is their focus on cultural values as a way to discern the experiences of Asian Americans. Many writers have described the various dimensions of Asian cultural values (e.g., Kitano & Matsushima, 1981; Sue & Sue, 2003). In particular, Kim, Atkinson, and Yang (1999) identified the following value dimensions that are salient for Asian Americans:

- Ability to resolve psychological problems
- Avoidance of family shame
- Collectivism
- Conformity to family and social norms and expectations
- Deference to authority figures
- Educational and occupational achievement
- Filial piety
- Importance of family
- Maintenance of interpersonal harmony
- Placing others' needs ahead of one's own

- Reciprocity
- Respect for elders and ancestors
- Self-control and restraint
- Self-effacement

To the extent that Asian Americans are in the Separation category and in the Resistance and Immersion stage of identity, we can expect them to have strong adherence to these cultural values.

> Michael feels that he is high acculturated and low enculturated, hence placing himself in the Assimilation status. He does not endorse any traditional Asian values, particularly values specific to the Filipino culture. He adheres principally to the mainstream U.S. values such as individualism and autonomy. He does not speak a Filipino language and does not participate in any Filipino cultural activities. Michael feels that he does not have any ties to his Filipino ancestry because he is far removed from immigration. Michael feels that he is in the Dissonance stage as a result of recently learning that in the past thousands of Filipinos bravely served in the U.S. Navy but were not eligible for U.S. citizenship. Consequently, he is beginning to have an appreciation for his ancestry.

> Phuong feels that she is high enculturated but low acculturated, hence placing herself in the Separation status. Because she entered the United States relatively recently, Phuong has been able to retain her proficiency in Cambodian and maintains her traditional values, including collectivism and humility. She has had difficulty fully grasping the English language and adapting to U.S. cultural norms. In terms of her identity, Phuong feels that she is in the Resistance and Immersion stage in which she completely endorses her traditional Cambodian values while rejecting mainstream U.S. values. Phuong admits that a part of the reason she rejects the mainstream U.S. culture is due to racist incidents at her work setting.

Social Factors Affecting Mental Health

It is also important for culturally competent psychologists and other mental health professionals to be familiar with environmental factors that may affect the mental health of Asian Americans. What follows is a description of three important factors, namely, the model minority stereotype, acculturative stress, and racial discrimination.

Model Minority Stereotype. One stereotype that has long affected Asian Americans is that of "the model minority." The notion of the model minority suggests that Asian Americans embody the American success story: They function well in society, are somehow immune from cultural conflicts and discrimination, and experience few adjustment difficulties. From a perspective of reflecting a central tendency, there is some truth to this model minority conception. Asian cultural values, such as emphasis on educational and occupational achievement and ability to resolve psychological problems, reinforce the stereotype (Kim et al., 1999). However, the model minority notion takes on a different appearance when these issues are evaluated in context. First, Asian Americans are a heterogeneous racial category comprising numerous ethnic groups with different educational, economic, and social characteristics. Second, Asian Americans earn significantly less income compared with White people with the same educational level (Bell, Harrison, & McLaughlin, 1997). In addition, the median income rate does not consider the fact that Asian Americans have a larger number of workers per family unit than other racial groups. Furthermore, Asian Americans are overrepresented among people who suffer from poverty (Reeves & Bennett, 2003).

The model minority stereotype has implications for the mental health of Asian Americans. The stereotype serves to alienate Asian Americans from other ethnic minority groups because of the inherent message: "If Asian Americans can succeed, other minority groups can too." Rosenbloom and Way (2004) found that teachers in an urban high school preferred Asian American students over Black and Latina/o students based on the model minority stereotype. As a result, the Black and Latina/o students physically and verbally harassed the Asian American students. Also, the myth places extreme pressure on Asian Americans to conform to high educational, economic, and occupational expectations. Failure to meet the expectations of the stereotype may lead to feelings of failure and inadequacy. In turn, these pressures and stresses may create psychological problems among Asian Americans (Crystal, 1989). Furthermore, the stereotype hinders the allocation of resources to the mental health needs of Asian Americans, because of the erroneous assumption that they tend not to suffer from psychological difficulties (Crystal, 1989). Therefore, it would be important to explore with Michael and Phuong their experiences with the model minority stereotype.

Acculturative Stress. When individuals make contact with a cultural environment that endorses norms that conflict with the internalized norms of their indigenous culture, they may experience stress. Berry and Annis (1974) noted that members of immigrant ethnic minority groups, including Asian Americans, are vulnerable to this type of stress, which they have labeled "acculturative stress." For Asian Americans, acculturative stress is a pervasive psychological response to their culturally different environment, because the European American norms that prevail in the United States tend to make traditional Asian norms ineffective. For example, a behavioral norm commonly observed in the United States is to voice one's opinion in the name of being honest and true to oneself, even at the risk of offending another person. Traditional Asian Americans who are engaged in these kinds of conversations may hesitate to respond to another person's strong and perhaps offensive remarks in an effort to maintain interpersonal harmony, a traditional Asian cultural value. This may leave these Asian Americans feeling dissatisfied, frustrated, and stressed. In terms of research on the effects of acculturative stress, several studies have documented the relationship between acculturative stress and depression (e.g., Constantine, Okazaki, & Utsey, 2004). Hence, it would be important to discuss how acculturative stress has affected Michael's and Phuong's lives.

Racial Discrimination. From the time of their first arrival to the present, Asian Americans have persevered through racism in the United States. Racism refers to the denigration and subordination of a group of individuals based on the perception that their racial and cultural characteristics are inferior (Uba, 1994). Chan (1991) pointed out that Asian Americans have faced racism through prejudice, economic discrimination, political disenfranchisement, physical violence, immigration exclusion, social segregation, and incarceration. The earliest accounts of racism toward Asian Americans goes back to 1871 when 15 Chinese Americans were hanged, 4 shot, and 2 wounded by a racist White mob in Los Angeles. More recently, in 1982, Vincent Chin, a Chinese American, intentionally was run down by a car and killed with a baseball bat by an unemployed auto worker who was frustrated by the competition from Japanese auto makers. Also, in 1992 in Philadelphia, where Asians comprised 4% of the population, 20% of hate crimes involved Asian American victims (Uba, 1994). From 1986 to 1989 in Los Angeles, where Asians comprise 10% of the population, 15.2% of hate crimes involved Asian American victims. Currently, 20% of Chinese Americans report that they have been discriminated against in their lifetime, 43% of them within the past year (Goto, Gee, & Takeuchi, 2002). In terms of effects of racism on mental health status, Fernando (1984) noted that racism may lead to low self-esteem, learned helplessness, and depression. Thus, it would be helpful to learn about any incidences of racial discrimination experienced by Michael and Phuong.

> Michael feels that his current difficulties regarding educational and career choice may have a lot to do with the model minority stereotype that he has internalized. Although he realizes that part of the pressure to obtain a degree in medicine comes from his parents and their traditional Asian values of academic and career achievement, he also feels that he can't see himself changing his major to one that may be perceived by others as

less prestigious. Furthermore, his difficulties with mathematics and science make him feel ashamed and a less-than-good student; he feels that he should be good in math and science regardless of whether he likes the subjects. As a result, he is struggling to stay in a major that he does not enjoy, while trying to cope with the psychological consequences.

Phuong reports that her ailments could be related mainly to the stresses from her job. She describes acts of prejudice and racism from her co-workers and customers. For instance, Phuong recalls several incidents in which she was called a name (e.g., "stupid Gook") by customers who were angry because she couldn't understand what they were looking for, and was asked to "go back to where [she] came from." Most recently, Phuong was bypassed for a night manager position in favor of a European American worker with less experience than she has. When Phuong asked the general manager why she was not selected, he told her that she might have difficulties managing the other workers because she is so "different." Even when Phuong is not working, she feels like an outsider. Because she lives in a predominantly European American community with very few Cambodian Americans, she has no sources of ethnic support. She notes that she has tried not to think about these problems as a way to cope with them.

GUIDELINE 5:
MULTICULTURAL COMPETENCE IN CLINICAL PRACTICE

The fifth APA Guideline recommends that psychologists become competent in their clinical practice with culturally different clients. To help psychologists and other mental health professionals gain this competence, the following section will describe clinical issues related to culturally competent treatment of Asian American clients.

Understanding Attitudes Toward Seeking Mental Health Services

Research in the past 3 decades has found that Asian Americans tend not to seek psychological services, and even if they enter treatment, they tend to terminate prematurely (e.g., Snowden & Cheung, 1990). More recently, a qualitative study found that Asian Americans would see a counselor only as the last resort (Kim, Brenner, Liang, & Asay, 2003). Hence, scholars have considered factors within or outside the Asian American group that limit Asian Americans' use of psychological services. Among the within-group factors, one possibility is that there may be other readily available therapeutic systems within Asian American communities. These systems may include a network of family members, respected elders, and practitioners of indigenous healing methods (Atkinson et al., 1998; Sue & Sue, 2003). In terms of outside factors, many multicultural scholars have pointed out that mainstream psychological service providers may lack cultural relevance and sensitivity, which may discourage Asian Americans from seeking help from them (e.g., Atkinson et al., 1998; Sue & Sue, 2003).

Recent theoretical and research work has focused on two other within-group factors: (1) Asian Americans' lack of familiarity with conventional Western forms of psychological help, and (2) Asian cultural norms that discourage seeking help from professional psychological service providers. As described above, acculturation is a within-group variable that reflects Asian Americans' familiarity with European American cultural norms in general, and specifically Western forms of psychological helping. Multicultural scholars have suggested that Asian Americans who are not acculturated might perceive conventional psychological services as overly foreign or even threatening (Atkinson et al., 1998; Sue & Sue, 2003). In terms of the second factor, enculturation is a within-group variable that reflects adherence to Asian cultural norms. Multicultural scholars have suggested that Asian Americans who are strongly enculturated may feel ashamed about having mental health problems and hesitate to reveal their problems to individuals outside their family, such as a psychologist (Atkinson et al., 1998; Sue & Sue, 2003).

In general, the results of studies examining the relationship between acculturation and attitudes toward seeking professional psychological help have indicated consistently that less acculturated Asian Americans tend to have less favorable attitudes toward seeking professional psychological services than their more acculturated counterparts (e.g., Atkinson & Gim, 1989). This finding supports the idea that Asian Americans' underutilization of psychological services is related to their lack of familiarity with Western norms. In terms of enculturation, a study by Kim and Omizo (2003) found that high adherence to Asian cultural values was associated with both less positive attitudes toward seeking professional psychological help and less willingness to see a counselor. Hence, the results support the idea that underutilization of psychological services among Asian Americans is related to Asian cultural norms. In the cases of Michael and Phuong, given Michael's high level of acculturation, it can be expected that he would have more favorable attitudes toward seeking psychological help than would Phuong.

Conducting Psychological Assessment

Despite the general reluctance among many Asian Americans to seek mental health services, many of them still do enter therapy. However, they may do so with a great deal of skepticism and culture-related concerns, which, if left unattended, could lead to prematurely terminating from service.

Hence, it is important for therapists to conduct a thorough assessment of clients at the beginning of the therapy relationship. As with any other clients, therapists should assess the nature, severity, and duration of the problem, and the ways in which it had been addressed in the past. In addition, it is very important for therapists to obtain information about factors related to clients' cultural background, which could lead to more relevant and helpful therapy relationships and interventions. Such cultural factors for assessment include (1) acculturation, enculturation, and racial and ethnic identity, (2) attitudes about therapy, (3) experiences with stereotypes, acculturative stress, and oppression, and (4) availability of other sources of support. For both Michael and Phuong, this type of assessment would be especially important given their experiences with oppression.

Drawing on Indigenous Healing Methods

Based on the results of a psychological assessment, therapists might consider taking one of two treatment routes: (1) conventional therapy that integrates culturally relevant and sensitive interventions, and (2) referral to practitioners of indigenous healing methods. If traditional Asian American (i.e., high enculturated) clients might not do well with conventional forms of therapy, even with the augmentation of culturally relevant and sensitive interventions, therapists could consider referring the clients to practitioners of indigenous healing practices. One type of indigenous healing method is acupuncture. Acupuncture treatments are based on principles of Chinese medicine in which health and illness are viewed in terms of a balance between the *yin* and the *yang* forces (Meng, Luo, & Halbreich, 2002). Acupuncture involves inserting small pins on specific points on the body to improve the circulation of energy that may be associated with psychological difficulties. Acupuncture has been used to successfully treat depression, anxiety disorders, and alcoholism and other substance abuse (Meng et al., 2002). For Michael, given that he is strongly acculturated and low enculturated, it may be appropriate to offer conventional therapy that integrates cultural sensitivity. But for Phuong, therapists might need to consider referring her for indigenous methods of healing given that she is highly enculturated but low acculturated.

Recognizing Areas of Conflict Between
Asian Cultural Values and Conventional Psychotherapy Theories

Multicultural scholars suggest that the match or mismatch among a client's cultural values, a therapist's cultural values, and the values inherent in the clinical interventions could influence the therapy process and outcome (Sue & Sue, 2003). There are numerous mismatches of this type. Some therapy theories (e.g., Gestalt Theory) posit the notion that emotional expressions are beneficial and even curative to clients' problems. However, for Asian American clients, like Phuong, who adhere to traditional Asian values and believe that stoicism and reticence are signs of psychological strength, being forced to express their emotions might leave them feeling embarrassed. Being forced to treat therapists in an egalitarian manner, as often is called for by humanistic theories, may lead clients to feel uncomfortable in the relationship because traditional Asian values emphasize hierarchical relationships, particularly in the doctor–patient context. Hence, traditional Asian American clients, who adhere to the value of deference to authority figures, may look to therapists to provide guidance and possible solutions to problems. Psychoanalytic theories posit the importance of exploring the underlying unconscious dynamics causing clients' problems, which often include unresolved issues with family members or other significant figures in one's early life. For traditional Asian Americans who value avoiding family shame, however, such exploration may be threatening and leave them feeling disloyal to their family. Furthermore, for clients who adhere to Asian values of self-effacement, having to openly describe their achievements and accomplishments perhaps as a way to dispute their negative self-concepts, as may be done in cognitive therapies, may be counterproductive and leave the clients feeling arrogant.

However, there also may be positive interactions between conventional therapy approaches and adherence to traditional Asian cultural values. For example, the value of interpersonal harmony may lead clients to work as hard as the therapists to form a good working alliance, a key ingredient in humanistic theories. In addition, the value of deference to authority figures may give therapists increased credibility, with which they can increase their helpfulness to Asian American clients. Phuong might perceive therapists as having a high level of credibility, given her adherence to traditional values.

Modifying Conventional Therapy

If the psychological assessment shows that clients can benefit from conventional forms of therapy, care must be taken to augment the treatment with culturally relevant and sensitive strategies. There have been a number of research studies on therapist types and therapy interventions that may be effective with Asian American clients. As summarized in Kim, Ng, and Ahn (2005), the findings using analogue designs suggest that Asian American clients favor ethnically similar therapists over ethnically dissimilar ones, and therapists who are older and have similar attitudes and personality to their own and more education. Asian American clients also prefer a logical, rational, and directive therapy style over a reflective, affective, and nondirective one, especially if the therapist is Asian American. The findings also suggest that Asian American clients view culturally sensitive therapists as being more credible and culturally competent than less sensitive therapists, and judge culturally responsive therapists as more credible than culturally neutral therapists. As summarized in Kim and colleagues (2005), research results suggest that bicultural Asian Americans perceive therapists as being more attractive than do Western-identified participants, and that acculturated Asian international students view authoritative peer counselors as being more credible than collaborative peer counselors.

Among studies that have employed real clients in actual therapy, the results suggest that Asian American clients favor the goal of looking for immediate resolution of the problem, rather than the goal of exploring the problem to gain insight about its source (Kim, Li, & Liang, 2002). Asian Americans prefer a directive counseling style to a nondirective style (Li & Kim, 2004). Asian American clients perceive therapists who disclose personal information about successful strategies they used in similar situations to be much more helpful than therapists who disclose other types of personal information (Kim, Hill, et al., 2003). Also, Asian American clients prefer therapists who try to match the client's worldview in terms of a possible cause of the problem over therapists who do not match the worldview (Kim et al., 2005). In terms of the relations between values adherence and the therapy process, studies have suggested that Asian American clients who have high adherence to Asian cultural values perceive therapists more positively than clients who are low in adherence to Asian values (Kim et al., 2002; Kim et al., 2005). This is especially true if the therapists are Asian Americans (Kim & Atkinson, 2002).

In general, many of these research findings are consistent with Sue and Zane's (1987) notion of "gift giving." The authors theorized that, for counselors to be perceived as culturally responsive and to reduce clients' premature termination, counselors should focus on helping clients to experience immediate and concrete benefits of therapy in the initial sessions; they termed this strategy "gift giving." Examples of "gifts" are, in general, a resolution of a presenting problem, and, in particular, anxiety reduction, depression relief, cognitive clarity, normalization, and skills acquisition. Sue and Zane pointed out that ethnic minorities in general and Asian Americans in particular have the need to attain some type of meaningful gains early in therapy and that "gift giving demonstrates to clients the direct relationship between working in therapy and alleviation of problems" (p. 42). For both Michael and Phuong, implementing these ideas may be very helpful.

Utilizing Additional Sources of Mental Health Support

Whether therapists use conventional counseling or facilitate the provision of indigenous healing methods with Asian American clients, therapists might consider referring Asian American clients, like Michael and Phuong, for adjunctive support services to agencies or organizations serving Asian Americans. For example, it has been well documented that Korean Americans, who are Christian, tend to seek support from church clergy and other parishioners (Park, 1989). Hence, when working with a traditional Korean American Christian client, a therapist may do well to help establish a connection between the client and a local Korean church in the community. Similarly, therapists might refer traditional Vietnamese American Buddhist clients to temples in which priests can provide supportive services. One inherent benefit of utilizing existing sources of support found within the ethnic communities is that service providers may be able to speak the native languages of the clients. Although using culture-based sources of support may be useful, care should be taken that clients do not experience shame and embarrassment as a result of having people from the same ethnic background learn about their psychological difficulties. To avoid such situations, therapists should work closely with their clients to identify support sources with which the clients feel comfortable.

> During the first session with Michael, the therapist learns that he has no qualms about coming in for therapy. As the therapist further assesses Michael, the therapist discovers that he is highly acculturated but low enculturated, which then inclines the therapist to turn to conventional therapy methods. Because the therapist is aware of the beneficial effects of gift giving, the therapist works with Michael to come up with some concrete ideas on how Michael might be able to communicate with his parents about his career uncertainty. At the end of the session, Michael has a number of strategies to help him communicate more effectively with his parents, including pointing out to them that other majors could still lead him to a well-paying and prestigious job. In terms of his internalized sense of model minority, Michael agreed to work with the therapist on this issue in future sessions.

> During the first session with Phuong, the therapist learns that she is quite nervous about coming in for therapy and feels ashamed that she can't resolve her problems by herself. Hence, the therapist spends time in the beginning to help Phuong cope with the feelings of embarrassment. Then, the therapist further assesses Phuong and learns that she is highly enculturated but low acculturated, which suggests that the therapist could either refer her to an indigenous healer or modify conventional counseling methods to address the fact that a big part of Phuong's functioning involves traditional Asian norms. Because there are no Cambodian healers nearby, the therapist decides to modify the service to be more culturally relevant and sensitive by being more directive, using appropriate self-disclosures, and looking for

more immediate ways to address Phuong's symptoms. In addition, the therapist contacts the nearest Cambodian Mutual Association in the next city to find out how Phuong might be able to access its support network.

STRATEGIES FOR FURTHER INCREASING
MULTICULTURAL COMPETENCE WITH ASIAN AMERICANS

This chapter provided a brief discussion about ways in which psychologists and other mental health professionals can become multiculturally competent in their clinical work with Asian Americans. The following is a list of strategies that can be used to become further competent with this population.

1. Consult the literature on working with Asian Americans. Here are examples

    Atkinson, D. R. (Ed.). *Counseling American minorities* (6th ed.). Boston: McGraw-Hill.

    Hall, G. C. N., & Okazaki, S. (2002). *Asian American psychology: The science of lives in context*. Washington, DC: American Psychological Association.

    Hong, G. K., & Ham, M. D. (2001). *Psychotherapy and counseling for Asian American clients: A practical guide*. Thousand Oaks, CA: Sage.

    Lee, L. C., & Zane, N. W. S. (Eds.). (1998). *Handbook of Asian American psychology*. Thousand Oaks, CA: Sage.

    Sue, D. W., & Sue, D. (2003). *Counseling the culturally diverse: Theory and practice* (4th ed.). New York: Wiley.

    Uba, L. (1994). *Asian Americans: Personality patterns, identity and mental health*. New York: Guilford Press.

2. Establish strong connections with the local Asian American community organizations to learn about the unique issues facing the community. Given the vast diversity among Asian Americans, many community organizations may be structured according to Asian ethnic groups.

3. Attend community events focusing on Asian American issues.

4. Learn from colleagues who have experience and expertise working with Asian American clients.

5. Visit websites related to clinical work with Asian Americans. Here is one for the Asian American Psychological Association: http://www.apaonline.org/ .

6. Most important, continue to evaluate and refine your own clinical work with respect to multicultural competence.

CONCLUSION

Based on the APA Guidelines, this chapter offers specific ideas and concrete suggestions to help psychologists become culturally competent in their clinical work with Asian Americans. Information on within-group cultural variations among Asian Americans and important social factors related to Asian American mental health were described in an attempt to help raise awareness and knowledge that leads to multicultural competence. Also, issues related to the provision of multiculturally competent service were discussed. To illustrate these ideas and suggestions, the cases of Michael and Phuong were used to bring to life how the information could be applied to various Asian Americans. It is hoped that reading this chapter represents just the beginning in your attempt to increase your multicultural competence in working with Asian Americans.

REFERENCES

American Psychological Association. (2003). Guidelines on multicultural education, training, research, practice, and organizational change for psychologists. *American Psychologist, 58,* 377–402.

Atkinson, D. R., & Gim, R. H. (1989). Asian-American cultural identity and attitudes toward mental health services. *Journal of Counseling Psychology, 36,* 209–212.

Atkinson, D. R., Morten, G., & Sue, D. W. (Eds.). (1998). *Counseling American minorities* (5th ed.). Boston: McGraw-Hill.

Barnes, J. S., & Bennett, C. E. (2002). *The Asian population: 2000.* Retrieved May 18, 2005, from http://www.census.gov/prod/2002pubs/c2kbr01-16.pdf

Bell, M. P., Harrison, D. A., & McLaughlin, M. E. (1997). Asian American attitudes toward affirmative action in employment: Implications for the model minority myth. *Journal of Applied Behavioral Science, 33,* 356–377.

Berry, J. W., & Annis, R. C. (1974). Acculturative stress: The role of ecology, culture and differentiation. *Journal of Cross-Cultural Psychology, 5,* 382–406.

Berry, J. W., Kim, U., Power, S., Young, M., & Bajaki, M. (1989). Acculturation attitudes in plural societies. *Applied Psychology: An International Review, 38,* 185–206.

Chan, S. (1991). *Asian Americans: An interpretative history.* Boston: Twayne.

Constantine, M. G., Okazaki, S., & Utsey, S. O. (2004). Self-concealment, social self-efficacy, acculturative stress, and depression in African, Asian, and Latin American international college students. *American Journal of Orthopsychiatry, 74,* 230–241.

Crystal, D. (1989). Asian Americans and the myth of the model minority. *Social Casework, 70,* 405–413.

Fernando, S. (1984). Racism as a cause of depression. *International Journal of Social Psychiatry, 30,* 41–49.

Goto, S. G., Gee G. C., & Takeuchi, D. T. (2002). Strangers still? The experiences of discrimination among Chinese Americans. *Journal of Community Psychology, 30,* 211–224.

Herskovits, M. J. (1948). *Man and his works: The science of cultural anthropology.* New York: Knopf.

Kim, B. S. K., & Abreu, J. M. (2001). Acculturation measurement: Theory, current instruments, and future directions. In J. G. Ponterotto, J. M. Casas, L. A. Suzuki, & C. M. Alexander (Eds.), *Handbook of multicultural counseling* (2nd ed., pp. 394–424). Thousand Oaks, CA: Sage.

Kim, B. S. K., & Atkinson, D. R. (2002). Asian American client adherence to Asian cultural values, counselor expression of cultural values, counselor ethnicity, and career counseling process. *Journal of Counseling Psychology, 49*, 3–13.

Kim, B. S. K., Atkinson, D. R., & Umemoto, D. (2001). Asian cultural values and the counseling process: Current knowledge and directions for future research. *The Counseling Psychologist, 29*, 570–603.

Kim, B. S. K., Atkinson, D. R., & Yang, P. H. (1999). The Asian values scale: Development, factor analysis, validation, and reliability. *Journal of Counseling Psychology, 46*, 342–352.

Kim, B. S. K., Brenner, B. R., Liang, C. T. H., & Asay, P. A. (2003). A qualitative study of adaptation experiences of 1.5-generation Asian Americans. *Cultural Diversity and Ethnic Minority Psychology, 9*, 156–170.

Kim, B. S. K., Hill, C. E., Gelso, C. J., Goates, M. K., Asay, P. A., & Harbin, J. M. (2003). Counselor self-disclosure, East Asian American client adherence to Asian cultural values, and counseling process. *Journal of Counseling Psychology, 50*, 324–332.

Kim, B. S. K., Li, L. C., & Liang, C. T. H. (2002). Effects of Asian American client adherence to Asian cultural values, session goal, and counselor emphasis of client expression on career counseling process. *Journal of Counseling Psychology, 49*, 342–354

Kim, B. S. K., Ng, G. F., & Ahn, A. J. (2005). Effects of client expectation for counseling success, client–counselor worldview match, and client adherence to Asian and European American cultural values on counseling process with Asian Americans. *Journal of Counseling Psychology, 52*, 67–76.

Kim, B. S. K., & Omizo, M. M. (2003). Asian cultural values, attitudes toward seeking professional psychological help, and willingness to see a counselor. *The Counseling Psychologist, 31*, 343–361.

Kitano, H. H. L., & Matsushima, N. (1981). Counseling Asian Americans. In P. B. Pedersen, J. G. Draguns, W. J. Lonner, & J. E. Trimble (Eds.), *Counseling across cultures* (2nd ed., pp. 163–180). Honolulu: University of Hawaii Press.

Li, L. C., & Kim, B. S. K. (2004). Effects of counseling style and client adherence to Asian cultural values on counseling process with Asian American college students. *Journal of Counseling Psychology, 51*, 158–167.

Meng, F., Luo, H., & Halbreich, U. (2002). Concepts, techniques, and clinical applications of acupuncture. *Psychiatric Annals, 32*, 45–49.

Park, K. (1989). "Born again": What does it mean to Korean-Americans in New York City? *Journal of Ritual Studies, 3/2*, 287–301.

Redfield, R., Linton, R., & Herskovits, M. J. (1936). Memorandum on the study of acculturation. *American Anthropologist, 56*, 973–1002.

Reeves, T., & Bennett, C. (2003). *The Asian and Pacific Islander population in the United States: March 2002*. Retrieved May 18, 2005, from http://www.census.gov/prod/2003pubs/p20-540.pdf

Rosenbloom, S. R., & Way, N. (2004). Experiences of discrimination among African American, Asian American, and Latino adolescents in an urban high school. *Youth & Society, 35*, 420–451.

Snowden, L. R., & Cheung, F. H. (1990). Use of inpatient mental health services by members of ethnic minority groups. *American Psychologist, 45*, 347–355.

Sue, D. W., & Sue, D. (2003). *Counseling the culturally diverse: Theory and practice* (4th ed.). Hoboken, NJ: Wiley.

Sue, S., & Zane, N. (1987). The role of culture and cultural techniques in psychotherapy: A critique and reformulation. *American Psychologist, 42,* 37–45.

Uba, L. (1994). *Asian Americans: Personality patterns, identity and mental health.* New York: Guilford Press.

U.S. Bureau of the Census. (2004). *U.S. interim projections by age, sex, race, and Hispanic origin.* Retrieved May 18, 2005, from http://www.census.gov/ipc/www/usinterimproj

3

African American Populations

Juanita K. Martin

African Americans are a diverse group who represent 13% of the U.S. population, or approximately 38 million people (U.S. Bureau of the Census, 2003). Many African Americans have families whose roots in this country may be traced back more than 200 years to slavery. Others may be more recent immigrants from places such as the West Indies, South America, and many countries in Africa. Some people who are biracial or multiracial also may identify as African American. Most of the African American population lives in the South (55%), and a little more than half (52%) is located in major metropolitan areas (U.S. Bureau of the Census, 2003).

The African American population contributes greatly to the diversity of the United States. As a people, African Americans have experienced years of oppression in this society. The resulting Civil Rights and Black Power movements of the 1960s and 1970s were major sociopolitical actions that spurred policy changes related to the treatment of minorities in many organizations and social institutions, including the field of psychology. The changes, beginning in the 1970s, included the suggestion that cultural issues be addressed in psychology graduate programs (Korman, 1974). Guidelines for clinical practice with ethnic, linguistic and culturally diverse populations were developed initially in 1990 (APA, 1993).

Taking the field a step further, the APA "Guidelines on Multicultural Education, Training, Research, Practice, and Organizational Change for Psychologists" were published in 2003. As explained in Chapter 1, these Guidelines encouraged psychologists to integrate principles of multiculturalism and diversity into all areas of the profession of psychology. Although the Guidelines are an excellent resource for culturally centered practice, they do not provide concrete examples or strategies for their implementation. This chapter, therefore, focuses on applying the Guidelines when working with African Americans, with the primary emphasis on developing cultural awareness and knowledge, and improving clinical practice and psychology education. First, I present information about historical factors and psychological constructs that affect African Americans' use of mental health services. Implementation of the Guidelines will then be illustrated through two case vignettes. This chapter will conclude with suggested strategies to enhance cultural competence when working with African Americans.

BARRIERS TO MENTAL HEALTH TREATMENT

African Americans are less likely to seek mental health services and more likely to terminate services prematurely than the general population (Snowden, 2003; Wallace & Constantine, 2005). One barrier to mental health treatment for African Americans is historically due to cultural bias in the field of psychology. Thomas and Sillen (1972) report a long history of what they call "scientific racism" in psychology. During slavery, Black mental health was associated with subservience and faithfulness, while the desire to rebel or live in freedom was considered a sign of mental illness (Guthrie, 1998). In the early 20th century, several prominent psychologists believed that African Americans had smaller brains and less complex minds than Europeans (Guthrie, 1998). Many psychologists therefore believed that African Americans did not develop or need to be treated for mental illness.

Until the 1960s, a genetic deficit model frequently was used to portray African Americans as intellectually inferior to European Americans (Jensen, 1969). Publication of the book *The Bell Curve* (Herrnstein & Murray, 1994) revived this theory and produced much controversy about this model. In the 1960s, some theorists attempted to move away from questionable biological explanations of differences and developed models of cultural deprivation and cultural deficiency to explain African American behavior (Samuda, 1998). These models imply that African Americans lack a culture or have a deviant culture that negatively affects their intellectual development, behavior, and mental status. This history of cultural bias in psychology has negatively influenced mental health professionals so that they may hold stereotypes about African Americans that can result in differential treatment and diagnosis. The mental health system, as an institution, also has been negatively affected in that it is often unresponsive to African Americans' mental health needs (Lawson & Kim, 2005). Approximately half of mental health professionals in two surveys reported that they did not feel competent to treat African Americans (Dana, 2002).

African Americans' beliefs and attitudes about mental illness and the mental health system also can pose potential barriers to seeking services. One such barrier is cultural mistrust. Terrell and Terrell (1981) defined "cultural mistrust" as Black Americans' suspiciousness of European American institutions such as the educational, legal, and mental health systems. Research has suggested that higher levels of cultural mistrust were associated with reluctance to seek help from and self-disclose to European American therapists (Nickerson, Helms, & Terrell, 1994; Poston, Craine, & Atkinson, 1991).

There are additional beliefs held by many African Americans that may contribute to their resistance to identifying or seeking treatment for mental illness. Many African Americans believe they should not "air dirty laundry" in public and that mental health problems, when identified, should be addressed within the family (Boyd-Franklin & Franklin, 2000). Due to the importance of religion in the lives of many African Americans, some individuals may prefer to resolve problems through spirituality, prayer, or religious faith. Another potential barrier to seeking treatment, suggested by Pouissant and Alexander (2000), is that African Americans, due to their history of oppression in the United States, have been raised to be resilient and ready to withstand hardship. Anecdotally, I have heard African Americans in therapy proudly describe themselves as a "strong Black man" or a "strong Black woman." Thus, mental illness may be viewed as "weakness" or a sign of being "crazy," which are the antitheses of projecting strength. There also may be some stigma and/or shame associated with mental illness and treatment (Cooper-Patrick, Power, Jenckes, Gonzales, Levine, & Ford, 1997).

IMPLEMENTING THE MULTICULTURAL GUIDELINES:
TWO CASE VIGNETTES

Development of Cultural Awareness and Knowledge: The Case of Tanisha

Tanisha is a 19 year-old African American sophomore at a medium-sized Midwestern college. She was raised by her parents along with two younger brothers. Her father is a factory worker and her mother is a secretary. She came to the college counseling center because she felt depressed.

In her initial interview, Tanisha reports that she went to neighborhood schools until high school. Her parents disliked the neighborhood high school and arranged for her to attend a high school in another neighborhood. Tanisha says that she did well academically in high school and that she was one of only five African American students in her predominately White high school class to take accelerated courses. She has earned good grades in college and is involved in several campus organizations. She knows many people, but most of her close friends are people she knew in high school. Despite her campus involvement, she sometimes feels depressed and isolated from other students. She compares herself with her college friends, most of whom are White women, and feels she is fat. She believes that many African American women are happy to be plus-sized, but she does not want to look like them. She practices the Seventh Day Adventist faith and adheres to her church's dietary rules of vegetarianism. When depressed, however, she procrastinates on schoolwork, watches television, and eats junk food.

Due to her presenting problem, she is referred to a new counselor whose dissertation and clinical interests revolve around eating and body image concerns. The counselor, Dr. Lake, is a White American woman who focuses on Tanisha's depression and eating issues. After several sessions, Dr. Lake was concerned about Tanisha's lack of progress in therapy and presented her case in the counseling center's clinical case meeting. An African American colleague asked Dr. Lake whether she had explored the client's remarks that associated being African American with being overweight. Dr. Lake had not explored this issue and assumed that many African American women were comfortable with their weight. The colleague suggested that Dr. Lake ask questions about the client's level of racial identity development and offered to provide Dr. Lake with readings about racial identity.

When Dr. Lake began to explore the racial identity and body size association with Tanisha, the counselor was surprised and saddened to hear her eventually say, "I don't like being Black" and begin to cry. Tanisha reported that her parents stressed the importance of education and that they felt that "many Black people do not have the right values." One of the reasons they had given her for selecting her high school was to ensure that she "spend time with the right people."

Racial Identity. In addition to demographic factors, levels of racial identity contribute to the heterogeneity of the African American population. African Americans often are viewed by some mental health professionals (and by laypeople) as a homogeneous group. For example, Dr. Lake assumed all African American women had similar feelings about body image. However, to reduce stereotyping and develop accurate, culture-centered diagnoses and treatment strategies, it is important to examine within-group differences in racial identity development. It is therefore important for Dr. Lake to help Tanisha recognize her level of racial identity and to explore the psychological impact of associated feelings and behaviors. Through consultation with her colleagues and the suggested readings, Dr. Lake was able to improve her competence to provide these services.

Religion and Spirituality. Religion and spirituality historically have been very important in the lives of many African Americans; this population reports more involvement with religious institutions than most other U.S. groups (Chatters, Taylor, & Lincoln, 1999; Constantine, Lewis, Conner, & Sanchez, 2000). "Religion" refers to an organized institution of beliefs, whereas spirituality is more broad and encompasses a sense of universal connectedness. Several African American psychologists, noting the importance of spirituality in the lives of many African Americans, have developed African-centered models of psychological functioning, all of which incorporate a sense of spirituality (Akbar, 1995; Azibo, 1989).

It often is helpful to ask about the importance of religion, faith-based organizations, or spirituality in the lives of African American clients. Some counselors are uncomfortable discussing these issues for a variety of reasons, including a lack of training in their graduate programs and/or a worldview that does not value religion (Queener & Martin, 2001). Acknowledgment of this aspect in clients' lives may help establish rapport between client and counselor, provide the therapist with additional information, and assist clients in the generation of coping strategies. Therefore, it would benefit culture-centered mental health practitioners to examine their beliefs about the role of spirituality in their own lives (Cervantes & Parham, 2005). In many African American churches, ministers not only provide traditional spiritual guidance but also serve as counselors to their congregants. The churches also may sponsor in-house and community-based programs to help congregants and other members of the African American community. Collaborations among psychologists, mental health systems, and Black churches have been developed to enhance the psychological well-being of African Americans in a culture-centered manner (Helms & Cook, 1999; Queener & Martin, 2001).

During consultation, Dr. Lake's colleague suggested that she further investigate the role of religion and spirituality in Tanisha's life. Dr. Lake had asked little about Tanisha's religious or spiritual affiliation and decided to explore the issue further. Tanisha said that her parents wanted her to attend a college affiliated with their religion but that they did not have the money to send her to the school. Tanisha feels that her religion and spirituality are important and generally give her a sense of direction and comfort. She misses the community of her church and sometimes feels isolated from her college peers. They do not understand why she is unavailable for some weekend activities and why she declines to drink alcohol when offered.

Tanisha does not know anyone at her school who is Seventh Day Adventist and has made no African American friends. She becomes depressed when she feels guilty about drinking beverages and eating food that she believes would be frowned on by her church. Tanisha thinks about making more contact with African American students. She has seen a flier for a group called "The Sistahood" that meets at the Black Culture Center on campus, but does not know whether she would feel comfortable or be accepted.

Dr. Lake had seen few African American clients prior to Tanisha and felt unsure of how to deal with these new issues. This case was different from the body image cases she had in the past. Although she felt some discomfort about these issues, she believed they were important to Tanisha and probably would help her to progress in therapy. As Dr. Lake continued to work with Tanisha, she again took her case to a clinical case meeting, consulted individually with her African American colleague, and wondered whether she should sign up for a continuing education workshop on "Counseling Diverse Clients."

Analyzing the Case. Many of the Guidelines are relevant to this case. The first two Guidelines encourage psychologists to commit to developing cultural awareness and knowledge of themselves and others. Like many other European American individuals, Dr. Lake has little awareness of herself as a racial being. She does not think about race as a major psychological variable and simply strives to treat everyone in a fair and equitable manner. She has had few African American clients and feels that the client's race should not affect her mode of conducting therapy. Her worldview is typical of what has been called "color-blind" (Doan & Bonilla-Silva, 2003). The Guidelines suggest, however, that psychologists acknowledge that all people, including themselves, are racial/ethnic beings.

Dr. Lake has little knowledge about African Americans. When she began her work with Tanisha, she assumed Tanisha's concerns were similar to those of most of the women with whom she previously had worked. Regarding eating issues and body image concerns, Dr. Lake had read some studies that suggested that many African American women were fairly comfortable with a larger body size compared with White women. She generalized from her reading that African American women were a fairly homogeneous group, and she tended to stereotype their issues around body image. Dr. Lake has no close African American friends and has little interaction with the African American community. She has little knowledge of the heterogeneity that exists in that community. She was exposed briefly to racial identity models in graduate school, but has not thought about their application to her work.

As Dr. Lake's colleague suggested, she read about Black racial identity development and discussed it in therapy. Dr. Lake then changed her initial focus and began to explore racial identity issues with Tanisha. Neither the therapist nor Tanisha had ever talked about racial identity with anyone. Dr. Lake, concerned about her competence to address this issue, spent more time with her African American colleague, consulting about her client and asking questions about her colleague's experience with race. She also decided to make an appointment to meet staff from the college's Black Culture Center. She had never been there and believed it might be helpful to have information about "The Sistahood" and other programs in the department.

Dr. Lake has seen African American gospel choirs on television, but that is the extent of her knowledge about the Black church. She is not a particularly religious person and has noticed in her reading that several authors indicate that spirituality is important for many African Americans. Realizing that religion has a major impact on Tanisha's life, Dr. Lake began to strategize with her on specific ways in which to maintain connections with her religious community.

Dr. Lake had given Tanisha personality tests to assess her level of depression and eating concerns. She went back to the manuals and realized that the test she used for assessing eating concerns contained no African Americans in the normative sample. This suggests that the test is culturally biased and/or that the pattern of scores may be interpreted differently for diverse racial groups. Therefore, she went over the test with Tanisha a second time and asked for more in-depth explanations of her responses in order to assess the impact of culture on the results. Tanisha feels comfortable with Dr. Lake, and although they discuss some difficult issues, she continues to engage in treatment.

Dr. Lake's experience with Tanisha also is leading her to her own self-introspection regarding race. Dr. Lake asked her brother if he ever thought about being White. When he told her, "No," she initiated discussions with him and other family members. Such an exercise might provide White American therapists with a starting point for understanding how racial and ethnic issues may have been dealt with in their families. These explorations could prove fruitful in helping them to examine their current level of racial identity development.

Examination of Multicultural Issues in Psychology Courses: The Case of John

John is a 40-year-old African American man who lives on the East coast. He is one of two African American students in a group therapy class in the graduate program of the counseling department. The class instructor asked if someone was willing to discuss a concern with the group to help him show the class a new therapy technique. Although a little hesitant, John described a series of incidents that had upset him. The police recently had stopped him while he was driving on his way to pick up his aunt from the hospital. The officer told him he was driving too fast and asked to search his car. Although unhappy with the request, he agreed. When nothing illegal was found, John was allowed to continue. Six miles down the highway, he was stopped by another officer who said that he was driving too slowly and who also asked to search the vehicle. John allowed the search, although he was angry. He picked up his aunt and on the way back to her house was

stopped a third time by an officer who stated that he was driving a dangerous vehicle because of a crack on his windshield. John told the officer that
the crack occurred when a rock, thrown by a truck, hit the windshield and
that he intended to fix it next week. He also pointed out that the crack was
low on the windshield and did not impair his vision. The officer looked
carefully inside the vehicle, saw the elderly aunt, and let him go with a
stern warning to fix the windshield within a week.

Racism. It is very important for therapists to address the role of racism
in the lives of African Americans. In at least one study (Williams & Morris-
Williams, 2000), 50% of European Americans held stereotypic beliefs about
African Americans (e.g., that they are lazy, violent, want to live on welfare,
and so forth). Racism is believed to take a physical toll on African Americans
as its effect has been linked to chronic stress and related diseases (Pierre &
Mahalik, 2005). Pouissant and Alexander (2000) noted high rates of hyper-
tension, heart disease, and chronic stress in African Americans. Research
also has found racism to be associated with psychiatric symptoms in African
Americans (Klonoff, Landrine, & Ullman, 1999). Therapists must be willing
to inquire about and address this issue with African American clients.

However, this issue may be difficult for some mental health professionals
to address, particularly European Americans. They may deny that racism
still exists. They may have little awareness of racism, due to White privilege,
and initially might resist dealing with issues of discrimination. They may feel
a sense of incompetence if they have had little experience with racial oppression. Working on issues of racism means that the therapist must have knowledge of or become involved with African American advocacy organizations.
As suggested in the Guidelines, this involves participation in organizational
change. Many psychologists and other mental health professionals do not
view this as part of their role in treatment. However, it is an important role
for culture-centered practitioners. Research suggests that dealing assertively
with racist situations positively affects mental health in some African Americans (Pierre & Mahalik, 2005).

> John's instructor and several classmates asked him how fast he was driving
> and if he had a history of speeding, and suggested that he may have been
> rushing in his attempt to pick up his aunt by the time she was discharged.
> The instructor mentioned that he traveled that highway several times a week
> and had never been stopped by the police. A student thought that speed
> traps may be set up routinely on that highway. One student wondered
> whether race had anything to do with what she perceived to be harassment.
> Another classmate responded that this was "the same as my sister who
> was stopped once for speeding." Several class members asked about John
> speaking in an assertive vs. passive-aggressive manner with his wife when

he took out his frustration on her. The class discussion ended fairly q
John became quiet, and the instructor noticed he was withdrawn and
tant during the remainder of the class. After the class ended, the instru
walked down the hallway and overheard John talking to another African
American student. He heard him mention that he was, "tired of White people" and did not "want to go to that racist class again!" The instructor, who
prided himself on his ability to be empathic and understand group dynamics, was surprised and angry to hear these comments.

Analyzing the Case. The Guidelines may be used to analyze this incident.
Many African American men have been stereotyped as violent criminals and
drug dealers (White & Cones, 1999). The United States has a long history of
discrimination and prejudice toward African Americans in the legal system.
Many African Americans, particularly males, have been pulled over by the
police for fallacious reasons while driving. These incidents have happened
so frequently throughout the nation that they have been called "DWB" or
"Driving While Black" situations. The second Guideline encourages psychologists to have knowledge of racially diverse individuals. This knowledge
includes understanding the oppression that many African Americans have
encountered. The response of John's classmates and instructor suggests that
they have little awareness of the frequent stereotyping and discrimination
many African American men face.

Guideline 3 encourages psychologists to employ constructs of diversity
in psychological education. When John brought up his incident, the group
therapy instructor missed an opportunity to facilitate a discussion on sociopolitical issues for African Americans and their potential impact on clinical
practice. Discussing racial issues in a classroom setting can be uncomfortable
for both European American students and students of color. Multicultural
discussions in a graduate psychology class may be met by all students with
several levels of resistance (Jackson, 1999). The Guidelines suggest, however, that instructors develop the knowledge and skills to lead productive
discussions.

CONCLUSION: STRATEGIES TO ENHANCE
MULTICULTURAL COMPETENCE WITH AFRICAN AMERICANS

This chapter presented a brief overview of ways in which mental health professionals might use the Guidelines with African Americans. The following
list of strategies is provided to reinforce some of the suggestions previously
mentioned and to provide additional means of increasing cultural competence with African American individuals.

1. *Explore your racial identity.* This may be particularly useful for some White therapists who, due partly to racial privilege, may not have thought about themselves as cultural or racial beings. (I recall the blank looks I received from many European American graduate students in a multicultural counseling class after I asked them to do this. Their initial responses included denying they were White, refusing to see any salience of race, and fear of being stereotyped.) Most African Americans are very conscious of their race. Initiate conversations with European American family, friends, and colleagues about what it means to be White in this society. You might read and discuss the book *White Out: The Continuing Significance of Racism* (Doan & Bonilla-Silva, 2003), which explores White racial identity and concepts such as color-blindness and White privilege.

2. *Acknowledge the fact that racism exists in this society and learn how to ask and talk about it with your African American clients.* For example, ask, "Do you believe you've experienced any racial prejudice or discrimination that has had an effect on your life and concerns?" Although not all problems presented by African Americans are due to prejudice, most African Americans can recount incidents where they believe racism was involved. Projecting a color-blind worldview ("I don't see race. We are all the same.") will cause you to immediately lose credibility with many African American clients. They will be better served by your ability to help them cope, work on a variety of responses, and provide community resources when issues of racism arise.

3. *Explore your spiritual identity.* Religion and/or spirituality can be very important for some African Americans. How do you view religion? Do you feel a sense of connectedness with others, nature, or a creator? How might these perspectives affect what you do in therapy? *Integrating Spirituality into Multicultural Counseling* (Fukuyama & Sevig, 1999) includes African American clinical case examples and questions for your own self-exploration.

4. *When meeting African American clients for the first time, remember that for some people there may be an element of mistrust and that you may be tested.* Developing rapport, as well as presenting yourself in a very genuine manner, is important even when clients do not seem mistrustful. Ask how the client prefers to be addressed, especially if he or she is older than you. Calling older African Americans by their first name in an attempt to be informal and friendly may be perceived as insulting.

5. *Learn to ask questions.* If your African American client makes reference to a word or custom with which you are not familiar, ask for information. It is better and more ethical to tactfully ask for clarification ("I'm not quite sure what you meant when you said . . .") rather than to suffer in silence or, worse, make an incorrect diagnosis because you did not understand what the person was saying.

6. *Read professional books and journal articles.* Journals may include the *Journal of Black Psychology, Journal of Counseling Psychology, Journal of Multicultural Counseling and Development,* and *Cultural Diversity and Ethnic Minority Psychology.* Take workshops and talk to people who have expertise in working with this population.

7. *Learn about Afrocentrism and African-centered psychotherapies.* The term *Afrocentric* sometimes is perceived to be "militant" or threatening by persons not familiar with these beliefs. Gaining an understanding of African consciousness, however, will increase your cultural competence in working with African Americans. Books such as *The Psychology of Blacks: An African Centered Perspective* (Parham, White, & Ajamu, 1999) and *Understanding an Afrocentric Worldview: Introduction to an Optimal Psychology* (Myers, 1988) are classics. Also, obtain information about African-centered community interventions like Rites of Passage, a process some adolescent African Americans participate in as a means of attaining adulthood. Rites of Passage will expose you to the Afrocentric principles of Nguzo Saba, which are also a basis for Kwanzaa, a holiday celebrated by many African Americans. You may obtain more information by reading *Kwanzaa: Origin, Concepts, Practice* (Karenga, 1997).

8. *Become familiar with general-purpose African American magazines* such as *Ebony, Jet,* and *Essence.* Within the past 5 or 6 years, many such magazines have begun to include articles about mental health. Consider keeping them in your waiting area and/or referring articles to your African American clients. It is no longer uncommon to find information about stress or depression in these publications. The personal testimonies in these articles often include a spiritual component that is culturally congruent for many African Americans. Also read and refer to books written by African American mental health professionals for the general public, such as *Soothe Your Nerves* (Neal-Barnett, 2003), which deals with anxiety; *Shifting: The Double Lives of Black Women in America* (Jones & Shorter-Gooden, 2003); and *Boys into Men: Raising Our African American Teenage Sons* (Boyd-Franklin & Franklin, 2000).

REFERENCES

Akbar, N. (1995). *The community of self* (Rev. ed.). Tallahassee, FL: Mind Productions & Associates.

American Psychological Association. (1993). Guidelines for providers of psychological services to ethnic, linguistic, and culturally diverse populations. *American Psychologist, 48*, 45–48.

American Psychological Association. (2003). Guidelines on multicultural education, training, research, practice, and organizational change for psychologists. *American Psychologist, 58*, 377–402.

Azibo, D. (1989). African-centered theses on mental health and a nosology of Black/African personality disorder. *Journal of Black Psychology, 15*, 173–214.

Boyd-Franklin, N., & Franklin, A. J. (2000). *Boys into men: Raising our African American teenage sons*. New York: Dutton.

Chatters, L. M., Taylor, R. J., & Lincoln, K. D. (1999). African American religious participation: A multi-sample comparison. *Journal for the Scientific Study of Religion, 38*, 132–145.

Cervantes, J. M., & Parham, T. A. (2005). Toward a meaningful spirituality for people of color: Lessons for the counseling practitioner. *Cultural Diversity and Ethnic Minority Psychology, 11*, 69–81.

Constantine, M. G., Lewis, E. I., Conner, I. C., & Sanchez, D. (2000). Addressing spiritual and religious issues in counseling African Americans: Implications for counselor training and practice. *Counseling and Values, 45*, 28–39.

Cooper-Patrick, L., Power, N. R., Jenckes, M. W., Gonzales, J., Levine, D. M., & Ford, D. E. (1997). Identification of patient attitudes, and preferences regarding treatment in depression. *Journal of General Internal Medicine, 12*, 431–438.

Dana, R. H. (2002). Mental health services for African Americans: A culture centered perspective. *Cultural Diversity and Ethnic Minority Psychology, 8*, 3–18.

Doan, A. W., & Bonilla-Silva, E. (2003). *White out: The continuing significance of racism*. New York: Routledge.

Fukuyama, M. A., & Sevig, T. D. (1999). *Integrating spirituality into multicultural counseling*. Thousand Oaks, CA: Sage.

Guthrie, R. V. (1998). *Even the rate was White: A historical view of psychology*. Needham, MA: Allyn & Bacon.

Helms, J. E., & Cook, D. A. (1999). *Using race and culture in counseling and psychotherapy: Theory and process*. Needham Heights, MA: Allyn & Bacon.

Herrnstein, R., & Murray, C. (1994). *The bell curve: Intelligence and class structure in American life*. New York: Free Press.

Jackson, L. (1999). Ethnocultural resistance to multicultural training: Students and faculty. *Cultural Diversity and Ethnic Minority Psychology, 5*, 27–36.

Jensen, A. (1969). How much can we boost I.Q. and school achievement? *Harvard Educational Review, 39*, 1–123.

Jones, C., & Shorter-Gooden, K. (2003). *Shifting: The double lives of Black women in America*. New York: HarperCollins.

Karenga, M. (1997). *Kwanzaa: Origin, concepts, practice*. Los Angeles: Kawaida.

Klonoff, E. A., Landrine, H., & Ullman, J. B. (1999). Racial discrimination and psychiatric symptoms among Blacks. *Cultural Diversity and Ethnic Minority Psychology, 5*, 329–339.

Korman, M. (1974). National conference on levels and patterns of professional training in psychology. *American Psychologist, 29*, 441–449.

Lawson, E. J., & Kim, Y. J. (2005). Collaborators: Mental health and public health in the African American community. In D. A. Harley & J. M. Dillard (Eds.), *Contemporary mental health issues among African Americans* (pp. 205–222). Alexandria, VA: American Counseling Association.

Myers, L. J. (1988). *Understanding an Afrocentric worldview: Introduction to an optimal psychology.* Dubuque, IA: Kendall/Hunt.

Neal-Barnett, A. (2003). *Soothe your nerves: The Black woman's guide to understanding and overcoming anxiety, panic and fear.* New York: Simon & Schuster.

Nickerson, K. J., Helms, J. E., & Terrell, F. (1994). Cultural mistrust, opinions about mental illness and Black students' attitudes toward seeking psychological help from White counselors. *Journal of Counseling Psychology, 41,* 378–386.

Parham, T. A., White, J. L., & Ajamu, A. (1999). *The psychology of Blacks: An African centered perspective.* Saddle River, NJ: Prentice Hall.

Pierre, M. R., & Mahalik, J. R. (2005). Examining African self–consciousness and Black racial identity as predictors of Black men's psychological well being. *Cultural Diversity and Ethnic Minority Psychology, 11,* 28–40.

Poston, W. C., Craine, M., & Atkinson, D. R. (1991). Counselor dissimilarity confrontation, client cultural mistrust, and willingness to self-disclose. *Journal of Multicultural Counseling and Development, 19,* 65–73.

Poussaint, A. F., & Alexander, A. (2000). *Lay my burden down: Suicide and the mental health crisis among African Americans.* Boston: Beacon Press.

Queener, J. E., & Martin, J. K. (2001). Providing culturally relevant mental health services: Collaboration between psychology and the African American church. *Journal of Black Psychology, 27,* 112–122.

Samuda, R. J. (1998). *Psychological testing of American minorities.* Thousand Oaks, CA: Sage.

Snowden, L. R. (2003). Bias in mental health assessment and interventions: Theory and evidence. *American Journal of Public Health, 93,* 239–243.

Terrell, F. & Terrell, S. (1981). An inventory to measure cultural mistrust among Blacks. *Western Journal of Black Studies, 5,* 180–185.

Thomas, A., & Sillen, S. (1972). *Racism and psychiatry.* New York: Brunner/Mazel.

U. S. Bureau of the Census. (2003). *Population profile of the United States.* Washington, DC: U.S. Government Printing Office.

Wallace, B. C., & Constantine, M. G. (2005). Africentric cultural values, psychological help-seeking attitudes, and self-concealment in African American college students. *Journal of Black Psychology, 31,* 369–385.

White, J. L., & Cones, J. H. (1999). *Black man emerging: Facing the past and seizing the future in America.* New York: Routledge.

Williams, D. R., & Morris-Williams, R. (2000). Racism and mental health: The African American experience. *Ethnicity and Health, 5,* 243–269.

4

Latina/o American Populations

Cynthia de las Fuentes

The ethnic and historical heritages of Latina/os are diverse, and the socio-political histories of Latina/os are as varied as the diversity within Latino cultures. For example, the history of Latin America includes conquests by the Spanish, French, Portuguese, and Dutch; land seizures by the United States; a legacy of slavery; *mestizaje* (a blending of indigenous and European people, cultures, values, beliefs, and languages); communism; and despots of the likes of Fidel Castro, Augusto Pinochet, and Manuel Noriega.

Latin America's racial heritage is also very diverse. Although most U.S. Americans know that Africans were forcibly brought to the United States as slaves, few know that one-third of all Africans on slave ships were sent to Brazil. Even fewer U.S. Americans know about the millions of Asian peoples from China, Japan, and elsewhere who arrived centuries ago and continue to arrive in the Americas, augmenting earlier waves of immigration. For instance, Brazil received thousands of Japanese immigrants in the 20th century. Their descendants represent the largest community of Japanese outside of Japan and Hawaii (*Asians in Latin America: A Guide to Resources*, n.d.). As another example of Asian immigration to Latin America, the oldest established Chinatowns in the Western hemisphere are found in Lima, Peru, and Havana, Cuba (*Chinatowns in Latin America*, n.d.).

Although most Latina/os immigrated to the United States in the past century, Latina/os have been in what is now the United States since before William Bradford and Edward Winslow set sail on the Mayflower for the New World. Mexicans account for just over one-fourth of all immigrants arriving since 1970 (Rumbaut, 1994), and one-third of all immigrants are Latina/os (U.S. Bureau of the Census, 2001). According to the 2000 U.S. Census, there were over 35 million Latina/os living in the United States, a number that likely underrepresents many undocumented workers and their families. By 2050, one-fourth of all persons in the United States, or approximately 96 million people, are predicted to be ethnic Latina/os of all races (Zavala, 1999).

This chapter focuses on the development of cultural competence when working with Latina/o[1] Americans and discusses pertinent issues, including immigration and acculturation, language, and culture-based values and beliefs. I use the APA Multicultural Guidelines (2003) as a framework for this discussion. Examples from my own teaching strategies and clinical practice will be used to illustrate certain concepts. (The names and identifying characteristics of my students and clients have been changed to protect their identities.)

RELEVANT MULTICULTURAL GUIDELINES

An understanding of cultural context is vital in the planning and delivery of mental health services for Latina/o Americans and their families. Multicultural Guideline 1 invites us to be aware and knowledgeable of ourselves and others as cultural beings. Because every person is the product of unique cultural experiences and backgrounds, Guideline 1 encourages psychologists to become aware of how their own culture(s) contribute to attitudes and biases about others. It also emphasizes that culturally competent psychologists recognize, assess, validate, and employ their own cultures and backgrounds as well as those of their clients in their practice.

In an attempt to prevent harm to consumers of mental health services (e.g., clients, students, and agencies), many writers have placed great emphasis on mental health professionals being aware of their own beliefs and values (Atkinson, Morten, & Sue, 1998; Pedersen & Ivey, 1993). In this context, one way that harm can occur is by holding an ethnocentric view toward culturally different clients. For example, if a counselor espouses individuality as a foundation for psychological well-being, Latina/o clients accepting this premise run the risk of creating conflict with and alienation from their families who are generally more allocentric (i.e., group and family oriented) than European American families.

Multicultural Guideline 2 asks that psychologists gain knowledge of other cultures. Psychologists therefore must increase their knowledge of the diverse cultural heritages that inform the lives of their diverse clients. Taken together, Guidelines 1 and 2 inspire mental health professionals to study their own cultural heritages and appreciate how cultural attitudes and values influence every interaction they have with their clients.

As noted above, culturally competent professionals strive to transform their attitudes and beliefs to prevent them from damaging the culturally different consumers of their practice. Multicultural Guideline 3 urges psychology educators and trainers to facilitate this transformation. The next section of this chapter focuses on the development of cultural awareness and self-knowledge in graduate training, through the use of a cultural family genogram.

Finally, Multicultural Guideline 5 implores psychologists, therapists, and counselors to deliver services in culturally appropriate and relevant ways. It synthesizes Guidelines 1 and 2 by requiring practitioners to use their knowledge of themselves and their consumers as cultural beings and to apply this knowledge in their work. The application of this knowledge includes an understanding of the environmental and institutional contexts that harm individuals through exclusion, bias, and discrimination.

GUIDELINE 3: USING THE
CULTURAL FAMILY GENOGRAM TO DEVELOP SELF-AWARENESS

Over a decade ago, Hardy and Laszloffy (1995) complained that training programs in family therapy that included multicultural courses relied too heavily on survey courses that taught students how to treat clients from different cultures rather than to explore their own cultural selves. This strategy of training for multicultural competence has been criticized more recently by other writers (Keiley et al., 2002) as a "cookbook" approach that denies students' affective explorations and experiences necessary for cross-cultural interactions in clinical settings. To address this concern, Hardy and Laszloffy (1995) developed the cultural genogram as a didactic-experiential training tool.

I have used this strategy for many years in training counselors, social workers, psychotherapists, and psychologists to be aware and knowledgeable of their own culture, as well as that of others. A genogram is a map of three or more generations of a family that illustrates relational patterns, demographic data, and the personal history of its members (McGoldrick & Gerson, 1985; McGoldrick, Gerson, & Shellenberger, 1999). It is useful in therapy to illuminate and track patterns and events that influence the psychological functioning of a family. In my class, I use a variation of the genogram, the cultural genogram, to track culturally based values and their transformation as evidenced in the students' articulated cultural organizing principles and pride and shame issues.

What makes the cultural genogram an exciting tool for training psychotherapists to be culturally competent is the assertion that the family is the principal mode by which people learn and develop an understanding about their cultures and ethnicities (McGoldrick, 1982; Preli & Bernard, 1993). By studying the cultural heritages and transitions of their own families, students can discover the origins of their own values, beliefs, and biases. In the classroom setting, the experience of constructing a cultural family genogram is further enhanced by the sharing of genograms with other students and simultaneously learning about others' cultural values and behaviors, as well as their families' adaptations and transformations. This experiential work helps us all learn about general cultural frameworks of different groups, while understanding unique family and community variations (Rigazio-DiGilio et al., 2005).

In my class, I require graduate students to construct a cultural genogram of their own families by interviewing family members about the ethnic and cultural heritages of the family, and then to create a representative genogram comprising the levels of structure, relationships, and culture-specific information (organizing principles and pride and shame issues). After conducting their research, students present their genograms in a "poster session" format, and finally write a synthesis paper on this research, their findings, their experiences, and the value this has on their training as mental health professionals.

Constructing the cultural genogram involves six steps. A student first defines his or her culture(s) of origin by determining the major ethnic group(s) from which he or she has descended. This task generally is accomplished by identifying the earliest known generations of the family. Next the student determines the organizing principles as well as the pride and shame issues for each ethnic group that makes up his or her culture(s) of origin. According to Hardy and Laszloffy (1995), "Organizing principles are fundamental constructs which shape the perceptions, beliefs, and behaviors of members of a group. They are the basic structures upon which all other aspects of a culture are predicated" (p. 229).

For example, a powerful organizing principle of Latina/o cultures is that of *La Familia. Familismo* is a relational orientation toward the family that emphasizes the primacy of the unit over the needs or concerns of any individual family member. Large extended families are a significant source of strength and support for many Latina/os. Pride and shame issues are those specific attitudes and behaviors, related to the organizing principles, that are culturally sanctioned as distinctively negative or positive. Therefore, if *La Familia* is an organizing principle of Latina/o cultures, then a pride issue is having and taking care of a large extended family. Shame issues, on the other hand, such as infidelity, divorce, and neglectful care of family, detract from the organizing principle of *La Familia.*

Another organizing principle of Latina/o cultures is religion. Although there were many pre-Columbian religions practiced in the Americas, since the Spanish conquest Catholicism has been a ubiquitous presence in the lives of many Latina/os (Cervantes & Ramírez, 1992). If the organizing principle is religion, then being an observant follower and counting priests and nuns as members of one's family are examples of pride issues. Failure to observe the tenets of that faith (e.g., violation of commandments, divorce and remarriage without an annulment, blaspheming) is considered shameful.

Engaging in the steps of exploring culture-specific organizing principles and pride and shame issues requires students to use a number of information sources, such as personal knowledge, interviews with family members, and reference materials. I encourage my students to interview the elders in their families using a "cultural interview" we create in class. Examples of cultural interview questions include:

- How do you identify your race, ethnicity, and culture? How do (did) your parents (and children) identify?
- (For non-Native American Indians) How long has your family been in the United States? What was the motivation for immigration? Who was left behind? How were these decisions made? (For American Indians, the questions can be revised to inquire about life on and off a reservation.)
- What is (are) your native language(s)? What language(s) do you speak at home? With your elders? With your children?
- What aspects of your culture are most important to you (e.g., family structures, norms and values, feast days, traditions, faith)? What are those things in your culture that you are most proud of? Are there aspects of your culture that bother you or that you find less attractive? What are they?
- Did (would) you raise your children in the same way that you were raised? Explain. Are (would) your children raising (raise) your grandchildren in the same way? Elaborate.
- To what extent can you follow your culture's way of life here in the United States?

The next step involves creating symbols to represent the identified pride and shame issues. These symbols are then placed on the cultural genogram to visually represent the occurrence of pride and shame issues and to draw attention to their influence on the family's attitudes, values, and beliefs (Hardy & Laszloffy, 1995). Next, colors are assigned to represent the student's primary ethnic group(s). To illustrate, although I identify ethnically as a Latina and culturally as Mexican and Mexican American, in my own cultural family genogram I am five-eighths Mexican or Mexican American (red), one-eighth Italian (green), one-eighth German (blue), and one-eighth Spanish (yellow). Therefore, the circle (women are circles and men are squares in genograms) that identifies me on my genogram is color coded five-eighths red, one-eighth green, one-eighth blue, and one-eighth yellow. My father's square, however, is one-half red, one-fourth yellow, and one-fourth blue, while his father's square is one-half yellow and one-half blue (although his culture was Mexican as he was born, raised, and died in Saltillo, Nuevo Leon, Mexico), and his father's (my paternal great grandfather's) square is yellow. There is a small town in Spain called *Cuidad* (city) *de las Fuentes*, where that line of my family heritage may have originated. Interestingly, only one-eighth of my Mexican heritage is from what is now Mexico (Vallecillo, Nuevo Leon). I have been able to trace the majority of my Mexican heritage (maternal lineage) to the 1600s in what is now Texas.

Intercultural marriages are then identified since they serve as indicators of the hybridization of races, ethnicities, cultures, organizing principles, and pride and shame issues. In addition to identifying these marriages, the student investigates, via interviews with family members, how differing cultural values were negotiated in these marriages and maps out the intergenerational consequences of these marriages. For example, in constructing my own genogram, I learned that intercultural marriages (and unions) in my paternal lineage are likely to end in divorce (seven of eight across three generations), leading me to believe that intercultural differences have not been successfully negotiated. What might this mean for future generations in my family? How will the children of these failed intercultural marriages define themselves? Who will they choose as partners and what will happen to these unions?

The student next creates a legend that provides keys for interpreting the genogram. It lists the major organizing principles and the pride and shame issues with their corresponding symbols, and the culture(s) in question with their corresponding color(s). The final step involves putting it all together in a genogram format, representing at least three generations (the student, parents, and grandparents), on a poster board to present in class.

The class presentation begins with a review of the legend describing the symbols and colors, followed by a detailed discussion of students' culture(s), organizing principles, and pride and shame issues, and of specifically how these are exemplified in their families from the oldest generations to the youngest. This process is the most exciting to the students as they now have an opportunity to discuss their experiences and findings with one another. Some of the findings my students shared with me from their synthesis papers will be peppered throughout this chapter. For example:

> As a result of this project, I learned that I am not only Cuban and Peruvian, but that my paternal grandfather has Hebrew and Spanish heritages and my paternal grandmother has Inca and Arab heritages; and my mother has a grandmother who said her mother was brought here as part of the slave trade!

I now feel my academic as well as my professional experiences are making me [into] an individual that is aware of my own cultural background and experiences, attitudes, values, and biases that may influence psychological processes. I am making efforts in my life to recognize and correct my prejudices and biases. I feel I am learning everyday about myself and will continue to improve my level of self-awareness.

Unlike other psychology classes I teach, the multicultural work this class requires goes beyond theoretical and didactic instruction. In this class we discuss material many students have never known about (e.g., boarding school experiences in American Indian lives), may not care about because they do not yet appreciate the relevance to our work (e.g., cultural beliefs about disease and disability), and may have resistance to engage in (e.g., White students studying "Whiteness as privilege" in U. S. society). As a White (third-generation Anglo American) student wrote: "I never did think of myself as being ethnic, and honestly always felt . . . guilty for the oppression other ethnics have experienced. I think the two are related. Because of the guilt, I would not allow myself the privilege of knowing my own ethnicity."

GUIDELINE 2:
GAINING KNOWLEDGE AND UNDERSTANDING OF LATINA/OS

Since Latina/os come from allocentric cultures, their presenting problems in psychotherapy typically reflect conflicts and concerns about one or more members of their family. Therefore, it behooves psychotherapists to view Latina/os in therapy within the context of *La Familia*, even when they come alone. To facilitate an understanding of the presenting problem, our role as counselors and therapists includes exploring the immigration experience and determining the degree of acculturation of the family, including discrepancies in acculturation among family members (de las Fuentes, 2003).

The Immigration Experience

Exploring the immigration stories of Latina/o families provides psychotherapists with an invaluable opportunity to learn about the country, culture, and people that were left behind, as well as the reasons for leaving (Falicov, 1998). Mental health professionals and their Latina/o clients can then discuss issues about preimmigration experiences, immigration decision making, and changes in how *La Familia* functions as a result of acculturation to the United States. As implied through these explorations, it is important to assess psychological problems that may have predated, originated in, or resulted from this period of cultural transition (Vasquez, Han, & de las Fuentes, 2005). Below is an excerpt from a student's synthesis paper, followed by a client's telling of immigration experiences.

> I didn't know that the reason my father left Mexico is that when [he] renounced Catholicism at the age of 16 his father stripped him of his name and gave him his mother's last name to wear in shame and to avoid any inheritance. . . .

> One day my mother brought all her children together and told us that they were having trouble making the mortgage payment and that we were about to lose our home. She then asked us, "Who would be willing to travel to El Norte to find work and send money home so we wouldn't lose our house?" I was 19 when I left Mexico. . . . I had no intentions of coming to this country and becoming a part of it, but because of the need that my parents had, I left Mexico to never return. My parents were able to keep their home, but I had to create a new one. [translated]

Yearning for their countries and cultures of origin becomes more profound when Latina/os are unable to return because of political turmoil, immigration laws, fear of deportation, and expense (McGoldrick, Giordano, & Pearce, 1996). Many Latina/os experience acute feelings of loss—missing the family, smells, and sights of who and what was left behind and fear they may never be able to see them again. Below a student explained her "immigration grief."

> I was born and raised in Puerto Rico and my family on both sides is Puerto Rican. We moved to Germany when I was 12 because my dad was transferred there. I cried for months! I missed my family, my friends, and the smells and tastes of home. The coldness of winter became a metaphor for how I eventually saw Germans and by extension all White people. My people, my language, my home, was always summer.

Experiences of Acculturation

Because a culture's organizing principles influence and shape an individual's and a family's lifestyles, the choices they make, and the pride and shame they feel as a result, acculturation becomes a critical variable when working with Latina/os in the United States (de las Fuentes, 2003). Acculturation is the transition and blending of values, customs, languages, and behaviors between two or more cultural groups (Atkinson et al., 1998). A student illustrated this concept in her description of whether she was going to have a *quinciñera* (a "coming out" party for a 15-year-old Latina girl that traditionally involves a church ceremony and a formal dance). "I was given the choice of having a quinciñera or a sweet sixteen party. Even though my mother had a quinciñera and she wanted me to have one, too, I chose a sweet sixteen party because we were Americans now. She still made me wear white, though!"

Adaptation to U.S. culture depends on the reasons for immigrating and goals regarding returning to the homeland or remaining, the perceived support received from loved ones, ability to accommodate new beliefs and values while retaining the strengths of the old culture, and cultural similarities between the culture of origin and the new culture. For example, a client of mine emigrated from northern Mexico to San Antonio seeking work, and initially adjusted well here because he had extended family here, found work easily, and did not have to learn English. His son was referred to counseling by his school; he was failing because of too many absences due to extended trips to Mexico to visit his elderly and ailing grandparents. This client often lamented, "Why don't they [the school officials] understand that we have to do this; we have to pay respect to my parents?"

Throughout discussions with Latina/o clients, it is important for mental health professionals to bear in mind that the Latina/o family has strengths and resources they can tap to deal with their acculturative challenges (Garcia-Preto, 1994). We can assist Latina/o clients in negotiating the acculturative process by facilitating understandings of cultural similarities and differences, and of what attitudes, beliefs, and behaviors from each culture they like as well as those they do not like. In therapy, discussions about how their lives have been changed by living in this country will help Latina/os and their families see themselves and their concerns in relation to the "normal family process" of acculturation. As one student described:

> I now know I embody a bicultural way of life. I value my Colombian heritage yet I have adapted to an American lifestyle, the process of which was very difficult for me and my family when I was growing up. . . . Although I have successfully blended the two cultures, I sometimes struggle in maintaining one identity.

Acculturative stress is an affective response to stressors that occur as a result of the process of acculturation. Lack of familiar networks and prejudice and discrimination are some issues that Latina/os experience as contributing to acculturative stress. Families in cultural transition often experience stress and conflict because of the acculturation process. For example, children in school and adults in the work force tend to acculturate more quickly than family members and peers who are not similarly involved. These factors and conditions may lead an individual or family to experience acculturative stress, a "particular set of stress behaviors that occur during acculturation, such as lowered mental health status (especially confusion, anxiety, depression), feelings of marginality and alienation, heightened psychosomatic symptom level, and identity confusion" (Berry, 1990, pp. 246–247). As a student illustrated:

> Because my father worked outside the home, and because we were in school, we acculturated faster than my mom. She was a stay-at-home mother and wife and did not have the same acculturative opportunities that we had. That created some schisms in our relationship that persist today when we disagree about my child-rearing practices, the fact that I do not attend church or make homemade papusas.

Language Competence

According to the 2000 U.S. Census, most Latinos (about 17 million) in the United States do not speak English in the home (U.S. Bureau of the Census, 2001). Knowledge of the Spanish language is indispensable in therapy with many Latina/os, given that cultural issues often are articulated through language (McGoldrick et al, 1996). As I have shared with my students, members of my own family have not had to assimilate to U.S. culture or learn English to succeed in this country. For example, although my maternal grandmother was born in Texas and lived here all her life, she was not fluent in English. She did not have to learn English because she lived in a community that validated and reinforced Spanish, her Mexican culture, and her traditions. Even some of her children, all of whom were born in the United States, are not completely fluent in English. Yet they, too, are raising successful and educated, and now bilingual, children.

Mental health providers who do not communicate in the dominant language of their Latina/o clients cannot possibly deliver competent services because language dissonances cause misinterpretations and barriers to accurate communication and understanding (Altarriba & Santiago-Rivera, 1994). Indeed, the Surgeon General's report on culture and mental health found that "cultural misunderstanding or communication problems between clients and therapists may prevent minority group members from using services and receiving appropriate care" (U.S. Department of Health and Human Services, 2001, p. 42). As a former client of mine complained, "Even though he was nice and tried to talk in Spanish, he didn't understand me. There were times he would be quiet, and I thought, maybe my problems aren't important after all; so I didn't return."

Fundamental to cultural competence, especially in our work with Latina/os, language competence entails "being able to say the right thing at the right time in the right manner" (Cheng, 1996, p. 10). In the delivery of mental health services to Latina/os, extricating language competence from cultural competence is as unfathomable as separating gender from ethnicity. Yet, language fluency is not indicative of cultural competence. Cultural and linguistic competence requires an understanding of the meaning of words, word usage, as well as the meaning of concepts and nonverbal communication (Acevedo, Reyes, Annett, & López, 2003). For example, a therapist must be able to assess a Latina's culturally preferred approach to communication with elders in her family as well as with her White American peers. She may communicate indirectly and with *simpatía* (a strong cultural value that involves being polite, avoiding ill-mannered behavior in all situations, and preventing interpersonal discord) in the context of her family but in more direct and assertive ways with her White American peers.

LA FAMILIA LUNA: A CASE VIGNETTE

The following case study, of the "Luna" family, is a good illustration of how the relevant Multicultural Guidelines, use of the cultural family genogram, and specific knowledge about Latina/os can all come together to effect a transformation in the concerns presented by a Latino family.

> "Sr. Jose" and "Sra. Paula Luna," both age 52, presented in therapy because of concerns about how to raise their only child, a daughter ("Isabella"), age 21. Isabella had always been "sheltered" and raised "close to home and church." She had few friends outside of the extended family, and was working with her father in his small business. The concerns they expressed about Isabella involved the fact that she was "a slow learner" and had not graduated from high school. A copy of the last intellectual and educational testing (when Isabella was in 10th grade) revealed low borderline intellectual functioning. Now that Isabella was 21, she was pressuring her parents to allow her to drive at night, go "clubbing" with friends, and date. Paula was very resistant to those ideas, while Jose was much more open to permitting Isabella these liberties. This caused some alliances and conflicts in the family that they had not experienced previously.
>
> The second session revealed that Jose had immigrated to the United States with his family when he was 12 years old. His father and mother both worked outside the home, and Jose and his older sister attended private Catholic schools through graduation. Neither attended college. Paula was a third-generation San Antonioian and had a fairly traditional upbringing in that her mother stayed at home and raised two sons and two daughters. Paula attended a local Catholic university, earned a bachelor's degree in education, and became an elementary school teacher. She was the first college-educated person in her family.

Jose and Paula met through some friends, fell in love, and married within a year of meeting each other at the age of 23. After many years of infertility, the couple decided to adopt a child who became available through friends from their church. In a meeting with the birth mother, Paula and she decided that the birth mother would register in the hospital under Paula's name and social security number. The day after Isabella was born, the birth mother and Paula met in the hospital parking lot and the newborn was relinquished.

Although Isabella was slower than average in reaching her developmental milestones, she was the joy of Jose and Paula's lives. She was described as being a "good" baby and an "easy" child to rear. The only thing remarkable about Isabella's childhood was that, although she tried very hard in school, she was held back in 1st grade, and again in 7th grade, and did not complete high school. Her primary friends were cousins and other extended-family members.

Believing the nature of their concerns was connected to their families of origin and cultural values, I introduced the idea of creating a cultural family genogram as a tool to help us better understand their situation. Interestingly, Paula had already done some genealogical work on their families a few years earlier and had even constructed pedigree genograms (paternal and maternal lineages with birth and death dates) of both sides of the family. I asked her to bring a copy of them to the third session.

With copies of the genograms in hand, we set our focus first on illuminating patterns of relationships in the families and then on organizing principles and pride and shame issues. Together we learned that Jose had an especially close relationship with his mother, while his sister had an especially close relationship with their father. We also learned that Paula's brothers had especially close relationships with their mother, while she and her sister were equally close to both of their parents. We created symbols to illustrate these relationships, and then used those symbols on their nuclear family with Isabella. This visual imagery generated rich discussions about how Paula sometimes had felt excluded from the attention and affection her mother gave her brothers and how she sometimes felt similarly with Jose and Isabella. Jose reflected that he was "permissive" with Isabella, because that was a pattern he was raised with in his family. He witnessed his father's permissiveness with his sister (*"la princesa"*), while his mother was more strict with him. After learning where the "alliance" pattern originated, we next turned our attention to why it was occurring at this point in time and in these circumstances.

We spent the next couple of sessions discussing organizing principles and pride and shame issues. There was remarkable concurrence in both of their genograms with regard to these constructs. What was fascinating to learn, however, was *how* these organizing principles (family, religion, and feast days where family, religion, and food were all celebrated) were exemplified. Jose believed that the ultimate role for a woman was to be a wife and a mother; Paula concurred, believing that her ultimate role was to nurture and protect her daughter, herself, and her husband. However, Jose worried that if he and Paula continued to be "overprotective" of Isabella, *"jamás se haría mujer"* ("she would never become a woman"). Paula, on the other hand, was petrified about what could happen to her daughter if she was permitted to "go clubbing," drive at night, or date. While Jose admitted these were also fears of his, he was more afraid of his daughter never realizing her role as a mother and wife. Then, at one point he tearfully asked, *"Quien la cuidara cuando nos muérenos nosotros si no un esposo o hijos?"* ("Who would take care of her when we die if not her husband or children?") His ultimate role was as a provider and protector. He could not envision doing that adequately for Isabella after his death if she remained unmarried. He did not want to fail in his role of taking care of Isabella either.

Over the next few sessions, we spent our time focusing on the dual issues of negotiating ways to permit Isabella to have successive trials of increasing liberty within parameters set by her parents (e.g., going "clubbing" with cousins and church friends, abstaining from alcohol, calling at the top of every hour), while consulting with financial planners and lawyers so that they could leave an estate and a trust for their daughter upon their death (something neither side of their families had ever done).

My work with the Luna family was unremarkable in that any trained therapist could have worked with them, performed a genogram with them, and negotiated the parents' fears and their daughter's desire for more independence. What made my work with them successful was the culturally and linguistically congruent service I provided while using techniques any trained therapist can employ. Guideline 5 implores psychologists, therapists, and counselors to deliver services in culturally appropriate and relevant ways. Would Jose have disclosed his fears in Spanish if he knew I was not fluent in his preferred language? Would he have disclosed at all? If I were more Eurocentric in my approach and believed in separation and individuation of adult children, would I have treated this family as if they were pathologically enmeshed?

SUMMARY

Although the areas reviewed above are certainly not exhaustive, I have focused on them as a way of presenting (1) a strategy, as in the case of the cultural genogram, to operationalize Guidelines 1 and 3; and (2) illustrations of acculturation, acculturative stress, and cultural and language competencies that I believe are particularly important in the competent delivery of mental health services to Latina/os, making Guidelines 2 and 5 come alive. I have endeavored to convey a strong belief that competent delivery of mental health services with Latina/os begins with the therapist's studied introspection of the self, as well as gaining culture-specific knowledge and skills. Therefore, mental health providers not only must know their cultural selves, but also must evaluate their theories, assumptions, and practices and enhance their own clinical skills to incorporate multicultural awareness and culturally resonant interventions to accommodate the ethnic, linguistic, and cultural perspectives of Latina/os.

NOTE

1. In describing people whose cultures of origin include countries of Latin America, I prefer to use the more pan-ethnic and geographically situated term Latina/o.

REFERENCES

Acevedo, M. C., Reyes, C. J., Annett, R. D., & López, E. M. (2003). Assessing language competence: Guidelines for assessing persons with limited English proficiency in research and clinical settings. *Journal of Multicultural Counseling and Development, 31,* 192–204.

Altarriba, J., & Santiago-Rivera, A. L. (1994). Current perspectives on using linguistic and cultural factors in counseling the Hispanic client. *Professional Psychology: Research & Practice, 25,* 388–397.

American Psychological Association. (2003). Guidelines on multicultural education, training, research, practice, and organizational change for psychologists. *American Psychologist, 58,* 377–402.

Asians in Latin America: A guide to resources (n.d.). Retrieved May 22, 2005, from http://lacic. fiu.edu/library/fi

Atkinson, D. R., Morten, G., & Sue, D. W. (Eds.). (1998). *Counseling American minorities* (5th ed.). Boston: McGraw-Hill.

Berry, J. W. (1990). Psychology of acculturation: Understanding individuals moving between cultures. In R. W. Brislin (Ed.), *Applied cross-cultural psychology* (pp. 232–253). Newbury Park, CA: Sage.

Cervantes, J. M., & Ramirez, O. (1992). Spirituality and family dynamics in psychotherapy with Latino children. In L. Vargas & J. Koss-Chioino (Eds.), *Working with culture: Psychotherapeutic interventions with ethnic minority children and adolescents* (pp. 103–128). San Francisco: Jossey-Bass.

Cheng, L. L. (1996). Beyond bilingualism: A quest for communicative competence. *Topics in Language Disorders, 16,* 9–21.

Chinatowns in Latin America. (n.d.). Retrieved May 26, 2005, from http://www.answers. com/topic/chinatowns-in-latin-america

de las Fuentes, C. (2003). Latino mental health: At least you should know this. In J. S. Mio & G. Y. Iwamasa (Eds.), *Culturally diverse mental health: The challenges of research and resistance* (pp. 159–172). New York: Brunner-Routledge.

Falicov, C. J. (1998). *Latino families in therapy: A guide to multicultural practice.* New York: Guilford Press.

Garcia-Preto, N. (1994). On the bridge. *Family Therapy Networker, 18,* 35–37.

Hardy, K. V., & Laszloffy, T. A. (1995). The cultural genogram: Key to training culturally competent family therapists. *Journal of Marital and Family Therapy, 21,* 227–237.

Keiley, M. K., Dolbin, M., Hill, J., Karuppaswamy, N., Liu, T., Natrajan, R., Poulsen, S., Robbins, N., & Robinson, P. (2002). The cultural genogram: Experiences from within a marriage and family therapy training program. *Journal of Marital and Family Therapy, 28,* 165–178.

McGoldrick, M. (1982). Ethnicity and family therapy: An overview. In M. McGoldrick, J. K. Pearce, & J. Giordano (Eds.), *Ethnicity and family therapy* (pp. 3–30). New York: Guilford Press.

McGoldrick, M., & Gerson, R. (1985). *Genograms in family assessment.* New York: Norton.

McGoldrick, M., Gerson, R., & Shellenberger, S. (1999). *Genograms: Assessment and intervention* (2nd ed.). New York: Norton.

McGoldrick, M., Giordano, J., & Pearce, J. K. (Eds.). (1996). *Ethnicity and family therapy* (2nd ed.). New York: Guilford Press.

Pedersen, P. B., & Ivey, A. (1993). *Culture-centered counseling and interviewing skills.* Westport, CT: Praeger.

Preli, R., & Bernard, J. M. (1993). Making multiculturalism relevant for majority culture graduate students. *Journal of Marital and Family Therapy, 19,* 5–16.

Rigazio-DiGilio, S. A., Ivey, A. E., Kunkler-Peck, K. P., & Grady, L. T. (2005). *Community genograms: Using individual, family, and cultural narratives with clients.* New York: Teachers College Press.

Rumbaut, R. G. (1994). The crucible within: Ethnic identity, self-esteem, and segmented assimilation among children of immigrants. *International Migration Review, 28,* 748–794.

U.S. Bureau of the Census. (2001). *Overview of race and Hispanic origin: Census 2000 brief.* Retrieved August 16, 2006, from http://www.census.gov/prod/2001pubs/c2kbr01-1.pdf

U.S. Department of Health and Human Services. (2001). *Mental health: Culture, race and ethnicity–A supplement to Mental health: A report of the Surgeon General.* Rockville, MD: U. S. Department of Health and Human Services, Public Health Office, Office of the Surgeon General.

Vasquez, M. J. T., Han, A .L., & de las Fuentes, C. (2005). Adaptation of immigrant girls and women. In C. Goodheart & J. Worell (Eds.), *Handbook of girls' and women's psychological health* (pp. 439–446). Oxford: Oxford University Press.

Zavala, A. E. (1999). *Anuario Hispano–Hispanic Yearbook.* McLean, VA: TYIM Publishing.

5

American Indians
and Alaskan Native Populations

John J. Peregoy
and Alberta M. Gloria

The treatment of American Indian/Alaskan Native peoples by Whites throughout history (beginning with Columbus) is codified in and riddled with inaccuracy and falsehoods. Propagating continued oppressions, this history is taught as fact to children throughout their educational tenures, particularly in middle and high school, and well into postsecondary education. It is within this distorted historical perspective and disruptions of social systems and life patterns (LaFromboise, Heyle, & Ozer, 1999) that many people view American Indians and Alaskan Natives. For example, common stereotypes include seeing Indians/Natives as solely belonging in the past, depicting them as noble savages (as per popular movies), or connecting them to reservations. History and educational books have failed to address how Indian/Native people have been systematically abused as individuals–removed from their homelands, children torn from their parents and culture and relocated, and men and women sterilized without their consent into the late 1970s (Vernon, 2002). Atrocities continue today and are evident in the U.S. Department of the Interior. This federal agency has lost trillions of dollars that had been held in trust for Indians/Natives because they were deemed incompetent to manage the monies earned from the sale of natural resources, or from lands leased to farmers and ranchers. Such abuse continues as Department of the Interior administrators are held in contempt repeatedly for refusing to be present in court despite multiple subpoenas (Indian Trust, 2005).

Given long-standing legal and political conditions within the United States, Indians/Natives have a distinguished history and unique delineation from other ethnic groups, particularly as they are the only group in the United States that has been legally defined and has legal relationships and obligations based in treaty and law (Trimble, Fleming, Beauvais, & Jumper-Thurman, 1996). From historical and cultural genocide to ongoing present-day assaults and attempts by U.S. society to usurp and erase indigenous culture (Juntunen & Morin, 2004), Indians/Natives have exhibited incredible strength to survive and, in many cases, thrive. Prior to European contact, the Indian/Native population was estimated to include between 5 and 40 million indigenous inhabitants in the contiguous North and South Americas (Peregoy, 1991). However, by the 19th century, the indigenous population had declined to approximately 250,000 (Gone, 2004) after entire tribes and bands were intentionally and systematically eradicated. Currently, a total of 2.5 million people in the United States, or .9% of the population, report being Indian/Native, and an additional 1.6 million report a multiracial identity of Indian/Native and at least one other race (Ogunwole, 2002). Important to note is that governmental estimates of Indians/Natives are often lower than those identified by Indian/Native researchers. Currently, 67% of all Indians/Natives live off the reservation (Peregoy, 2004), residing in towns and cities where employment, housing, and educational opportunities are more abundant (Gone, 2004).

In the 21st century, the needs of Indians/Natives for mental health services continue to be disregarded despite legislation and calls to the profession to be more systematic in providing culturally integrative and effective services (Gone, 2004; Peregoy, 1999). Recognizing the vast heterogeneity of individuals, tribes, and communities, we nonetheless intend this chapter to provide a primer for mental health professionals who have had little contact with Indians/Natives. In doing so, we provide concrete and practical recommendations about service delivery to Indians/Natives. Specifically, the Multicultural Guidelines as set forth by the American Psychological Association (APA, 2003) are addressed relative to awareness and knowledge of and skills for working with American Indians and Alaskan Natives. Next, salient empirical and conceptual areas relevant to Indians/Natives are briefly presented. For each area, four questions for reflection are provided. Case vignettes also are included that elucidate various needs and concerns, while integrating suggested strategies for use by mental health professionals. The online resources listed at the end of the chapter can be consulted for additional information. It is important that the reader continuously be mindful that this chapter is a starting point and that no "recipe" or singular approach exists for working with Indians/Natives. Each tribe varies in culture, language, spirituality, level of acculturation, and commitment to their Indian/Native heritage and subsequent identity.

KEY ELEMENTS OF THE MULTICULTURAL GUIDELINES

It is commonly accepted that multicultural counselor-training models employ the tripartite framework of cultural competence: beliefs and awareness, knowledge, and skills (Sue, Arredondo, & McDavis, 1992). It is from within the tripartite framework that the Guidelines are presented specific to Indian/Native populations.

Guideline 1: Personal Awareness

Each community possesses unique values, preferred communication styles, and spiritual orientations that can support psychological and spiritual healing. When stepping into a community, individuals bring with them their own psychological mindedness (i.e., professional assumptions) and personal biases and stereotypes. These biases and assumptions are directly influenced by media and exposure to a history that glosses over the issues affecting Indian/Native peoples both in the past and the present. Quite often, self-discovery challenges the biases and stereotypes we harbor, requiring us to change how we view and interact in the world. This notion encompasses Guideline 1.

Guideline 2: Content Knowledge

The life-long journey toward competence requires learning content knowledge (e.g., sociopolitical history) and current issues, as well as the interplay between the two (Guideline 2). The importance of multicultural sensitivity and responsiveness in building knowledge and understanding of Indians/Natives goes beyond experiencing an occasional Pow Wow, Indian/Native-focused movie (e.g., *Smoke Signals*), or classroom activity. Although such activities are relevant, acquiring content knowledge also involves becoming known in the community by attending social functions and seeking out community members who can assist in the learning process.

With more than 562 federal and state recognized tribal governments, the terms "American Indian" or "Native American" aggregate the vast differences in traditions represented by hundreds of tribal nations (Garrett, 2006). Considered "generalized gloss," the terms are imposed ethnic categories that have no singular meaning or definition (Trimble et al., 1996).

Guideline 3: Education

Closely related to the learning process is Guideline 3, which directs educators to employ the constructs of multiculturalism and diversity in psychological training. Skillful teaching about Indian/Native populations requires more than having knowledge of these groups and the ability to approach teaching from multiple learning perspectives. That is, teaching about multiculturalism is insufficient; instead, teaching from a multicultural perspective about multicultural issues is warranted (Roberts et al., 1994). Challenging students to honestly identify their biases and assumptions about Indians/Natives and to unlearn, and subsequently relearn, about them is central to this Guideline. With few exceptions, it is likely that non-Indians/Natives will teach students about Indians/Natives in graduate training programs, forming the basis from which clinical services will be provided. As such, it is imperative that learning about Indian/Native culture be based on addressing and integrating core issues and values of this population.

Guideline 4: Research

Similar to teaching, development of research procedures and methods of study requires specific skills when working with Indians/Natives (Guideline 4). Many Indian/Native communities have been subjected to research investigation without perceived benefits. This exploitation results in a healthy cultural mistrust by Indians/Natives toward researchers. Tribal councils and Indian/Native communities are legitimately wary of "drive-by research." To circumvent inappropriate research with Indian/Native communities, the Society of Indian Psychologists (SIP), in 1997, unanimously endorsed a model for conducting culturally appropriate research in Indian country. This model later was published by the Council of National Associations for the Advancement of Ethnic Minority Issues (McDonald, 2002). SIP's directed guidelines can be tied specifically to curriculum (academic coursework) and teaching approaches (Guideline 3). For example, the SIP's guidelines advise researchers to work collaboratively with the tribe to gain entry and support or, when communities do not have a formal political structure, to identify key stakeholders and engage them in collateral research that will benefit the community or tribe (see LaFromboise, 1999; Peregoy, 1999, 2005; Trimble et al., 1996).

Guideline 5: Counseling

Within the counseling setting, it takes both practice and skill to develop appropriate interventions that are grounded in cultural values and worldviews (Guideline 5). Although there is great variability in values and in adherence and ultimate commitment to one's Indian/Native heritage, there are common, or pan-Indian, values and approaches to living in the world (Peregoy, 1999). As a result, the integration of values, beliefs, and traditions are core aspects to ensure effective and appropriate services. Currently, there are several culturally integrated counseling approaches that have been identified in the literature specifically for Indian/Native individuals. For example, Thomason (1991) provided initial considerations for non-Native counselors, with particular attention on the initial interview. Further, Herring (1992) proposed a new paradigm for non-Native counselors that emphasizes heterogeneity and specific values of Indians/Natives, and Juntunen and Morin (2004) recommended advocacy counseling to address community empowerment efforts. Specific counseling approaches also have been proposed for Indians/Natives with disabilities, two-spirited Indians/Natives, Indian/Native adolescents in educational settings, and those with substance-abuse concerns (Hawkins, Cummins, & Marlatt, 2004; Herring, 1996).

Guideline 6: Culturally Informed Practice and Social Justice

Finally, addressing organizational and larger societal structure for Indians/Natives requires a skill not that often is not taught in the classroom and necessitates personal and professional commitment to social justice advocacy (Guideline 6).

Entering into an Indian/Native community at its request, or requesting entry and having it approved, is an awesome responsibility. When referring to Tribal people on reservations today, there is a strong overlap between Tribal members, the community, and the Tribal government. Connecting the circles is a function of bringing systems together. Systems theory is a conceptual tool (theoretical guide) for entering into the community, ideally at the side of a cultural guide (a key stakeholder who serves as a cultural broker to the researcher/consultant). The navigation process begins with key stakeholders, followed by tribal bands or clans, Chapter Houses or Districts, and then representative tribal leaders (both formal and informal), resulting in a resolution of support for research by the Chapter House and/or Tribal Council/Government.

An example of this process is the *Five Drums Healthy Family Project* (a pseudonym applied for anonymity) on a reservation in the northwest, a project born out of a summer youth program. The principal investigator (a non-Indian/Native) saw a need for family strengthening and developed the concept through discourse and consultation with many tribal members and other key stakeholders. Prayed over in many Sweat Lodge and Pipe Ceremonies, the concept and subsequent program design were submitted to the Tribal Council and received approval. Funded by the Center for Substance Abuse Prevention, the grant ran successfully for 3 years, serving a number of Indian families. Before federal funding came to an end, the Tribal Council saw the need for and benefit of the project to the tribes and funded the program on a hard-budget line.

INDIAN/NATIVE IDENTITY AND SELECTED MENTAL HEALTH ISSUES

In preparing oneself to provide services for Indian/Native individuals and communities, there are several caveats that warrant consideration. In all likelihood the Indian/Native client will be away from his or her tribal provider of behavioral health services and likely will not have had experience with counseling. It will be necessary to provide the client with information about counseling expectations and relationship parameters. Indians/Natives may hold negative assumptions about counseling (Lokken & Twohey, 2004) or question or mistrust the counselor's sensitivities and abilities to appropriately and effectively respond to their culturally based needs and issues (Johnson & Cameron, 2001). Rurality, or the sociocultural impact of geographic isolation, also considerably affects Indians/Natives' access to mental health services.

Review of the literature on Indians/Natives reveals both a scope and breadth of issues, many of which are intertwined. Despite a growing literature base, it is evident that Indians/Natives are an understudied and underserved population. As there are countless areas of study and writing on Indians/Natives, the subsequent discussion of salient mental health concerns is not intended to be comprehensive. Instead, the areas of focus are proposed as entrée into the current literature that is likely to be referenced when working with Indians/Natives. For each of the areas, a brief review of the findings is presented, followed by four sample questions or areas of inquiry that service providers can consider to begin a thoughtful and intentional dialogue with their Indian/Native clients. For each set, the first three questions can be used with clients, and the last is designed for a counselor's own self-assessment.

Identity and Bicultural Identity

A salient area of investigation for Indians/Natives is identity, particularly for adolescents. Because they continually are given inconsistent messages about who they are from larger society, positive identity formation is a complex challenge (Trimble, 2000). The process of identity development for Indian youth has been identified as fraught with systematic struggles, yet also psychologically imperative (Newman, 2005). For example, research supports the concept that a positive view of one's identity and a strong commitment to one or more Indian/Native cultural groups serve to facilitate positive outcomes (e.g., academic achievement and persistence) and protect against negative outcomes (e.g., substance abuse and suicide) (LaFromboise & Howard-Pitney, 1995). The need to develop a strong identity or bicultural competence is critical for Indians/Natives, since they have to interact with non-Indians/Natives and their sociocultural values on a daily basis (Moran, Fleming, Somervell, & Mason, 1999), referred to as "walking in two worlds."

Although the need for bicultural ethnic identity is clear for Indians/Natives, the process of measurement is complicated due to the large number of tribes, languages, and intertribal and interracial marriages (Moran et al., 1999). Despite difficulties, critical strides in the development of ways through which to assess Indian/Native identity have emerged (see LaFromboise,

1999; Moran et al., 1999). Some questions mental health providers can consider with regard to identity are:

- What does it mean to you to be a member of your tribe?
- What does it mean to you to live or walk in two worlds?
- How have you been successful in the past in dealing with identity issues?

- As a counselor, how can I explore and become more aware of my own identity issues in order to help others with theirs?

Acculturation, Worldview, and Cultural Values

A closely related area is level of adherence to cultural values, acculturation, and specific values upheld for Indians/Natives. As a function of cultural genocide, numerous attempts have been instigated to strip Indians/Natives of their cultural values and spiritual beliefs (Tafoya & Del Vecchio, 1996). Yet, strong cultural value connections have been identified and remain across different disciplines as central aspects of Indian/Native daily life. For example, the Circles of Life energy surround, exist within, and make up the many relationships of existence. Each individual has a Circle comprising (1) elements of the self (e.g., mind, body, spirit, and surroundings); (2) family (e.g., immediate, extended, tribal, community, and nation); (3) relations with nature; and (4) universal surroundings. All life exists in an intricate system of interdependence (i.e., the universe exists in a dynamic state of harmony and balance) where the cycling of energy emanates from each life form into every other living being (Garrett & Carroll, 2000).

Within the inner Circle, the four components of spirit, natural environment, body, and mind represent "Medicine," or the essence of life. Being in balance is being in step with the sacred rhythms or harmony of the universe, also known as "Good Medicine." In contrast, being out of balance represents energies that are unfocused, when one loses sight of one's place in the universe, resulting in disharmony. To maintain harmony and balance of the individual, family, clan, and community, spiritual practices are central to every aspect of daily life. In effect, wellness through spirituality is life (Garrett & Carroll, 2000).

Connection and interdependence to family is at the core of balance and harmony. The greatest loss that an Indian/Native can have is the loss of family and community connection. Multigenerational disruption and disconnection from family (through physical and emotional means) consistently is identified as a source of conflict and stress for many Indians/Natives (Tafoya & Del Vecchio, 1996). Strong familial and tribal connections serve to maintain cultural "rootedness" in addition to sustaining ego strength (Trimble et al., 1996) and ultimately a sense of harmony. Relevant questions for service providers to consider include:

- How are you able to maintain familial and community connections?
- Where do you find your support here (while away from home)?
- What activities have you been able to bring with you from home (e.g., smudging)?

- As a counselor, how can I begin to understand the deep-rootedness of family and community for Indians/Natives?

Academic Nonpersistence and Dropout

One of the arenas in which disconnection of values is salient is U.S. educational settings (Herring, 1998; Tafoya & Del Vecchio, 1996). Although there is wide variability in the educational attainment of Indians/Natives by tribe, as a whole they tend to be the least well-educated ethnic group in the United States. High school dropout rates have been cited as high as 50% (Bellcourt, 2004) to 90% on some reservations (Campbell, Herbert, & Peregoy, 1999). Different tribes range in educational level completion rates: for high school from 29% (Miccosukee tribe) to almost 95% (Coos tribe); and for college less than 1% (Cupeno, Salinan, and Serrano tribes) to 32% (Chehalis tribe). Completion rates are attributable to resource availability and differing values and emphasis on formalized education (Pavel et al., 1998). The government historically has used education to "civilize" young Indians/Natives, where children as young as 4 and 5 years of age were taken from their homes and communities for a minimum of 8 continuous years and forced to attend government-supported and church-run boarding schools (Garrett & Pichette, 2000). Current-day mistreatments and lack of competence of teachers for working with Indians/Natives within the educational system remain a salient aspect of their education (Campbell et al., 1999).

The values of educational settings continue to be incongruent or in conflict with Indian/Native values (Gloria & Robinson-Kurpius, 2001), particularly for those tied more closely to their tribal communities (Garrod & Larimore, 1997). Many Indians/Natives consider emotional, physical, intellectual, and spiritual identities as integrated; however, in educational settings, only students' academic and social aspects (which are typically separate) are addressed (Montgomery et al., 2000). Educational research has shown that the integration of cultural values or traditional Indian/Native ways into all aspects of the educational experience is critical to academic progress (Montgomery et al., 2000) and academic persistence (Gloria &

Robinson-Kurpius, 2001), salient aspects driving the success of the 34 tribal colleges. Knowledge of educational challenges and barriers, and subsequent coping and navigation skills, is particularly important as increasing high school graduation rates suggest that an increasing number of Indians/Natives will be eligible for college enrollment (Pavel et al., 1998). Helpful questions to consider include:

- How have you been successful in balancing school with family and participating in ceremonies?
- Where and how often are you able to engage in your cultural and spiritual traditions?
- Is there an Indian/Native student organization on campus? Are you active in the organization? Are there any other students or faculty you hang with?

- As a counselor, how can I get into the Indian/Native student community to become a known and trusted person?

Substance Use

The issue of substance use for Indians/Natives is a critical mental health concern. However, this issue often is overgeneralized in reports that dismiss use differences that exist by gender and age within different tribes (Herring, 2004). Individual, community, and societal factors have been implicated as rationales for substance abuse, with more than 40 different theories for alcohol problems among Indians/Natives (Thomason, 2000). With no single explanation for substance use/abuse, economic (e.g., un- and underemployment, socioeconomic status), geographic (living on or off a reservation), cultural (e.g., acculturative stress, values conflict), physical (e.g., mortality rates, poor health, chronic disability), deculturative stress, and community aspects (e.g., disintegration of tribes) contribute to the complexity of risk factors for Indians/Natives (Gloria & Peregoy, 1996). Similarly, it has been suggested that drug use/abuse within Indian/Native communities has arisen, in part, as a coping mechanism (e.g., numbing of pain) needed to contend with the anger and anguish of cultural loss (Okamoto, Hurdle, & Marsiglia, 2001) and historical antecedents (Taylor, 2000).

Central to understanding substance use is the context of the particular community. For example, alcohol is often a drug of choice among Indians/Natives, particularly youth. Recent data of the Substance Abuse and Mental Health Services Administration (SAMSHA, 2002) show that for Indians/Natives 12 years of age and older, the percentage of "current drinkers" was much lower than for Whites or other groups. Also, binge drinking among

12–17-year-olds was highest for Indians/Natives (12.8% vs. 11.9% for Whites and 11% for Blacks).

"Heavy alcohol use" (defined as binge drinking 5 times a month or more) has declined significantly among Indian/Native youth, to about half as much as a decade ago. After age 26, however, the rate of heavy alcohol use is highest among Indians/Natives (7.4%), and is increasing, while most other groups' heavy-use rates are stable or declining (SAMSHA, 2002). Some studies indicate a decrease in alcohol consumption over an individual's lifetime. One study showed an inverse relationship of use and age, with Indian/Native use declining with age and White consumption increasing (Barker & Krammer, 1996). Substance abuse, and in particular alcohol use/abuse, takes a toll on Indian Country (Peregoy, 2005). Questions to consider with regard to substance use include:

- How does the community you grew up in view alcohol use?
- What activities have you participated in when drinking and not drinking?
- Can you help me understand how drinking has played a role in your family, from your great grandparents to you?

- As the counselor, do I differentiate between recreational drinking (e.g., adolescent binge drinking) and drinking in response to grief? How can I begin to understand the subtle differences between the two?

Health and Physical Concerns

Substance abuse cannot be separated from health concerns. Of the 10 leading causes of death identified in *Healthy People 2010* (National Center for Health Statistics, 2000), the six major causes of early death among Indians/Natives are accidents, cirrhosis of the liver, homicide, suicide, pneumonia, and diabetes complications. In fact, five of the six leading causes of death are intricately intertwined with alcohol use/abuse (Indian Health Service, 1997).

Specific areas of growing concern are the increasing prevalence of HIV and AIDS, intimate-partner violence, and physical violence among Indians/Natives. Although less than 1% of the Indian/Native population is reported to have HIV/AIDS, many speculate that the current count is a low estimate due to a lack of reporting or misreporting. Indians/Natives are considered at risk for acquiring HIV/AIDS due to risky alcohol behaviors in combination with economic, biological (e.g., poor health or diet), and social factors, with Indian/Native women having a slightly higher incidence and death rate than their male counterparts (Vernon, 2002). The legacy of distrust of the medical field (e.g., because of forced sterilization) contributes to the avoidance of medical diagnosis and treatment (Vernon, 2002).

For Indian/Native women in particular, the issue of intimate-partner violence is prominent. Defined as physical, sexual, or psychological harm from a current or past partner or spouse (regardless of partner/spouse gender), intimate-partner violence varies in frequency and severity, and is related to immediate and long-term health, social, economic, and psychological consequences. Although little empirical research has been conducted on intimate-partner violence within Indian/Native communities (Robin, Chester, & Rasmussen, 1998), prevalence data indicate that Indian/Native women encounter more intimate-partner violence than all other groups (Perry, 2004). In particular, Indian/Native women are identified as being at greater risk for violence than non-Indian/Native women; Indian/Native women are almost three times more likely to be killed by an intimate partner than Hispanics and Whites, and have twice the incidence rate of rape (Oetzel & Duran, 2004). Because intimate-partner violence often is portrayed as an individual concern, rather than a community or tribal issue, underestimated reporting and delineated risk factors remain unclear.

Finally, Indians/Natives experience per capita rates of violence twice those of other U.S. groups, with rates of violence higher in every age group. In particular, nearly a third of all victims of violence are between the ages of 18 and 24, and more than half are between 12 and 24. Also, Indians/Natives who live in urban areas are more likely to be victims of crime (Perry, 2004). Questions for service providers to consider include:

- In your lifetime, what types of violence have you experienced?
- Who in your family experienced direct or personal violence?
- Can you tell me about the last time you felt unsafe or threatened?

- Given the heightened exposure to violence (cultural, emotional, and physical) against Indians/Natives, as the counselor how do I begin to understand it rather than be appalled by it?

Suicide

Thought to be a result of multiple factors, including (but not limited to) substance abuse, poverty, a history of physical or sexual abuse, alienation from family or community, multigenerational disruption, violence, stress, and cultural loss and shame (Grossman, Milligan, & Deyo, 1991; Tafoya & Del Vecchio, 1996; Taylor, 2000), suicide is a mental health concern that is affected by sociohistorical and sociopsychological factors (Herring, 2004). Although the majority of Indians/Natives live off the reservation, suicide research overwhelmingly focuses on the behavior of those living on the reservation (Freedenthal & Stiffman, 2004). Although many reservations and tribal areas have a disproportionate number of risk factors for suicide (Frantz, 1999), proximity to cultural and tribal life consistently is acknowledged as helpful in the development of a strong and positive sense of self as an Indian/Native individual.

Sadly, cluster suicides (a phenomenon in which an initial suicide occurs and is followed by several other suicides within a finite time) are at epidemic proportions in Indian Country. Suicide is estimated to be 3 to 9 times greater for Indian/Native children and adolescents (aged 12–24) than for their peers in other groups, and overall suicide attempts are 250–350% greater than in the general population (Melmer, 2005). Evidencing this tragedy, 10 children and young adults committed suicide on the Standing Rock reservation (population estimated at 10,000) in the Dakotas in 2004 (Melmer, 2005). The "issue" of cluster suicide has been glossed over by the media and met by the federal government with inaction, representing another layer of oppression and adding to the government's belief that Indians/Natives are a disposable population. One can only wonder, if these acts of despair had happened in midtown Manhattan or Bellaire, California, would similar inaction occur? Questions for mental health professionals to consider with regard to suicide include:

- Has anyone close to you attempted or committed suicide?
- Are there any situations in which you have considered or would consider suicide?
- Who can you see right now that will stand by you and support you through this challenging time?

- As the counselor, how can I begin to understand the hopelessness and despair felt by Indians/Natives who experience suicide (directly or indirectly), while engendering genuine hope and empowerment?

Post Traumatic Stress Disorder

Post traumatic stress disorder (PTSD) is a common experience and diagnosis among Indians/Natives who have to contend with multiple events that have been devastating to them, their family, and their community. In addition to systematic cultural extermination (e.g., Trail of Tears, Wounded Knee Massacre) and the stripping of value and identity (e.g., boarding schools), Peregoy (1999) identified historical individual violence against Indians/Natives who were assigned to act in point patrol positions during wartime. In those positions, Indians/Natives endured tremendous stress as they were exposed to snipers, landmines, and other first-contact threats.

PTSD also occurs through direct and indirect witnessing or hearing about potentially life-threatening or violent acts or accidents and historical trauma (Duran, Duran, & Braveheart, 1998). For example, historical trauma is the passing of trauma from one generation to the next through stories and experiences. Community stories and family remembrances, which often are told in the oral tradition, lend to the continuation of trauma. Finally, more contemporary traumas include (but are not limited to) substance abuse (e.g., alcohol-related accidents, loss of individuals due to alcohol-related health issues), personal violations (e.g., rape, violence, suicide, sterilization without consent), and community abuses (e.g., co-opting of culture, exploitation through research, miseducation of students). All of these abuses have ongoing impacts on the mental health and well-being of Indian/Native individuals, families, and communities. Helpful questions with regard to PTSD include:

- How do you spend your time when your sleep is interrupted?
- How have the stories that you have been told affected your thinking?
- What kinds of traumas have you experienced?

- As the counselor, how can I begin to understand the array of events and influences that affect PTSD among Indians/Natives?

CASE VIGNETTES

The following vignettes are provided as starting points from which to consider issues and needs of Indians/Natives with whom counselors might work. Although the vignettes are integrated composites of individuals with whom we have worked, they are not intended to propagate stereotypes, but rather to offer a primer for practicing the specific skill development needed to provide appropriate and effective services.

Adolescent in Trouble: The Case of David

David, a 13-year-old Diné (Navajo) adolescent, lives in a large urban city in Arizona and attends a combined middle and high school. He lives part-time with his aunt and part-time with his second cousin. They live three city blocks from one another and within walking distance to his school. Having been continually tardy, disruptive, and truant from classes (he showed up to class drunk on several occasions), David is mandated to work with the school counselor as part of a school-developed truancy remediation program (4 weeks of individual counseling). David and his aunt are informed that this remediation program is his last opportunity to remain in school before he is suspended for a month. Several months ago, there were school suspicions that David recently attempted suicide (but was unsuccessful after having been found by his aunt) after his 14-year-old first cousin (his closest friend) killed himself. School officials, however, were unable to verify the attempt and believed that the best intervention would be to have him meet with the school counselor since his truancy and acting out had steadily increased.

Perhaps one of the greatest differentiations that David's school counselor will need to make is separating the source of his concerns from the symptoms or behaviors that he manifests (e.g., truancy, acting out, use of alcohol). The most critical aspect of the counseling relationship is the development of safety and trust. As David may already feel wary or distrusting of the counseling process (Herring, 1990; LaFromboise, Trimble, & Mohatt, 1990; Sutton & Broken Nose, 1996), the focus on relationship building will be central, particularly as the counselor likely will be seen as part of the system with which he is in trouble. That is, determining the degree to which David will be able to trust the counselor (who represents the enforcer of the school system's rules) can facilitate a mutually negotiated relationship. The school counselor can align with David by serving as an advocate, rather than a representative of the system that pathologizes his behaviors. If David perceives his counselor as an advocate, rather than the person responsible for the remediation program, he is more likely to benefit from the counseling process.

Only after a minimum level of trust has been established, can the school counselor begin to slowly investigate the reasons behind David's truancy and drinking behaviors. For example, there are a host of individual and system factors that warrant investigation. To begin, it is critical to investigate whether the truancy and acting out are a result of grief or not fitting in at school, or a means to escape a school setting or persons that are unwelcoming and unsupportive. Furthermore, providing meeting times that are fluid (have an end time that is not restricted to the hour) and counseling that is ongoing (beyond the mandated time) could be helpful and require the counselor to approach the counseling relationship differently. The school counselor can further advocate for David by working with his teachers to address his learning style and individual educational needs.

College Student Away from Home and Community: The Case of Jillian

Jillian, a Northern Cheyenne woman from Nebraska, is a freshman at a predominately White 4-year institution. Away from home for the first time, she has struggled with feeling comfortable in her surroundings. She has a few Indian friends with whom she hangs out and attends the Native student organization activities. Living in the residence hall, she also has a small group of non-Indian friends who increasingly have become a source of stress and tension for her. Because of her phenotype, Jillian's residence hall friends assume that she is White and thus she has been privy to stories, jokes, and disparaging talk about minority students. As a result, she feels uncertain as to whether she can disclose a core aspect of who she is to her "friends." Feeling lonely and questioning whether she should stay in school or return home and find work in her community (where she and her family are well known), she feels anxious about "passing" (as her Indians friends caution her not to "blend in") and nervous about how her friends will react in finding out that she is Cheyenne. Uncertain about how to negotiate her discomfort and lack of connections, her residence hall friends convince her to go to the university counseling center to get help with her "depression."

It could be helpful for Jillian's counselor to address her concerns as an advocate or psychoeducational mentor from a student services or student development approach, rather than from an individual psychotherapy perspective. Doing so would integrate the environment and multiple systems that surround the college student experience, rather than unduly focus on Jillian as the source of concern. It is not uncommon for Indians/Natives who are away from their families and communities to experience feelings of marginality and uncertainty as they negotiate two cultures. In particular, navigation of the university environment is difficult as the context has been described as hostile, racist, oppressive, and indifferent toward Indian/Native students (Huffman, 1991). As a result, helping Jillian to hone her bicultural identity will be critical to her feeling able to negotiate her Indian and university values. Although achieving balance is central, a disruption of values occurs for Indians/Natives who leave their community. Encouraging students to return home periodically to get regrounded, or to "reinfuse cultural strength" (Trimble et al, 1996, p. 191), most likely could be helpful.

Given that individuals will likely perceive Jillian negatively, teaching educational coping skills to navigate the university environment is warranted. For example, connecting students with other Indian/Native students in more advanced classes could help them derive value and personal meaning, honor the strength of others, and trust the wisdom of their student elders (Montgomery et al., 2000). Engaging in specific and intentionally developed events (e.g., Talking Circles, mentoring events), in which Jillian could be proud of her heritage and converse with others who have managed similar issues, is suggested. Similarly, working with Jillian to discover her own purpose and strengths, and to seek out choices that reflect harmony and balance in her school setting, would be useful (Garrett & Myers, 1996).

IMPLICATIONS AND STRATEGIES
FOR COUNSELING, SUPPORT, AND WELLNESS

Although several specific counseling strategies were addressed in the vignettes, providing broad-based approaches for counseling, support, and
wellness for Indians/Natives is complex. Indian/Native populations are far
too diverse to provide general counseling recommendations that would be
consistently effective (Herring, 1994). At the same time, there are shared cultural standards and meanings that stem from common core values across different Indian/Native communities that can be identified without detriment
or stereotype (Garrett & Myers; 1996; Peregoy, 1999). Similarly, there are
core counseling issues that mental health service providers must consider to
begin and maintain relationships with Indian/Native individuals who seek
help, and within Indian/Native communities in which service providers consult and conduct prevention and intervention programming.

Because the relationship between Indians/Natives and helping professionals (missionaries, teachers, social workers) historically has been marred
by racism, attending to the counseling relationship is critical. Having personal authenticity, genuine respect, and culturally empathetic concern for
Indian/Native clients is essential (Lokken & Twohey, 2004; Sutton & Broken Nose, 1996), particularly for White therapists (Herring, 1990; LaFromboise et al., 1990). Within the relationship, in order to earn the trust of clients, counselors must express positive attitudes, knowledge, and respect for
Indian/Native culture and extended-family systems (Peregoy, 1991), recognizing and understanding the unique stresses imposed by cultural conflict
(LaFromboise et al., 1990). It may take a year or more for a community
to understand the purpose of a counselor's role. Yet, as a result of becoming a known entity (both personally and professionally), a mutual awareness and trust between counselor and community members may develop
(Trimble et al., 1996). Counseling effectiveness depends on a counselor's
ability to develop and nurture trust and flexibility. In fact, scholars (e.g.,
Sutton & Broken Nose, 1996; Trimble et al., 1996) suggest that unsuccessful and ineffective counseling is due to counselors' lack of basic knowledge
(e.g., nature and history of Indian/Native communities) about the client's
ethnic background or inappropriate counseling style, or a combination of
the two.

Addressing the individual in relation to his or her family (nuclear and
extended) and community is central to effective services. Because identity is
defined in relation to community (LaFromboise & Jackson, 1996), and family
represents a unique component of living (Garrett & Garrett, 1994), understanding relationships (e.g., immediate and extended family, clan members,

tribal community, nature and the universe) should be a central aspect of counseling. In effect, concerns can be addressed and problems solved by mobilizing families and communities to work together (Sutton & Broken Nose, 1996). Because resources typically are shared and many Indians/Natives maintain cultural obligations to extended-family members, using networking and systems counseling to address concerns is warranted. The use of formal (e.g., counseling) and informal (e.g., tribal or community leaders) help-seeking pathways (Peregoy, 1991) for dealing with mental health concerns can ensure more spiritually based and comprehensive services, creating an open and supportive environment in which spiritual issues are addressed (LaFromboise, Choney, James, & Running Wolf, 1995).

Anyone who has genuine interest and concern for Indian/Native communities can, in effect, serve as a helper and empower those communities. For example, a high school teacher can help Indian/Native students who struggle with home concerns to write their stories of strength in journals. An academic advisor also could bring together a group of Indian/Native students to share time and food (e.g., make Indian tacos) and use a Talking Circle to gain clarity and validation for students within the university community. Similarly, an aunt, guardian, or community member could relay familial or community stories and experiences of strength to help individuals (regardless of age) through difficult times. Because healing and support can come from informal relationships (LaFromboise & Jackson, 1996), mental health professionals should seek to integrate such connections, particularly when there is a lack of specialized assistance available to address the needs and concerns of Indian/Native communities (e.g., in rural and potentially isolated areas).

In addition to interventions in Indian/Native communities, prevention approaches can be facilitated by accessing differing dimensions of the same system. Such efforts not only must be individualistic in approach, but also must consider the influence of family, tribe, and community. Any concern, whether intimate-partner violence, suicide, or substance use, affects multiple and larger systems beyond the individual. In effect, "all programming, from prevention to rehabilitation, needs to be developed within the context of the community and the individual" (Peregoy, 2005, p. 270). Because of the strong interrelationships of individual to family and community, disharmony and imbalance for one person translates into disharmony for the community. Such disharmony extends beyond current and future generations of Indians/Natives as it generally is symptomatic of some greater and long-standing concern. Finally, prevention efforts must address the comorbidity that often occurs with mental health concerns in Indian/Native communities.

CONCLUSION: COMING FULL CIRCLE

Multicultural competence is not an event; instead, it is a continuous and life-long process of knowing oneself in order to facilitate the healing and well-being of others in a manner that is compassionate, skillful, and effective. Such competence requires substantial unlearning and relearning about oneself and about Indian/Native individuals and communities. For example, Garrett and Garrett (1994) suggested that "if counselors first come as students, and second, as professionals" (p. 143), there would be forward movement for Indians/Natives and non-Indians/Natives alike. More specifically, if Indians/Natives are willing to come to counseling with expectations of practicing potentially different traditions, then counselors also should enter the relationship willing to learn new traditions (Herring, 1998).

Recognizing that each person has his or her own "way of life" or balance of spirit is a means to address each Indian/Native as an individual and as part of the larger community (e.g., family, tribe, universe). Ultimately, using the Guidelines to become a culturally competent counselor, healer, teacher, and change agent for Indian/Native communities is ensconced in planting seeds of hope and empowerment. Perhaps one of the greatest skills for a change agent is to recognize that the community has its own culturally prescribed ways of healing. Serving as a facilitator of individual growth and community healing requires fluid connections of the past and present for Indians/Natives, thus maintaining harmony, balance, and beauty of the Circle.

ONLINE RESOURCES

To increase awareness, knowledge, and skills in working with Indian/Native populations, the following online resources are provided for broadening perspectives and increasing access.

Government

- *American Indian Health* (http://americanindianhealth.nlm.nih.gov/). Sponsored by the National Library of Medicine. Provides general and specific information on health and medical resources and research and data for American Indians. Additional links to documents and other relevant websites are provided.
- *Bureau of Indian Affairs* (http://www.doi.gov/bureau-indian-affairs. html). Originally housed in the Department of War and now housed in the Department of the Interior. Responsible for the administration

and management of 55.7 million acres of land held in trust by the government for Indians/Natives.

- *Indian Health Services* (http://www.ihs.gov/). An agency within the Department of Health and Human Services. Provides health and behavioral services to Indians/Natives. These services are obligated by treaties as a result of the tribes' giving up land and the right to go to war.

Professional Associations

- *Association of American Indian Physicians* (http://www.aaip.com/). Dedicated to pursuing excellence in Native American health care by promoting education in the medical disciplines, honoring traditional healing practices, and restoring the balance of mind, body, and spirit.
- *Society of Indian Psychologists* (http://www.okstate.edu/osu_orgs/sip/). An organization for American Indian and Native people who are concerned with improving the mental well-being of their people. Through an exchange of skill, expertise, and experiences, creates opportunities for career development, positive inter- and intrapersonal relationships, and general personal enhancement of American Indian and Native peoples. Encourages all American Indian and Native people to become involved in improving the quality of their lives.

Informational Sites

- *American Indian and Alaskan Native Programs* (http://www.uchsc.edu/ai/index.htm). Promotes the health and well-being of all American Indians and Alaska Natives through research, training, continuing education, technical assistance, and information dissemination within a biopsychosocial framework.
- *Association on American Indian Affairs* (http://www.indian-affairs.org/). A nonprofit publicly supported organization. Seeks to promote the welfare of American Indians and Alaska Natives. Mission is to sustain and perpetuate cultures and languages; protect sovereignty, constitutional, legal and human rights, and natural resources; and improve health, education, and economic and community development.
- *Native American Nations* (http://www.nativeculturelinks.com/nations.html). An organizing page of links to different Native/Indian Nations' webpages.

Fellowships

- *American Indian College Fund* (http://www.collegefund.org/). Provides scholarships and other support for the Nation's 34 tribal colleges. Vital to educating students while keeping them in touch with their Indian culture.
- *American Indian Graduate Center* (http://www.aigc.com/). National nonprofit organization dedicated to aiding Indian graduate students in all fields of study.
- *National Indian Education Association* (http://www.niea.org/). Founded in 1969. The largest and oldest Indian education organization in the nation, whose purpose is to advance educational opportunities and equity for American Indian, Alaska Native, and Native Hawaiian students while protecting cultural and linguistic traditions.

Research Journals

- *American Indian and Alaska Native Mental Health Research: The Journal of the National Center* (http://www2.uchsc.edu/ai/ncaianmhr/journal_home.asp). Refereed publication. Publishes empirical research, program evaluations, case studies, dissertations, and other articles in the behavioral, social, and health sciences related to the mental health status of American Indians and Alaska Natives.
- *American Indian Culture and Research Journal* (http://www.books.aisc.ucla.edu/aicrj.html). Refereed quarterly research journal of American Indian Studies.
- *American Indian Quarterly* (http://muse.jhu.edu/journals/american_indian_quarterly/). Peer-reviewed, interdisciplinary journal of the anthropology, history, literatures, religions, and arts of Native Americans.
- *Journal of American Indian Education* (http://jaie.asu.edu/). Peer-reviewed scholarly journal addressing work specifically related to the education of American Indians and Alaska Natives.
- *Tribal College Journal of American Indian Higher Education* (http://www.tribalcollegejournal.org/). Culture-based publication that addresses journalistic and scholarly articles relevant to the future of American Indian and Alaska Native communities.

Newspapers

There are a number of tribal and state Indian/Native newspapers; however, three of the primary national Native/Indian news sources are:

- *Indian Country Today* (http://www.indiancountry.com/). The nation's leading American Indian news source, read by most tribal leaders, U.S. senators and representatives, officials in the Bureau of Indian Affairs, lawyers, educators, students, business professionals, and local and state politicians.
- *Indianz.com* (http://www.indianz.com/). Provides online news, information, and entertainment from a Native American perspective through daily news features.
- *Native American Times* (http://www.nativetimes.com/). The largest independently owned Native American newspaper in the United States. Coverage is tailored specifically to the Native American perspective, including issues such as sovereign rights, civil rights, and tribal relationships with the federal government.

REFERENCES

American Psychological Association. (2003). Guidelines on multicultural education, training, research, practice, and organizational change for psychologists. *American Psychologist, 58*, 377–402.

Barker, J. C., & Krammer, J. B. (1996). Alcohol consumption among older urban American Indians. *Journal of Studies of Alcohol, 57*, 119–124.

Bellcourt, M. A. (2004, February). Advising Native Americans in higher education. *NACADA Academic Advising News, 27*(1). Retrieved November 11, 2005, from http://www.nacada.ksu.edu/InterestGroups/C36/News-Article-Feb2004

Campbell, K., Herbert, M., & Peregoy, J. (1999). *Walking in two worlds: Issues in Indian education* [Video documentary]. KUED–Public Broadcasting Service & University of Utah.

Duran, B., Duran, E., & Braveheart, M. Y. H. (1998). Native Americans and the trauma of history. In R. Thornton (Ed.), *Studying Native America: Problems and prospects* (pp. 60–76). Madison: University of Wisconsin Press.

Frantz, K. (1999). *Indian reservations in the United States: Territory, sovereignty, and socioeconomic change.* Chicago: University of Chicago Press.

Freedenthal, S., & Stiffman, A. R. (2004). Suicidal behavior in urban American Indian adolescents: A comparison with reservation youth in a southwestern state. *Suicide and Life-Threatening Behavior, 34*, 160–171.

Garrett, J. T., & Garrett, M. T. (1994). The path of good medicine: Understanding and counseling Native American Indians. *Journal of Multicultural Counseling and Development, 22*, 134–144.

Garrett, M. T. (2006). When eagle speaks: Counseling Native Americans. In C. C. Lee (Ed.), *Multicultural issues in counseling: New approaches to diversity* (3rd ed., pp. 25–53). Alexandria, VA; American Counseling Association.

Garrett, M. T., & Carroll, J. J. (2000). Mending the broken circle: Treatment of substance dependence among Native Americans. *Journal of Counseling and Development, 78*, 379–388.

Garrett, M. T., & Myers, J. E. (1996). The rule of opposites: A paradigm for counseling Native Americans. *Journal of Counseling and Development, 24*, 89–104.

Garrett, M. T., & Pichette, E. F. (2000). Red as an apple: Native American acculturation and counseling with or without reservation. *Journal of Counseling and Development, 78,* 3–13.

Garrod, A., & Larimore, C. (1997). Introduction. In A. Garrod & C. Larimore (Eds.), *First person, first people: Native American college graduates tell their life stories* (pp. 1–19). Ithaca, NY: Cornell University Press.

Gloria, A. M., & Peregoy, J. J. (1996). Counseling Latino alcohol and other substance users/abusers: Cultural considerations for counselors. *Journal of Substance Abuse Treatment, 13,* 119–126.

Gloria, A. M., & Robinson-Kurpius, S. E. (2001). Influences of self-beliefs, social support, and comfort in the university environment on the academic persistence issues for American Indian undergraduates. *Cultural Diversity and Ethnic Minority Psychology, 7,* 88–102.

Gone, J. P. (2004). Mental health services for Native Americans in the 21st century United States. *Professional Psychology: Research and Practice, 35,* 10–18.

Grossman, D. C., Milligan, C., & Deyo, R. A. (1991). Risk factors for suicide attempts among Navajo adolescents. *American Journal of Public Health, 81,* 870–874.

Hawkins, E. H., Cummins, L. H., & Marlatt, G. A. (2004). Preventing substance abuse in American Indian and Alaska Native youth: Promising strategies for healthier communities. *Psychological Bulletin, 130,* 304–323.

Herring, R. D. (1990). Understanding Native American values: Process and content concerns for counselors. *Counseling and Values, 34,* 134–137.

Herring, R. D. (1992). Seeking a new paradigm: Counseling Native Americans. *Journal of Multicultural Counseling and Development, 20,* 35–43.

Herring, R. D. (1994). The clown or contrary figure as a counseling intervention strategy with Native American Indian clients. *Journal of Multicultural Counseling and Development, 22,* 153–164.

Herring, R. D. (1996). Synergetic counseling and Native American Indian students. *Journal of Counseling and Development, 74,* 153–164.

Herring, R. D. (1998). Native American Indian college students: Implications for college counseling practice. *Journal of College Counseling, 1,* 169–180.

Herring, R. D. (2004). Physical and mental health needs of Native American Indian and Alaska Native populations. In D. R. Atkinson (Ed.), *Counseling American minorities* (6th ed., pp. 171–192). New York: McGraw-Hill.

Huffman, T. E. (1991). The experiences, perceptions, and consequences of campus racism among Northern Plains Indians. *Journal of American Indian Education, 30,* 25–34.

Indian Health Service. (1997). *Trends in Indian health-1996.* Washington, DC: U.S. Government Printing Office.

Indian Trust. (2005, November). *Indian trust: Cobell vs. Norton.* Retrieved November 5, 2005, from http://www.indiantrust.com/

Johnson, J. L., & Cameron, M. C. (2001). Barriers to providing effective mental health services to American Indians. *Mental Health Services Research, 3,* 215–223.

Juntunen, C. L., & Morin, P. M. (2004). Treatment issues for Native Americans: An overview of individual, family, and group strategies. In D. R. Atkinson (Ed.), *Counseling American minorities* (6th ed., pp. 193–213). New York: McGraw-Hill.

LaFromboise, T. (1999). *The living in two worlds survey.* Unpublished test instrument, Stanford University, Palo Alto, CA.

LaFromboise, T. D., Choney, S. B., James, A., & Running Wolf, P. R. (1995). American Indian women and psychology. In H. Landrine (Ed.), *Bringing cultural diversity to feminist psychology: Theory, research, and practice* (pp. 197–239). Washington, DC: American Psychological Association.

LaFromboise, T. D., Heyle, A. M., & Ozer, E. J. (1999). Changing and diverse roles of women in American Indian cultures. In L. A. Peplau, S. C. DeBro, R. C. Veniegas, & P. L. Taylor (Eds.), *Gender, culture, and ethnicity: Current research about women and men* (pp. 48–61). Mountain View, CA: Mayfield.

LaFromboise, T. D., & Howard-Pitney, B. (1995). The Zuni life skills development curriculum: Description and evaluation of a suicide prevention program. *Journal of Counseling Psychology, 42,* 479–486.

LaFromboise, T. D., & Jackson, M. (1996), MCT theory and Native-American populations. In D. W. Sue, A. E. Ivey, & P. B. Pedersen (Eds.), *A theory of multicultural counseling and therapy* (pp. 192–203). Pacific Grove, CA: Brooks/Cole.

LaFromboise, T., Trimble, J., & Mohatt, G. (1990). Counseling intervention and American Indian tradition: An integrative approach. *The Counseling Psychologist, 18,* 628–654.

Lokken, J. M., & Twohey, D. (2004). American Indian perspectives of Euro-American counseling behavior. *Journal of Multicultural Counseling and Development, 32,* 320–331.

McDonald, J. D. (2002). *A model for conducting research with American Indian participants.* Washington, DC: American Psychological Association.

Melmer, D. (2005, May). Senate Committee addresses suicide. *Indian Country Today.* Retrieved November 5, 2005, from http://www.indiancountry.com

Montgomery, D., Miville, M. L., Winterowd, C., Jeffreis, B., & Baysden, M. F. (2000). American Indian college students: An exploration into resiliency factors revealed through personal stories. *Cultural Diversity and Ethnic Minority Psychology, 6,* 387–398.

Moran, J. R., Fleming, C. M., Somervell, P., & Mason, S. M. (1999). Measuring bicultural ethnic identity among American Indian adolescents: A factor analytic study. *Journal of Adolescent Research, 14,* 405–426.

National Center for Health Statistics. (2000). *Healthy People 2010.* Washington, DC: Department of Health and Human Services.

Newman, D. L. (2005). Ego development and ethnic identity formation in rural American Indian adolescents. *Child Development, 76,* 734–746.

Oetzel, J., & Duran, B. (2004). Intimate partner violence in American Indian and/or Alaska Native communities: A social ecological framework of determinants and interventions. *American Indian and Alaskan Native Mental Health Research: The Journal of the National Center, 11,* 49–68.

Ogunwole, S. U. (2002). *The American Indian and Alaska Native population: 2000.* Census 2000 Brief, U.S. Department of Commerce, C2KBR/01-15.

Okamoto, S. K., Hurdle, D. E., & Marsiglia, F. F. (2001). Exploring culturally-based drug resistance strategies used by American Indian adolescents of the southwest. *Journal of Alcohol and Drug Education, 47,* 45–59.

Pavel, D. M., Skinner, R. R., Cahalan, M., Tippeconnic, J., & Stein, W. (1998). *American Indians and Alaska Natives in postsecondary education.* National Center for Education Statistics (NCES 98-291).

Peregoy, J. J. (1991). *Stress and the sheepskin: An exploration of the Indian/Native perspective in college.* Unpublished doctoral dissertation, Syracuse University, Syracuse, NY.

Peregoy, J. J. (1999). Revisiting transcultural counseling with American Indians and Alaskan Natives: Issues for consideration. In J. McFadden (Ed.), *Transcultural counseling* (2nd ed., pp. 137–170). Alexandria, VA: American Counseling Association.

Peregoy, J. J. (2004). Working with American Indian/Alaskan Native clients: Perspectives for practitioners to start with. In E. Wellfeld & R. E. Ingersoll (Eds.), *The mental health desk reference: A practice-based guide to diagnosis, treatment, and professional ethics* (pp. 306–314). Upper Saddle River, NJ: Merrill Prentice Hall.

Peregoy, J. J. (2005). Working with diverse cultures: Revisiting issues in prevention and intervention. In. P. Stevens & R. L. Smith (Eds.). *Substance abuse counseling: Theory and practice* (3rd ed., pp. 266–271). Upper Saddle River, NJ: Pearson Education.

Perry, S. W. (2004). *American Indians and crime: BJS statistical profile, 1992–2002.* Washington, DC: U.S. Government Printing Office.

Roberts, H., Gonzalez, J. C., Harris, O., Huff, D., Johns, A. M., Lou, R., & Scott, O. (1994). *Teaching from a multicultural perspective.* Thousand Oaks, CA: Sage.

Robin, R. W., Chester, B., & Rasmussen, J. K. (1998). Intimate violence in a southwestern American Indian tribal community. *Cultural Diversity and Mental Health, 4,* 335–344.

Substance Abuse and Mental Health Services Administration. (2002). American Indians/Alaska Natives and substance abuse. *Prevention Alert, 5,* 1.

Sue, D., Arredondo, P., & McDavis, R. (1992). Multicultural counseling competencies and standards: A call to the profession. *Journal of Counseling and Development, 70,* 477–486.

Sutton, C. T., & Broken Nose, M. A. (1996). American Indian families: An overview. In M. McGoldrick, J. Giordano, & J. K. Pearce (Eds.), *Ethnicity and family therapy* (2nd ed., pp. 31–44). New York: Guilford Press.

Tafoya, N., & Del Vecchio, A. (1996). Back to the future: An examination of the Native American holocaust experience. In M. McGoldrick, J. Giordano, & J. K. Pearce (Eds.), *Ethnicity and family therapy* (2nd ed., pp. 45–54). New York: Guilford Press.

Taylor, M. J. (2000). The influence of self-efficacy on alcohol use among American Indians. *Cultural Diversity and Ethnic Minority Psychology, 6,* 152–167.

Thomason, T. C. (1991). Counseling Native Americans: An introduction for non-Native American counselors. *Journal of Counseling and Development, 69,* 321–327.

Thomason, T. C. (2000). Issues in the treatment of Native American with alcohol problems. *Journal of Multicultural Counseling and Development, 28,* 243–252.

Trimble, J. E. (2000). Social psychological perspectives on changing self-identification among American Indians and Alaskan Natives. In R. H. Dana (Ed.), *Handbook of cross-cultural and multicultural personality assessment* (pp. 197–222). Mahwah, NJ: Erlbaum.

Trimble, J. E., Fleming, C. M., Beauvais, F., & Jumper-Thurman, P. (1996). Essential cultural and social strategies for counseling Native American Indians. In P. B. Pedersen, J. G. Draguns, W. J. Lonner, & J. E. Trimble (Eds.), *Counseling across cultures* (4th ed., pp. 177–209). Thousand Oaks, CA: Sage.

Vernon, I. (2002). *Native American and HIV/AIDS.* University of Oklahoma Health Sciences Center. Retrieved November 10, 2005, from http://ccan.ouhsc.edu/AIDS.pdf

6

Arab American Populations

Sylvia C. Nassar-McMillan

The "Guidelines on Multicultural Education, Training, Research, Practice, and Organizational Change for Psychologists" define ethnic and racial minority groups as Asian and Pacific Islanders, sub-Saharan Black Africans, Latino/Hispanics, and Native American/American Indians. Within that definition, Arab Americans do not have a place. This discrepancy points to a larger series of dichotomies inherent in the ongoing tasks of defining and operationalizing culturally competent psychology. Although the spirit of the challenge may pose opportunity to broadly define, to be inclusive, and to see "outside the box," so to speak, the pressure to apply scientific rigor to our pursuit dictates a clear definition of terms. Thus, groups such as Arab Americans, whose descent spans 22 countries across the continents of both Asia and Africa, are categorized by default into the dominant European American culture, when in fact their cultural norms, values, and beliefs are in many ways diametrically opposed to those of the mainstream United States.

Moreover, although the Guidelines may acknowledge the importance of developing cultural competence within our domestic borders, cultural competence in working with Arab Americans may not be achievable without a global perspective. For example, many of the current crises and issues encountered by Arab Americans in contemporary U.S. society arise out of global issues, with which most, if not all, U.S. citizens are at least exposed to, and at best inundated with, on a daily basis (e.g., the New York City Twin Tower terrorist attacks of September 11, 2001, and the ongoing U.S. occupation of Iraq). Thus, the criticality of social, political, historical, and economic context suggested by the Guidelines is heightened with regard to culturally competent work with Arab Americans.

The two issues described will serve as an effective backdrop to this chapter. In the first section, I highlight key elements of the Guidelines as they pertain to the Arab American population. Relevant empirical and other literature on Arab Americans also will be summarized. Next, I present four case vignettes to illustrate the diversity within the population and provide effective strategies for culturally competent work with Arab Americans. Finally, a list of resources is provided to assist mental health professionals in developing multicultural competence in working with Arab Americans.

KEY ELEMENTS OF THE MULTICULTURAL GUIDELINES

Guideline 1: Awareness of Attitudes and Beliefs

Guideline 1 pertains to personally held attitudes and beliefs. Well before the contemporary post-9/11 climate, individuals of Middle Eastern descent were typologized as extremists, Islamic fanatics, and terrorists. Despite the lack of empirical support garnered by any of these views, present-day media and other inherent and sometimes subtle but powerful influences continue to uphold such a stereotype. Historically, the stereotypic images of Arabs as camel riding villains, ill-mannered and ill-meaning powerful sheikhs, enslaved maidens or harem girls, terrorists, and Egyptian caricatures permeated virtually all sources of American media (Shaheen, 1985, 1991, 1997, 2001). In other words, the contemporary trend has picked up where the historical has led it. Edward Said (1978), the late, distinguished Palestinian scholar, coined the term *Orientalism*, describing a process engaged in by the Western world to define anything unfamiliar or different from the common mores or culture as Oriental.

Some religious scholars attribute the perceived differences between cultures to the religious differences between the prevailing Christianity of the West and the predominant Islamism of the non-West, the Middle East in particular. However, it should be noted that the shared collectivist values of Arab and Islamic cultures have independent historical origins (Dwairy, 2006; Smith, 1991). Thus, although Arab and Muslim cultures are much intertwined, they are not synonymous.

In fact, the majority of Arab Americans are not of the Muslim faith (Arab American Demographics, n.d.). By the same token, the terms *Arab* and *Middle Eastern* are utilized interchangeably, although the Arab Middle East represents a subset of that geographic region (Nassar-McMillan, 2003a, 2003b, in press). Racial, or skin color, diversity among Arab Americans is prevalent as well (Jackson & Nassar-McMillan, 2006).

Changes in policy, despite their compulsory nature, in fact may facilitate attitudinal changes over time. The fact that Arab Americans are not among the four major population classes targeted in the Guidelines as minority groups, or as protected, also has historical roots, most likely relating to the concept of Orientalism and unfamiliarity and fear described earlier. Historically, the definitional problem has plagued the Arab American community since the beginning of its immigration history. Over their 100-plus year history, Arab Americans have been classified as being "from Turkey in Asia," "Syrian," neither White nor of African descent and thereby ineligible for citizenship, "Colored," and "White" (Samhan, 1999). Currently, there is some debate at federal levels about whether Arab Americans have minority status (Llorente, 2002). Although there are recognized advantages and disadvantages on either side of the argument, the fact that Arab Americans are not viewed as a minority, or protected group, may contribute on some levels to the attitude of free license by media and other officials to discriminate against them.

Guideline 2: Impacts of Multicultural Insensitivity

Guideline 2 addresses the importance of recognizing the impacts of multicultural sensitivity and responsiveness or lack thereof. For many Arab Americans, prejudice and discrimination represent daily facts of life (Abu El-Haj, 2002; Ammar, 2000; Arab American Institute, 2002; Arab American Institute Foundation, 2002; Bouffard, 2004; Sarroub, 2002). For others, oppression by the mainstream U.S. culture may be so internalized that prejudice becomes unrecognized or even operationalized within the population itself—perhaps by discrimination toward those most recently immigrated, those with darker skin, or those of Islamic faith (Ajrouch, 2000; Nassar-McMillan, in press; Nassar-McMillan & Hakim-Larson, 2003). Such internalized oppression serves to create and maintain hierarchical status both within and without the population, with Arab Americans seeking to "pass" as being White. These attempts may range from selective to permeating the social relationships of individuals or families. Relatedly, when terrorist acts or other acts of violence occur, because of the pattern of being linked, legitimately or not, to those of Arab descent, Arab Americans may be even more likely to deny their ethnic heritage for fear of discrimination or repatriation. Concurrently, the oppression of contemporary post-9/11 legislation that serves to target and profile those of Arab, Middle Eastern, and Muslim descent, while spurring some individuals toward community advocacy efforts (Nassar-McMillan, 2003b, in press), has effectively served to silence others (Sarroub, 2002).

Guidelines 3 and 4: Education and Research

Guidelines 3 and 4 refer to present states of psychological education and research, respectively. Throughout both these realms, Arab Americans have been both pathologized and presented as such. Behavior, both in terms of individual mental health contexts or in larger sociological contexts, has been explained primarily by religious bases—whereas historical and even sociological bases, ironically, have been largely ignored. For example, family honor and prescribed family roles have a tribalistic origin rather than a religious one. Culturally sensitive research is emerging in social science disciplines (e.g., Abu El-Haj, 2002; Bennett, 1994; Halliday, 1997; Read & Bartkowski, 2000; Sarroub, 2002), although scholarly clinical and community efforts focused on mental health issues are slower to emerge (e.g., Al-Krenawi & Graham, 2000; Erickson & Al-Timimi, 2001; Nassar-McMillan & Hakim-Larson, 2003; Nobles & Sciarra, 2000). Even trusted individuals, indigenous to local or national Arab American communities, attempting to conduct such research may be regarded with suspicion, given the hostile anti-Arab sentiment perceived in the post-9/11 era.

Guideline 5: Clinical Practice

Guideline 5 pertains to clinical practice. Here again, clinical assessment may yield pathology among Arab American clientele based both on non-Western-oriented client behaviors as well as Western models of psychological well-being and mental health. For example, collectivism values inherent in both Muslim and Arab cultures could lead to a clinical assessment of enmeshment or other dysfunctionality if measured by Western or U.S. criteria. In addition, without the sociological, historical, political, and economic context as a backdrop for appropriate clinical assessment and diagnoses, one could not accurately or adequately understand concepts of racism (whether or not reported by the client), clarify expectations for therapy, or determine appropriate and effective methods of intervention.

Guideline 6: Organizational Change and Policy Development

Finally, Guideline 6 addresses organizational change and policy development. Social justice, indeed, has become a focal point for psychologists and other mental health providers and educators, often in conjunction with cultural competence. This political role, although relatively new in the psychologist's job description, is of critical importance in working with Arab American individuals, communities, and families. In recent years, hundreds of individuals, predominantly Muslims, Arabs, and South Asians, have been required to participate in a special registration program designed to track specific minority groups; hundreds of others have been detained for weeks or longer without due process, legal representation, or contact with their families. Hundreds of others have been detained for minor violations such as not reporting a change of address. Effective, responsible, and culturally sensitive mental health treatment of Arab American individuals cannot occur without considering the current hostility against Arab countries. Nor can it occur if psychologists do not play an advocacy role to eradicate discriminatory legislation and violations of civil liberties at multiple levels.

EMPIRICAL AND CONCEPTUAL BACKGROUND

Immigration and Acculturation

According to the Census Information Center of the Arab American Institute (AAI, 2003), national population estimates of Arab Americans exceed 3.5 million, despite the 1.2 million recorded by the U.S. Bureau of the Census (2003). As with other ethnic groups, the dramatic undercounting of the Census is attributed to various factors. The largest Arab American populations are located in California, Florida, Michigan, New Jersey, New York, Illinois, Massachusetts, Ohio, Pennsylvania, and Texas (AAI, 2004). The substantial heterogeneity of this cultural group is related in part to its immigration history. Immigration from the Arab Middle East occurred in several distinct waves over the past approximately 125 years. The acculturation, and thus the mental health issues among Arab Americans, also may be associated with this immigration history (e.g., Abudabbeh, 1996; Ammar, 2000).

The first group came to the United States in pursuit of better economic opportunities, coupled with the desire to escape the oppression of the pan-Islamic Ottoman Empire (Naff, 1985). These individuals were primarily young, uneducated, Christian peddlers from Palestine, Syria, Lebanon, and Jordan (Orfalea, 1988). This group immigrated relatively eagerly, assimilated quickly, and excelled in educational and political arenas (Abudabbeh, 1996).

The next, post-World War II group represented a vastly different profile. Educated, economically successful, and Muslim, large numbers of individuals and families from Palestine, Egypt, Syria, Jordan, and Iraq and fewer ones from Lebanon and Yemen came to escape the political tensions and traumas in the region. This second wave of immigrants and their offspring, often referred to as the Brain Drain (Orfalea, 1988), tended to remain more tied to their ancestral roots and less inclined to adopt traditional American lifestyles and values (Abudabbeh, 1996).

In the 1960s, a similar demographic group emigrated: Some were Palestinians seeking to escape the Israeli occupation, while many others sought economic gain (Orfalea, 1988). Individuals in this third group have tended toward successful professional achievements, while personally and socially maintaining the cultures of their homelands (Abudabbeh, 1996).

Since the 1990s, a fourth wave has been identified, comprising primarily refugees and other immigrants from Iraq. Many of these individuals, fleeing the oppressive regime, have experienced trauma, disruptions in family relationships, and career and other economic instability (Nassar-McMillan & Hakim-Larson, 2003). This most recent group may psychologically consider their country of origin as home, perhaps even with plans to return. Given this phenomenon, they may be among those least likely to forsake or even compromise their ethnic traditions, lifestyles, and values (Nassar-McMillan, in press).

Collectivistic Values: Religion, Gender, and Family

Collectivistic values make up the fabric of Arab American belief systems. This value structure dates back to earliest civilizations, during which entire communities and societies were interrelated to the extent that nonadherence to a common goal could harm the entire community (Dwairy, 2006). All other values commonly attributed to Arab-culture parenting can be linked to such an overarching purpose and function.

Although most Arab Americans belong to non-Muslim faiths (AAI, n.d.; Shaheen, 1997; Zogby, 2001), Arab Americans across religious faiths and communities share similar values regarding modesty, intrafaith marriage, and gender and familial relationships. At the same time, however, those who actively practice Islam and its traditions, such as veiling, five times daily prayer, and the like, may be most visible as representing a different culture and lifestyle from the U.S. norm. So, on the one hand, religion may pose an additional challenge to evading ethnic/religious discrimination (Samhan, n.d.). On the other hand, some Muslims' religion is associated with their marital satisfaction and overall satisfaction with life in the United States (Faragallah, Schumm, & Webb, 1997).

Within the context of Islam, males and females share equal rights (Council on Islamic Education, 1995). In terms of actual gender roles and relationships, male and female roles are substantively differentiated in Arab American society by preadolescence (Ajrouch, 2000). Males are expected to interact with individuals outside their familial and community boundaries, while females are expected to stay within them. From a collectivistic perspective, males are learning behaviors geared toward successful economic adaptation, while females are believed to be preparing for effective family development and maintenance. Female behavior is scrutinized more by elders within communities, and in some ethnic enclaves in the United States, parents report being even more strict than they would need to be within their countries of origin due to the pressures on adolescents and their behaviors from sources external to their communities (Ajrouch, 1999). These typical roles notwithstanding, recent and current research indicates wide ranges in beliefs about gender ideology, spanning issues about veiling practices (Read & Bartkowski, 2000), feminism (Marshall & Read, 2003), and gender role identity development (Abu-Ali & Reisen, 1999).

Regarding family structure and relationships, multiple generations may reside together as a single unit. Male and female familial and parenting roles may be influenced as described earlier, although many egalitarian values are present within the family structure. For example, because Arab Americans place such a high value on education, both parents may take part in helping children with homework. Parents within Arab societies tend to practice authoritarian parenting strategies, which, in cultural context, have been shown to facilitate the mental health of both children and families (Dwairy, 2006). For Arab Americans in contemporary U.S. society, intergenerational and acculturation forces may cause stress on families or communities as their value system transitions (Meleis, 1991; Nassar-McMillan & Hakim-Larson, 2003).

Acculturation and Mental Health

Only a few small, exploratory studies have examined the critical issues related to acculturation for contemporary Arab Americans (Hakim-Larson & Nassar-McMillan, 2005). Exploratory empirical studies, representing interviews of community service officials (Paine, 1986), individual therapists (Hakim-Larson, Kamoo, & Voelker, 1998), and a focus group of therapists (Nassar-McMillan & Hakim-Larson, 2003), have yielded a number of salient variables for North Americans of Arab descent. Other scholars have explored some of these variables in greater depth, although more research is needed to generate broader generalizability of conclusions.

This preliminary research suggests that some of the most salient indicators of individuals' level of acculturation include country of origin, length of U.S. residency, reason for immigration, language use, and residence within or near a large Arab American community or enclave (Nassar McMillan, 2003a). Most of these variables can be linked to the earlier discussion of immigration history and waves. Although those from immigration waves tending toward maintaining their cultural heritage may constitute the majority within any given Arab American enclave, others may reside there as well. In addition, intraethnic discrimination may occur, even within such communities. Conflicts among youth from more versus less Westernized countries of origin have been cited as issues (Nassar-McMillan & Hakim-Larson, 2003), as well as conflicts among those more acculturated versus those more recently immigrated and less acculturated (Ajrouch, 2000).

Ethnic Discrimination and Contemporary Contextual Issues

Ethnic discrimination has been a salient issue for Arab Americans since the beginning of their immigration history, as detailed earlier in this chapter. Present-day forms of such discrimination have become alarmingly heightened by legislative acts, condoning and even supporting them. The AAI (n.d.)

cites the most critical issues among Arab Americans today as the 9/11 aftermath, discrimination and civil liberties, Iraq, and Palestine. Thus, once again, it should be clear that global issues are intertwined with the everyday lives of Arab Americans and potentially affect their level of acculturation, mental health, and well-being. Relatedly, recent refugee populations from the Arab Middle East who are likely to encounter the greatest legislative hurdles are those who need support most, as many suffer from post traumatic stress disorder (PTSD), anxiety, depression, and other maladies found among refugee populations from other parts of the world throughout U.S. history.

CASE VIGNETTES AND CONCRETE STRATEGIES

Postmigration Trauma: The Case of Ibrahim

Ibrahim is a graduate student in biochemistry at a major state university. He immigrated to the United States from Iraq with his family in the mid-1990s, via a refugee camp in Saudi Arabia, where he and his family lived for 5 years after fleeing the political regime in Iraq. His father had fought against the regime and allied with the U.S. forces during Desert Storm. Ibrahim did fairly well as an undergraduate student. Despite his positive performance, Ibrahim has had a number of health issues. During his years at the refugee camp, he began to develop chronic headaches and fatigue. These symptoms heightened after his immigration to the United States, and even more after September 11, 2001. He finally went to the physician at the health center on campus and was referred to the Counseling Center for psychotherapy.

The severity of Ibrahim's symptoms brought him in for treatment. As he began to tell his story, it seemed that he was experiencing, in addition to his physical symptoms, an array of psychological ones, including hallucinations and paranoia.

Recommended Considerations. Guideline 1 prescribes self-examination of attitudes and beliefs. The case of Ibrahim suggests a scenario in which an examination of this nature would be a particularly critical prerequisite for effective and multiculturally responsive practice. In a clinical situation such as Ibrahim's, it would be imperative to examine what one believes or perceives about the recent political history, particularly relative to the relationship between Iraq and the United States. Given that Middle Easterners historically have been perceived as terrorists, and that the vast majority of U.S. citizens are not well versed in current political events (Bennett, 1994; Halliday, 1997), it would not be unusual for psychologists to be unaware of the various roles played by Iraqis in the Gulf War. In addition, it would be important to research issues such as resultant psychological (e.g., PTSD, anxiety, depression) and physical (e.g., chronic fatigue syndrome, fibromyalgia) symptoms reported by U.S. veterans (Barrett et al., 2002; Haley & Kurt, 1997), Iraqi veterans (Gorst-Unsworth & Goldenberg, 1998; Jamil, Nassar-McMillan, & Lambert, 2004; Kira, 2002) and other refugees and immigrants from Iraq (Jamil et al., 2002), as well as by veterans, refugees, and immigrants from other combat-related or otherwise tumultuous environments (Blair, 2000, 2001; Gorman, 2001; Keyes, 2000; Lee et al., 2001). It also would be important to consider how those symptomologies might differ between immigrants originating from countries with harmonious versus troubled relationships with the United States. Coordinating assessments with a physician potentially would help inform this process.

Guideline 2 speaks to the importance of recognizing multicultural sensitivity and understanding. In working with Arab Americans, it is especially important to assess the ways in which individuals' and groups' experiences may be affected differentially via nurturing, or multiculturally sensitive, versus hostile, or insensitive, environments. For example, in Ibrahim's case, the issues of secondary trauma should be researched in working with a combat and trauma survivor, refugee, and immigrant. The postmigration trauma experienced by Ibrahim and his family must be considered in the context of the current sociohistorical, political, and economic climate of the United States, and should be examined during the course of his therapy. These contextual issues should include Gulf War and related issues, as well as 9/11 and subsequent federal legislation targeting individuals and communities of Middle Eastern descent. On the opposite side, federal legislation may serve as a support for providing specific services for qualified veterans and their offspring. Thus, Ibrahim's premigration (e.g., country of origin), migration (e.g., refugee camp experiences; entry into the United States), and postmigration (e.g., language barriers) issues all must be assessed fully in order to understand the overall impact of the trauma.

Guideline 5, pertaining to clinical practice, suggests the criticality of understanding Arab culture and its collective origins, lest one misdiagnose or develop an inappropriate treatment plan. For Ibrahim, also, one must consider his symptoms, such as paranoia and flashbacks. In his premigration as well as actual migratory experience of going first to a refugee camp and subsequently to the United States, it is likely that his family developed acute distrust within a regime that pitted family and community members against one another. Hallucinations, too, might be assessed as PTSD-related flashbacks if taken in context of premigration trauma. In terms of postmigration trauma, Ibrahim might have been targeted or profiled in the community or even at the university, such as being denied entrance to the laboratory facility or having university officials submit his personal file to federal government representatives.

Such experiences reasonably might lead to a level of paranoia. More research is needed on the results of secondary or vicarious trauma and resultant symptomologies. Relatedly, Arab Americans tend to somaticize their psychological symptoms, which would be evident upon learning about psychological theories developed among Arab cultures.

Strong Family Influence: The Case of Lily

Lily was born in the United States in the early 1980s. Her family, which is Greek Orthodox, had emigrated from Lebanon in the 1970s to escape the tensions of the civil war. Their immigration was sponsored by a close family relative. They quickly settled near an ethnic enclave comprising many Lebanese and other Arab Americans, in the same community as their relatives. Lily grew up with many Lebanese American cousins, and her family was active in the Greek Orthodox Church community. In both high school and college, Lily socialized with both Arab American and non-Arab American peers. She found the life of her non-Arab American peers intriguing—on the one hand, she found their freedoms enticing, while on the other, frightening and confusing. Although she experienced considerable latitude from her parents as far as actual rules, she was committed to upholding their wishes with regard to dating and cross-gender socializing in unchaperoned situations. After college, Lily became a CPA. Early in her career, she met a non-Arab American man she really liked, and she began to date him in secret. They soon fell in love. They spoke of marriage, and Lily truly believed that he would make a good partner in many ways. However, she knew that her parents would have a difficult time accepting her choice and she did not want to shame her parents or her family. One of her friends suggested that she utilize the company Employee Assistance Program to talk with an "expert" who could provide some guidance.

Recommended Considerations. In keeping with Guideline 2, recognizing multicultural sensitivity and individuals' and groups' experiences, it is critical that psychological theories and models of wellness be examined and adapted appropriately if utilized in therapy. For example, many models of identity development depict stages through which individuals ideally should matriculate. However, psychological or developmental theories normed and developed in Western cultures potentially could pathologize those of non-Western, or, specifically Arab American, origins. For example, Lily might be viewed as having traditional (nonprogressive) feminine versus feminist views and as being at low levels of her own cultural identity development because, through internalized oppression, she cannot fully accept the notion of partnering with an non-Arab American. She also might be viewed as enmeshed or nonindividuated, because even as an adult, she places a high value on parental approval. Thus, internalized oppression needs to be explored, as well as family dynamics in the context of immediate family roles (e.g., family responsibility, shame) and in a larger context (e.g., family of origin, community).

Guidelines 4 and 5, addressing cultural competence in research and clinical practices, respectively, are potentially problematic in this case, as there is an absence of theoretical models applicable to Arab American populations. Researchers both within and without the Arab American community are stepping up to conduct such research, despite the sometimes overwhelming obstacles created by the hostile post-9/11 climate. Until this knowledge base reaches a more substantial level, existing models must be utilized and applied with care. For example, as discussed earlier, while existing models might pathologize Lily in terms of her individual development in relationship to her parents, psychologists can critically examine the models they might utilize by default and make adjustments accordingly. In addition, both solution-focused and constructivistically oriented strategies may be particularly effective for working with Arab American clients. For example, in Lily's case, employing strategies such as values clarification, decision making, and narrative development might be helpful.

Examination of Attitudes: The Case of Bill

Nabil, also known as "Bill," is a master's student studying counseling psychology. He is in his early 20s, and has lived in the United States for most of his life. His father emigrated from Palestine to Egypt in 1967, where he met Nabil's mother. Nabil was born in Egypt in the early 1980s, and immigrated to the United States with his parents and older siblings. The family belongs to the Coptic Egyptian Church. All three of Bill's siblings, two brothers and one sister, have studied either engineering or computer technology. All of them have Anglicized names. He has always been interested in the migration of the various role models in his life, such as each of his parents and his family as a whole, as well as his cousins in various places around the United States whose origins are Palestinian. Bill is just becoming more aware of some of the circumstances surrounding their migration patterns. His parents and extended family do not speak of politics often, but Bill can sense that they have strong feelings about their countries of origin as well as about U.S. foreign policy. Some of these interests have prompted him, with an undergraduate major in sociology, to pursue psychology as a graduate degree. His parents do not particularly value his choice, but because he is the youngest sibling, and because others already represent fields that they view as more important in terms of economic viability, they have consented to economically support his graduate studies.

In his multicultural and other counseling classes, Bill often asks provocative questions. He sometimes gets frustrated in discussions, in which he challenges other students as well as instructors, about political issues that they may not see as relevant to the issues at hand. He makes good solid points, but his arguments are not always fully developed.

Recommended Considerations. In best nurturing Bill as a psychologist-in-training, it is imperative to self-examine attitudes and beliefs (Guideline 1) about Arab Americans (including sociohistorical and political beliefs about this group), as well as the origins of these beliefs. This "information" then should be researched further by utilizing as references both common U.S. media, media sources from identified "opposite" perspectives and viewpoints, and, finally, any neutral sources that exist. For example, Bill's Palestinian family perspective is likely to be vastly different from that portrayed in mainstream U.S. media sources. Palestinian or Arabic news sources could be accessed via the web. Books by Arab American authors, such as Edward Said (1978), might provide humanistic portraits of both the conflict as well as the resultant suffering of those involved. Finally, researching both Middle Eastern and Islamic history from non-U.S. sources and perspectives, and Arab American immigration history from well-regarded Arab American sources such as the Arab American Institute or the American Arab Anti-Discrimination Committee, will round out the knowledge base for educators and other practitioners.

In short, the Guidelines suggest that viewing individuals rather than groups might lead to more accurate, less stereotyped, and more culturally competent interactions and clinical practice. In researching the issues identified, one not only would become more competent to provide such culturally responsive training, per Guideline 3, but concomitantly would be perceived by student consumers as more caring, trustworthy, and credible. For Bill, it is important to understand the impact of his experiences with both overt and covert prejudice. Mainstream U.S. media sources have been criticized by many Arab American advocacy groups as portraying limited, if any, Palestinian victims in humanistic stories or accounts, as compared with their Israeli counterparts. Rather, Palestinians are demonized as terrorists and suicide bombers rather than as individuals with families striving and hoping for freedom from an occupation that has been condemned by the United Nations as well as many non-U.S. entities around the world. In Bill's level of self awareness and cultural identity development, he may possess a low level or even unconscious awareness of walking on eggshells—that is, a fear of his behavior being labeled or perceived as consistent with a prevalent stereotype of Palestinians as irrational or violent. Uncertain how to best present his case, Bill can be helped to examine his views through open, balanced, and skillfully moderated course discussions and provocative assignments, such as promoting well-researched debates or media analyses, or reports on domestic or foreign policy impacts on specific groups or individuals. Such discussions and assignments are designed to facilitate class and self-examination into broader contextual issues and to link self-identified attitudes and beliefs with an acknowledgment of individuals' experiences of discrimination. It also is important to note that Bill, alone, should not bear the burden of educating the class. With appropriate support, as suggested by Guideline 6 on advocacy and social policy, educators and other students should work with Bill in developing and implementing legislation and other advocacy measures.

Thus, various strategies could be employed with Bill, including incorporating socio-political, -historical, and -economic elements and assignments into class discussions (e.g., debates and presentations), exploring and discussing media influences on perceptions of social issues, encouraging personal growth through projects relating to selected populations of personal or professional interest, and facilitating explorations of internalized oppression.

Oppositional Adolescent: The Case of Rafik

> In the late 1960s, when he was 15 years old, Tarek immigrated to the United States from Sudan with two of his older brothers. Ten years later, he had not yet found a mate, so he consented to his parents finding him a suitable mate in Sudan. He went to Sudan to meet Jamilla, who was a distant cousin and his parent's and community's choice. The two decided to get married, and shortly thereafter returned to the United States. Within the next 10 years, the couple had four children. In addition, Tarek's mother, Nabila, becoming widowed, immigrated to the United States to live with them. The youngest of the four children, Rafik, is in high school. Since September 11, 2001, his behavior has become alarmingly angry and oppositional, and most recently he has made violent threats to his peers. The family lives in a community with a sizable Arab Muslim population, although it is not exclusively an enclave. Nabila has had many ideas about how to treat Rafik's problem, as has the Imam from their mosque; and Tarek and Jamilla have acquiesced to these treatments. Now, however, Rafik has been suspended from school, and the school officials have requested that he receive a psychological assessment and adhere to appropriate treatment before being readmitted to school.

Recommended Considerations. Guideline 2 speaks to the importance of recognizing multicultural sensitivity and responsiveness. For Rafik and his family, it would be important to assess the responsiveness of the local community in providing support for Arab Americans during and after the 9/11 crisis, when a flood of hate crimes toward the Muslim community were reported nationwide. Regarding multicultural implications for Rafik, it would be critical to ascertain whether this tragedy was indeed a catalyst for his behaviors, which seems to be suggested by the timing of their onset. Relatedly, it would be important to assess whether any family members have been targeted since the Patriot Act and other such legislative actions became law. Often, the observance of a family or community member being subject to such discrimination or profiling can serve to facilitate vicarious traumatization. From a clinical perspective (Guideline 5), family dynamics, roles, and experiences of each family member (e.g., Nabila, Tarek, Jamilla, Rafik, and other siblings) need to be explored; and community (e.g., Imam) and family (e.g., Nabila) members need to be involved in assessment, diagnosis, and treatment—in effect, dictating an expanded wraparound treatment approach that includes family and community in addition to the school and area mental health systems.

CONCLUSION

A few common themes are illustrated in the cases. For each case, it is imperative for the psychologist to identify whether any racism exists, and whether its origins are institutional versus socialized, so as to be better situated to counteract the effects. This measure also will help to ensure that the psychologist does not perpetuate the process of internalized oppression.

For all of the clinical case examples, it is important to establish and agree upon, early on, the desired outcomes. Within Arab cultures, helping professionals, including educators, are regarded as authority figures and thus, are looked upon to provide answers to dilemmas, resolutions to problems, and cessation of symptoms.

Finally, Guideline 6 addresses perhaps the most critical element in terms of large-scale intervention. Without appropriate legislation and policy change, the status of Arab Americans in terms of acculturation, mental health, and wellness is not likely to change. The contemporary post-9/11 climate has been analogized by some to the McCarthyism of past U.S. history (e.g., Beinin, 2004). Because we now realize, as a profession, the inextricability of the social, political, historical, and economic contexts of immigration from the subsequent adjustment of individuals, families, and communities, psychologists can and should advocate for these entities at both community or local as well as national and international levels. In doing so, both domestic and foreign policy changes ultimately will lead to a healthier and safer global context for all individuals.

RESOURCES

Select Websites on Arab Americans, Their Religion, and the Middle East

The following list of websites was excerpted directly from the website of the Arab American Institute (http://www.aaiusa.org/links.htm#On):

Arab Community Center for Economic and Social Services (http://www.accesscommunity.org)
> Includes cultural arts, employment and training, public health, and education.

Arab American Business Magazine (http://www.arabamericanbusiness.com)
> A magazine for Arab American businesses.

American-Arab Anti-Discrimination Committee (http://www.adc.org)
> Civil rights organization committed to defending the rights of people of Arab descent and promoting their rich cultural heritage.

The Union of Arab Student Associations (http://angelfire.com/or/uasa)
> Serves as an umbrella for 11 universities in the Washington, DC, area, working to form a national mobilization front uniting all Arab American student organizations.

Religion and the Arab World (http://www.aaiusa.org/links.htm#Religion)

Council on Islamic Education (http://www.cie.org/)
> A body of scholars that provides academic information about Islam, Muslims and world history.

Middle East Institute (http://www.mideast.org/)
> Founded in 1946, the Middle East Institute's principal objective is to increase Americans' knowledge and understanding of the region.

AMIDEAST (http://www.amideast.org/)
> Promoting understanding and cooperation between Americans and the people of the Middle East and North Africa.

Middle East Policy Council (http://www.mepc.org/)
> Nonprofit organization whose purpose is to contribute to an understanding of current issues in U.S.–Middle East relations.

For Further Reading

The following selected resources were excerpted directly from *Teaching About Islam & Muslims in the Public School Classroom: A Handbook for Educators*, (3rd ed.) produced by the Council on Islamic Education:

Introduction to Islam

Haneef, S. (1985). *What everyone should know about Islam and Muslims*. Chicago: Kazi Publications.
> A straightforward approach toward explaining the religion of Islam and its adherents. Particularly useful as it explores life for Muslims in the United States and the challenges that young Muslims face growing up in the American cultural milieu. ISBN: 0-935782-00-1

Maqsood, R. (1994). *Teach yourself Islam*. Chicago: NTC Publishing Group.
A straightforward and refreshing overview of Islam, with emphasis on contemporary issues and lifestyles. ISBN: 0-86316-155-3

Family and Gender Issues

Al-Faruqi, L. (1991). *Women, Muslim society, and Islam*. Plainfield, IN: American Trust Publications.
Discusses a wide range of issues, such as marriage, divorce, gender roles, feminism, legal rights, education, and the family model. ISBN: 0-89259-068-8
Kahf, M. (1999). *Western representations of the Muslim woman*. Austin: University of Texas Press.
The author has made an intriguing analysis of the ways in which the idea of the Muslim woman has figured in Western literature, plays, songs, and the popular imagination. ISBN: 0-2927-4336-X

Interreligious Studies

Peters, F. E. (1990). *Judaism, Christianity, and Islam*.
Takes the basic texts of the three monotheistic faiths and juxtaposes extensive passages from them to show the similarities and common issues facing the followers of each.

Legal Resources

This section on discrimination and civil liberties was excerpted in total from the website of the Arab American Institute (http://www.aaiusa.org/discrimination.htm)

Civil Rights

U.S. Commission on Civil Rights Hotline 1-800-552-6843
The Department of Justice, Civil Rights Division's Initiative to Combat the Post-9/11 Discriminatory Backlash: http://www.usdoj.gov/crt/nordwg.html
How to file a complaint about an alleged civil rights violation by a Department of Justice employee, including employees of the FBI, the Drug Enforcement Administration, the INS, the Federal Bureau of Prisons, and the U.S. Marshals Service: http://www.usdoj.gov/oig/hotline2.htm
Brochure on federal protections against national origin discrimination in
English: http://www.usdoj.gov/crt/legalinfo/natlorg-eng.htm
Arabic: http://www.usdoj.gov/crt/legalinfo/natlorg-ar.pdf
Civil Liberties Restoration Act of 2004 (pdf): http://www.immigrationforum.org/documents/TheDebate/DueProcessPost911/CLRAsecbysec.pdf

Immigration

Information about the rights of INS detainees: http://www.immigration.gov/graphics/lawsregs/guidance.htm

Employment

Workplace rights of Muslims, Arabs, South Asians, and Sikhs under the Equal Employment Opportunity Laws (updated May 2002): http://www.eeoc.gov/facts/backlash-employee.htm
Employer responsibilities concerning the employment of Muslims, Arabs, South Asians, and Sikhs (updated July 2002): http://www.eeoc.gov/facts/backlash-employer.html

Religious Freedom

Protecting the Religious Freedom of All Americans: Federal Laws Against Religious Discrimination, A brochure published by the U.S. Department of Justice's Civil Rights Division (September 2002): http://www.usdoj.gov/crt/religdisc/religionpamp.htm

REFERENCES

Abudabbeh, N. (1996). Arab families. In M. McGoldrick, J. Giordano, & J. K. Pearce (Eds.), *Ethnicity and family therapy* (pp. 333–346). New York: Guildford Press.

Abu-Ali, A., & Reisen, C. A. (1999). Gender role identity among Muslim girls living in the U.S. *Current Psychology: Developmental, Learning, Personality, Social, 18*, 185–192.

Abu El-Haj, T. R. (2002). Contesting the politics of culture, rewriting the boundaries of inclusion: Working for social justice with Muslim and Arab communities. *Anthropology and Education Quarterly, 33*, 308–316.

Ajrouch, K. J. (1999). Family and ethnic identity in an Arab American community. In M. Sulciman (Ed.), *Arabs in America: Building a new future* (pp. 129–139). Philadelphia: Temple University Press.

Ajrouch, K. J. (2000). Place, age, and culture: Community living and ethnic identity among Lebanese American adolescents. *Small Group Research, 31*, 447–469.

Al-Krenawi, A., & Graham, J. R. (2000). Culturally sensitive social work practice with Arab clients in mental health settings. *Health and Social Work, 25*, 9–22.

Ammar, N. H. (2000). Simplistic stereotyping and complex reality of Arab-American immigrant identity: Consequences and future strategies in policing wife battery. *Islam and Christian-Muslim Relations, 11*, 51–70.

Arab American Demographics. (n.d.). Retrieved May 25, 2005, from www.aaiusa.org/demographics.htm

Arab American Institute. (2002). *Healing the nation: The Arab American experience after September 11.* Washington, DC: Arab American Institute Foundation.

Arab American Institute. (2003). *First Census report on Arab ancestry marks rising civic profile of Arab Americans.* Retrieved February 1, 2005, from http://www.aaiusa.org/pr/release12-03-03.htm

Arab American Institute. (2004). Retrieved December 2, 2005, from www.aaiusa.org

Arab American Institute. (n.d.). Retrieved December 2, 2005, from www.aaiusa.org

Arab American Institute Foundation. (2002). *Profiling and pride: Arab American attitudes and behavior since September 11.* Washington, DC: Author.

Barrett, D. H., Doebbeling, C. C., Schwartz, D. A., Volker, M. D., Falter, K. H., Woolson, R. F., et al. (2002). Post-traumatic stress disorder and self-reported physical health status among U.S. military personnel serving during the Gulf War period: A population-based study. *Psychosomatics, 43*, 195–205.

Beinin, J. (2004). The new American McCarthyism: Policing thought about the Middle East. *Race & Class, 46,* 101–115.

Bennett, S. E. (1994). The Gulf War's impact on Americans' political information. *Political Behavior, 16,* 179–201.

Blair, R. G. (2000). Risk factors associated with PTSD and major depression among Cambodian refugees in Utah. *Health and Social Work, 25,* 23–31.

Blair, R. G. (2001). Mental health needs among Cambodian refugees in Utah. *International Social Work, 44,* 179–196.

Bouffard, K. (2004, October 22). Arab American teens struggle with rising stress. *The Detroit News.*

Council on Islamic Education. (1995). *Teaching about Islam and Muslims in the public school classroom* (3rd ed.). Fountain Valley, CA: Author.

Dwairy, M. (2006). *Culturally sensitive counseling and psychotherapy: Working with Arabic and Muslim clients.* New York: Teachers College Press.

Erickson, C. D., & Al-Timimi, N. R. (2001). Providing mental health services to Arab Americans: Recommendations and considerations. *Cultural Diversity and Ethnic Minority Psychology, 7 ,* 306–327.

Faragallah, M. H., Schumm, H. R., & Webb, F. J. (1997). Acculturation of Arab-American immigrants: An exploratory study. *Journal of Comparative Family Studies, 28,* 182–203.

Gorman, W. (2001). Refugee survivors of torture: Trauma and treatment. *Professional Psychology: Research and Practice, 32,* 443–451.

Gorst-Unsworth, C., & Goldenberg, E. (1998). Psychological sequelae of torture and organised violence suffered by refugees from Iraq: Trauma-related factors compared with social factors in exile. *British Journal of Psychiatry, 172,* 90–94.

Hakim-Larson, J., Kamoo, R., & Voelker, S. (1998, July). *Mental health services and families of Arab ethnic origin.* Poster session presented at the annual meeting of the Family Research Consortium II, Blaine, WA.

Hakim-Larson, J., & Nassar-McMillan, S. (2005). *Middle Eastern Americans and counseling.* Unpublished manuscript.

Haley, R. W., & Kurt, T. L. (1997). Self-reported exposure to neurotoxic chemical combinations in the Gulf War. *Journal of American Medical Association, 277,* 231–237.

Halliday, F. (1997). Neither treason nor conspiracy: Reflections on media coverage of the Gulf War 1990–1991. *Citizenship Studies, 1,* 157–172.

Jackson, M. L., & Nassar-McMillan, S. (2006). Counseling Arab Americans. In C. C. Lee (Ed.), *Multicultural issues in counseling: New approaches to diversity.* (3rd ed., pp. 235–247). Alexandria, VA: American Counseling Association.

Jamil, H., Hakim-Larson, J., Farrag, M., Kafaji, T., Duqum, I., & Jamil, L. (2002). A retrospective study of Arab American mental health clients: Trauma and the Iraqi refugees. *American Journal of Orthopsychiatry, 72,* 355–361.

Jamil, H., Nassar-McMillan, S. C., & Lambert, R. (2004). Aftermath of the Gulf War: Mental health issues among Iraqi Gulf War veteran refugees in the United States. *Journal of Mental Health Counseling, 26,* 295–308.

Keyes, E. F. (2000). Mental health status in refugees: An integrative review of current research. *Issues in Mental Health Nursing, 21,* 397–410.

Kira, I. A. (2002). Torture assessment and treatment: The wraparound approach. *Traumatology, 8,* 23–51.

Lee, Y., Lee, M. K., Chun, D. H., Lee, Y. K., & Yoon, S. J. (2001). Trauma experience of North Korean refugees in China. *American Journal of Preventive Medicine, 20,* 225–229.

Llorente, E. (2002, August 12). Arabs debate need for minority status. *North Jersey News.*

Marshall, S. E., & Read, J. G. (2003). Identity politics among Arab-American women. *Social Science Quarterly, 84,* 875–891.

Meleis, A. I. (1991). Between two cultures: Identity, roles, and health. *Health Care for Women International, 12,* 365–377.

Naff, A. (1985). *Becoming American: The early Arab immigrant experience.* Carbondale and Edwardsville: Southern Illinois University Press.

Nassar-McMillan, S. C. (2003a). Counseling Arab Americans. In N. A. Vacc, S. B. DeVaney, & J. M. Brendel (Eds.), *Counseling multicultural and diverse populations* (4th ed., pp. 117–139). New York: Brunner-Routledge.

Nassar-McMillan, S. C. (2003b). *Counseling Arab Americans: Counselors' call for advocacy and social justice.* Denver: Love.

Nassar-McMillan, S. C. (in press). *Counseling Arab Americans.* Boston: Houghton Mifflin.

Nassar-McMillan, S., & Hakim-Larson, J. (2003). Counseling considerations among Arab Americans. *Journal of Counseling and Development, 81,* 150–159.

Nobles, A., & Sciarra, D. (2000). Cultural determinants in the treatment of Arab Americans: A primer for mainstream therapists. *American Journal of Orthopsychiatry, 70,* 182–191.

Orfalea, G. (1988). *Before the flames: A quest for the history of Arab Americans.* Austin: University of Texas Press.

Paine, P. (1986). *A study of the Middle East community in the Detroit metropolitan area.* Detroit, MI: United Community Services of Metropolitan Detroit.

Read, J. G., & Bartkowski, J. P. (2000). To veil or not to veil? A case study of identity negotiation among Muslim women in Austin, Texas. *Gender & Society, 14,* 395–417.

Said, E. (1978). *Orientalism.* New York: Random House.

Samhan, H. (1999). Not quite white: Race classification and the Arab American experience. In M. Suleiman (Ed.), *Arabs in America: Building a new future* (pp. 209–226). Philadelphia: Temple University Press.

Samhan, H. (n.d.). *Arab Americans.* Retrieved May 25, 2005, from www.aaiusa.org/definition.htm

Sarroub, L. K. (2002). From neologisms to social practice: An analysis of the wanding of America. *Anthropology and Education Quarterly, 33,* 297–307.

Shaheen, J. (1985). Media coverage of the Middle East: Perception and foreign policy. *Annals of the American Academy, 482,* 160–175.

Shaheen, J. (1991). The comic book Arab. *The Link, 24,* 1–11.

Shaheen, J. (1997). *Arab and Muslim stereotyping in American popular culture.* Washington, DC: Center for Muslim–Christian Understanding.

Shaheen, J. G. (2001). *Reel bad Arabs: How Hollywood vilifies a people.* Brooklyn, NY: Interlink.

Smith, H. (1991). *The world's religions: Our great wisdom traditions.* San Francisco: Harper.

U.S. Bureau of the Census. (2003). *The Arab population: 2000.* Retrieved August 26, 2006, from www.census.gov/prod/2003pubs/c2kbr=23.pdf

Zogby, J. J. (2001). *What ethnic Americans really think: The Zogby culture polls.* Washington, DC: Zogby International.

7

Biracial Populations

Angela R. Gillem,
Sean Kathleen Lincoln,
and Kristen English

Our purpose in this chapter is to depathologize biracial psychology by discussing the psychotherapeutic needs of biracial people within a framework provided by the "Guidelines on Multicultural Education, Training, Research, Practice, and Organizational Change for Psychologists" (APA, 2003), hereinafter referred to as the Guidelines. During most of the 1900s, the social scientific community examined the experiences of mixed race people from a racist perspective, and only since the late 1980s have researchers and clinicians begun to repair this distorted lens. Literature in the late 1980s and early 1990s focused on challenging constructions of biracial identity based on hypodescent (identifying with the parent with the lowest social status) and the one-drop rule (one drop of non-White blood makes one non-White), both of which forced biracial people to identify with only part of their heritage. Because mixed race people challenge our understanding of racial identity, their efforts to claim their entire heritage often are characterized as naive and pathological. Guideline 1 encourages psychologists to recognize that "they may hold attitudes and beliefs that can detrimentally influence their perceptions of and interactions with individuals who are ethnically and racially different from themselves" (APA, 2003, p. 382). Being a minority within minorities, biracial people are different from others around them, including their own parents. Thus, it is important that psychologists work to overcome the tendency to pathologize the perspectives of biracial people, by learning about this population and debunking the historical myths that surround them.

In the literature, authors often do not distinguish among the specific racial mixtures of biracial individuals. Psychology is slowly growing toward an understanding that people from different races have developmental and psychological issues that may not be shared across groups. Thus, we acknowledge that not all biracial combinations are the same–an Asian/White person, for example, has very different social sequelae from a Black/White person.

We conceptualize race as an historically evolved construct for the maintenance of White privilege. Anthropological and biological studies report greater variation within racial groups than between them, suggesting that races are not biologically distinct (Gillem, Cohn, & Throne, 2001). Within this social constructionist perspective, consistent with the Guidelines, we employ the following terms to designate racial differences. *Monoracial* individuals have parents of the same socially defined race, while the parents of *biracial* people represent two different races. This biracial designation includes Latino ethnicity as a "race" (e.g., a person with a Latino and a Black parent will be considered biracial as well as bicultural). *Bicultural* designates individuals whose parents come from distinct cultural heritages (e.g., Vietnamese/Chinese, Puerto Rican/Mexican). An individual with more than two socially defined racial backgrounds (e.g., Filipinos or Latinos) will be referred to as *multiracial.* We use *mixed race* to refer to both biracial and multiracial people, with context determining its meaning. In this chapter, we primarily will be discussing biracial people. Some authors employ *biracial* and *biethnic* synonymously; however, using our definitions, children from parents of two cultures or ethnicities can be monoracial (e.g., monoracial Asians can be biethnic if their parents are Japanese and Chinese). We use *interracial* to refer to relationships in which individuals of two or more races interact.

Guideline 2 emphasizes the development of multicultural knowledge and sensitivity in understanding racially different people (APA, 2003). In the next section, we review the literature on biracial identity development as a foundation for competent and sensitive approaches to treatment. Then, addressing Guideline 5's emphasis on applying culturally appropriate skills in clinical practice, we discuss psychotherapy approaches with biracial individuals. Finally, we address Guideline 3, on employing multiculturalism in psychological education, by discussing training and education for cultural competence with this population.

IDENTITY DEVELOPMENT

Research in this field has focused on three main areas: identity, self-concept/self-esteem, and psychological adjustment. With few exceptions (e.g., Bracey, Bamaca, & Umana-Taylor, 2004; Brown, 2001; Herman, 2004; Rockquemore & Brunsma, 2002), most studies are qualitative, using small, region-bound samples. Despite these limitations, there is enough consistency across studies to allow tentative generalizations and treatment recommendations. Applying Guideline 2 to this population, it is essential to understand the identity development of biracial individuals in order to provide them with culturally competent services.

Identity Models

Racial identity is defined narrowly by social categories, yielding monoracial models that do not capture the complexity of biracial identity development (Gillem et al., 2001; Poston, 1990; Root, 1990). Root (1990) posited that monoracial identity models are inappropriate for mixed race people because they idealize a rejection of White values, which would be internally oppressive to individuals who are part White. She suggested that the most consistent and intense conflict in biracial development involves "the tension between racial components within oneself" (p. 198). Social, family, and political systems perpetuate these tensions.

Since the 1990s, biracial models (see Collins, 2000; Henriksen, 2001; Henriksen & Trusty, 2004; Jacobs, 1992; Kerwin & Ponterotto, 1995; Kich, 1992; Poston, 1990) have indicated that healthy identity moves from a nonracially defined personal identity (color-blind), through immersion in one or more externally motivated monoracial identities, to an internally defined multiracial one. This often involves identity ambivalence, questioning, experimenting, and struggle (Gillem et al., 2001; Thompson, 1999). For biracial people, it is common to have fluid, situational, or simultaneous identities (Root, 1995; T. K. Williams, 1995). Unfortunately, this fluidity has been pathologized in some of the monoracial- and early biracial identity literature.

In a personal narrative, C. B. Williams (1999) described herself as having concurrent identity statuses and processes—one in the White model and one in the Black model. This "combined consciousness" (p. 34) does not mesh with the monoracial models imposed on biracial people (e.g., Helms & Cook, 1999). Williams discussed how "racial identity, especially for mixed people, is centered in the person, not in societal constructions . . . there is no one 'correct' identification for mixed race people—it is the person herself or himself who gets to name her or his experience" (p. 34). This notion is not easily digested within current constructions of race.

Identity Resolutions

As alternatives to stage models of biracial identity, Root (1990, 1999, 2001) and Rockquemore and Brunsma (2002) have moved toward ecological frameworks. Root (1999) based her model on three premises: No identity resolution is inherently superior or problematic, racial identity is dynamically rooted in history and social context, and people have multiple statuses influencing racial identity and affecting its salience at any given time. Similarly, Rockquemore and Brunsma (2002) refused to privilege biracial identity as an ideal, considering the multifaceted ways that biracial people understand their identities and grounding their model in the lived experiences of biracial people. They saw social validation and invalidation as the overarching influences on racial identity resolution. Invalidation occurs when self-understanding is different from how others perceive and respond to biracial individuals, and as a result, they experience a push away and/or a pull from others about who and what they are. Given the similarity of Root's and Rockquemore and Brunsma's models, we discuss them together.

Monoracial or *singular* identity involves identification with one part of one's heritage. It can involve passive acceptance of socially assigned identity or active experience-based choice (Root, 1990, 2001). Acceptance from the extended family with which one identifies is crucial for healthy identity (Root, 1990). If appearance does not match the chosen identity group, biracial individuals must be prepared to cope with opposition from others (Rockquemore & Brunsma, 2002).

Biracial or *border* identity involves identification as a new racial group resulting from a strong connection with other biracial people (Root, 1990). Borders identify with both heritages, resisting social dichotomy and hierarchy (Rockquemore & Brunsma, 2002). This is positive as long as it is not an attempt to escape or hide one's racial heritages (Root, 1990).

Symbolic or *transcendent* identity involves refusing to capitulate to society's pressure to use race to understand the social world and biracial individuals' place in it (Rockquemore & Brunsma, 2002). Distant from both sides of their family, individuals acknowledge race and ethnicity but without cultural competence or attachment (Root, 2001). They recognize racism's negative impact, but it is not an important issue for them (Rockquemore & Brunsma, 2002).

Situational or *protean* identity is dependent on the situation or circumstance (Rockquemore & Brunsma, 2002; Root, 2001). Individuals feel connected to both sides of their family and are culturally savvy in several social worlds, moving fluidly from one to another. This identity is positive if they maintain a sense of personal integrity across groups and if both groups accept them, which they often do (Rockquemore & Brunsma, 2002; Root, 1990).

Researchers have found some consistent patterns in biracial identity development. Biracials show higher ethnic identity (EI) levels and place more importance on race than do Whites, but evidence lower levels of

EI and racial salience than do monoracial people of color (Bracey et al., 2004; Grove, 1991; Herman, 2004; Jaret & Reitzes, 1999; Jones, 2000; Mass, 1992). However, rather than suggesting lower levels of racial/ethnic salience, these findings might suggest a lengthier process of identity development for biracials, given the broad range of issues they have to manage. Brown (2001) found that most of her 119 participants resolved racial identity conflicts postadolescence, and Root (1998) suggested that the biracial identity process is more active and prolonged than that for monoracials, possibly lasting 20 years. It is noteworthy that many researchers recruited their participants from college-based monoracial organizations (e.g., Asian student associations and Black student associations). Given that biracials often feel more invalidated by their minority heritage group than by Whites (Grove, 1991; Rockquemore & Brunsma, 2002), one might anticipate more racial/ethnic ambivalence and prolonged struggle in these samples.

Brown (2001) found that most of her participants had Black public identities, often due to social pressure or internal conflict involving guilt, shame, or loyalty to Black family and community. Private identities, revealed only when asked and when not pressured to identify as Black, were primarily biracial and only secondarily Black or White. White private identity allowed individuals to avoid denying their White parent. Suyemoto (2004) had similar findings with her 50 Japanese/European American participants. When not pressured to choose, they primarily identified as multiracial, but when forced to choose to identify with a Japanese, a White, or a racially different biracial person, most (52%) chose a Japanese person based on shared culture or connection with the community. Those who chose a racially different biracial person (32%) did so because of the salience of their multiracial experience or in response to minimal acceptance from monoracial people. The few who chose White (16%) were raised among Whites.

Identity validation or invalidation often is related to physical features. Brown (2001) found that darker skinned Black/White biracials were questioned about their race less frequently and had stronger Black identities. However, lighter skinned Black/White biracials encountered more difficulties with others accepting their racial designation. Rockquemore and Brunsma (2002) also found that the more one's physical features aligned with the expected phenotype of a particular group, the more one tended to be treated as a member of and to identify with that group. Social invalidation results when individuals' racial identity differs from society's view of their phenotype and what others believe they should be (Rockquemore & Laszloffy, 2003).

A number of authors have identified marginal status as a primary fate of biracials (Baptiste, 1990; Deters, 1997; Gibbs, 1989; Gibbs & Moskowitz-Sweet, 1991; Grove, 1991); however, a number of quantitative research studies found no indicators of marginalization for biracial participants

(Aldarondo, 2001; Field, 1993; Johnson & Nagoshi, 1986; Kerwin, Ponterotto, Jackson, & Harris, 1993; Phinney & Alipuria, 1996; Stephan & Stephan, 1991). The key to healthy, nonmarginalized biracial identity is to accept both parts of one's heritage, to identify in a way that feels comfortable regardless of appearance and approval from others, and to develop coping strategies to defend against challenges to identity (Root, 1990, 1997).

Self-Concept/Self-Esteem

Biracial people face two major identity tasks: distinguishing how others see them from how they see and experience themselves, and developing a genuinely felt place of belonging. In reconciling these reactions and molding a positive self-concept, they must resolve the painful experience of being different from everyone around them.

Awareness of "otherness" begins at approximately 3 years of age when children notice skin-color differences (Morrison, 1995; Root, 1990). Over time, biracial people experience strange looks as others try to figure out what they are, express surprise at their parentage, or express disapproval. These "interactional invalidations" (Rockquemore & Brunsma, 2002) initiate biracial children's education on the meaning of racial difference. The feeling of outsider status due to perceived (by self and others) differentness (Gibbs & Moskowitz-Sweet, 1991; Pinderhughes, 1995; Roberts-Clarke, Roberts, & Morokoff, 2004; Root, 1990) may be exacerbated in adolescence when dating and peer approval become important. This appears to be a more difficult time for females than for males, as definitions of attractiveness and beauty are assessed (Gibbs & Moskowitz-Sweet, 1991; Gillem, 2004; Roberts-Clarke et al., 2004; Root, 1998).

Brown's (2001) research suggests that conflict is the best predictor of self-esteem. In her sample, those who encountered identity and group membership conflicts had lower self-esteem. Her Black/White biracial participants tended to cope with internal conflict and protect their self-esteem in a number of ways: public versus private identity compartmentalization, denial of one racial part, rationalization of a monoracial identity, sublimation through educational and professional achievement, or compartmentalization of societal negativity. It is important to take these things into account when exploring the relationship between racial identity and self-esteem.

Adjustment and Well-Being

Biracials face social challenges that complicate identity resolution in ways not encountered by monoracials. Many report feeling guilty, confused, and disloyal when they identify with the heritage of only one parent, often feeling as if they are rejecting the other parent (Baptiste, 1990; Bowles, 1993; Brown, 2001; Gibbs & Moskowitz-Sweet, 1991; Gillem et al., 2001; Winn & Priest, 1993). Sometimes there is shame at denying their heritage (Bowles, 1993; Brown, 2001) and anxiety about the discrepancy between their sense of themselves as biracial and their public assertion, under social pressure, of a monoracial identity (Bowles, 1993). Also, the pressure to identify with one heritage can imply negative messages about the other.

Several researchers have reported that their participants experienced rejection from both races (often including family), resulting in a sense of isolation and a lack of a sense of belonging (e.g., Bowles, 1993; Brown, 2001; Collins, 2000; Gibbs & Moskowitz-Sweet, 1991; Grove, 1991; Phillips, 2004; Root, 1998; Thompson, 1999). Sometimes they were criticized for not acting enough like their racial group of color. Because they usually had no biracial reference group with which to identify and from which to seek social support, biracial individuals often struggled to figure out where they belonged (Collins, 2000; Grove, 1991; Thompson, 1999).

Positive interracial family environments do not attach self-worth to race, ignore race, or denigrate racial groups. If a parent's racial group is denigrated and the child is expected to identify with that heritage, it can negatively affect his or her identity development and lead to feelings of inferiority. It also can lead the child to reject that parent, reflecting internalized oppression (Root, 1990). Particularly problematic are a lack of conversation and limited preparation in the family for dealing with racism and prejudice (Buckley & Carter, 2004; Root, 2001; Winn & Priest, 1993), which leave biracial individuals unequipped to cope with their racialized social environment and negative messages about their heritage (Gillem, 2004).

Negative messages from family can lead to identity development difficulties. For example, being racially mixed in some Asian cultures might mean bringing shame on immediate and extended families as well as ancestors. This can result in the mixed race child being treated differently by relatives. Also, if dysfunction in the family is racially encoded, the child will develop a distorted understanding of race, even if a parent does not explicitly speak negatively about the partner's race. If the family does not speak openly and positively about race, negative social messages might be used to explain family problems (Root, 2001).

White neighborhoods and schools might inflict racial trauma, affecting self-esteem, body image, and emotional well-being. They also may enhance the likelihood of a White racial identity because of the expectation of assimilation into the White cultural environment (Brown, 2001). This expectation often is coupled with less positive attitudes toward the minority heritage and racial identity conflict (Brown, 2001; Herman, 2004). However, perceiving racial discrimination in the context of receiving positive racial messages from the family and having a racial peer group is associated with a non-White identification and less racial identity conflict (Brown, 2001; Gillem et al., 2001; Herman, 2004). Thus, the family is the most effective means of defending against racial confusion (Motoyoshi, 1990).

Within minority communities, many biracials are subjected to "racial legitimacy tests" in which their authenticity and loyalty are challenged (Root, 1997, 2001). For example, Fukuyama (1999) discussed the "racial Catch-22" exemplified by her experiences in college. Hawaiian students recognized her biraciality, yet derogatorily labeled her half-White status. During a counseling center staff discussion on affirmative action, she was called "half a minority" by colleagues and was deemed "not ethnic enough" by other women of color. Thus, the minority community cannot be assumed to be a social haven for biracial people (Brown, 2001). As a result, many display immersion behavior and dress or adopt ethnic names to prove racial authenticity (Brown, 2001; Gillem et al., 2001; Root, 1998; Storrs, 1999), especially if physical appearance betrays their mixed race. Although integrated neighborhoods and schools may foster acceptance of biraciality through more role models, less isolation and sense of differentness, and less identity conflict, there still may be pressure to choose sides (Brown, 2001).

In the past decade, researchers have provided a more balanced picture of biracials' race-related psychological health, finding biracial youngsters to be no different psychologically from monoracial children in adjustment (Johnson & Nagoshi, 1986) and in symptomatic distress, self-esteem, and self-concept (Harrison, 1997). Phinney and Alipuria (1996) concluded, from comparisons of biracials and multiracials with monoracials, that their results contradicted popular views and clinical impressions that mixed race individuals are "troubled, marginal people" (p. 152). Several quantitative research studies of biracial and mixed race children and young adults have reached similar conclusions: Biracials may have difficulties finding acceptance due to their dual ethnic/racial heritage within rigidly monoracial societies; however, being biracial does not predispose them to pathology (e.g., Johnson & Nagoshi, 1986; Kerwin et al., 1993; McKelvey & Webb, 1996; Phinney & Alipuria, 1996; Stephan & Stephan, 1991).

COUNSELING BIRACIAL INDIVIDUALS: CULTURALLY APPROPRIATE SKILLS

In Guideline 2, as noted previously, psychologists are urged to be knowledgeable of and sensitive to the needs of racially different clients (APA, 2003).

Issues specific to biracial people must be considered so as to avoid the imposition of a monoracial perspective, which could produce secondary racial traumatization (see Root, 2001). On the other hand, we must not assume that everything presented in therapy by biracial people relates to being biracial or to identity conflicts or confusion (Deters, 1997). Biracial people have normal developmental issues and reactions to life challenges that sometimes require therapeutic attention (Looby, 2001). Many clinicians are guilty of attributing to biracial status anything from reactions to sexual, physical, or psychological abuse, to adjustment problems related to divorce, abandonment, or death.

An example of this misattribution of causation is the case of Ryan, which, according to Hart-Webb (1999), demonstrates how "mixed race identity complicates the development of a cohesive well-integrated self-concept" (p. 117):

> Ryan's White mother got pregnant out of wedlock by a Black man who was "run out of town" by his mother's family when Ryan was an infant. Thus, Ryan never knew his father, and his mother never told him that he was biracial until junior high when his peers started calling him names.

The author attributed Ryan's sexual-orientation conflicts, sex-role-identification conflicts, and rage at White women to his biracial status. She seemed to ignore the possibility that the sexual and physical abuse by the men that his White mother brought home and married might be related to his substance abuse, academic problems, identity issues, and social marginalization. The racial identity issues for this young man more than likely were related also to his rejecting his White extended family and his mother's inability to deal with or discuss his biracialness. This case is a good example of misattributing problems to biracial status, a dangerous approach a number of authors have warned against (e.g., Cooney & Radina, 2000; Deters, 1997; Gibbs, 1989, 1998; Pinderhughes, 1995; Root, 1999). Therapists must rule out other stressors before attributing issues to dual-racial heritage.

It is also important not to pathologize normal biracial identity development when it does not follow monoracial models. Biracial identity development is a different process, and we must understand its complexity in order to distinguish healthy from unhealthy development (Deters, 1997). Therapists should not pathologize the simultaneous endorsement of multiple identities—both multiracial and monoracial identities as well as separate ethnic identities and other intersecting identities—as they are normal, psychologically healthy identity processes and resolutions for biracial people. With clients who are in treatment for identity conflicts, it is important to explore various identities in order to find resolutions that are comfortable for them (Suyemoto, 2004; see also Brown, 2001; Rockquemore & Brunsma, 2002; Root, 2001).

Clinicians must distinguish social (reference group) from personal meanings, and racial from ethnic meanings within the client's identity (Aldarondo, 2001; Suyemoto, 2004), as in this example:

Monica is an 18-year-old Black/White college freshman who identifies as Black and Italian. She described her Italian identity: "When people ask me, the first thing I say is, I'm Italian, just because my grandfather was from Italy, so I'm totally Italian." Monica also asserted a Black identity: "I think that it might be, in part, because I was always with them [her Italian family] and they were all White. I was with my dad every other weekend and that was it. I was [always] with White people. I looked different, so it was always obvious—I wasn't White."

Her racial differentness shaped her Black racial identity, and her social/familial reference group shaped her Italian/White identity. Therapists must recognize these complexities in order to provide competent treatment to this population.

It is also important not to pathologize or idealize situational/protean identity or symbolic/transcendent identity (Root, 2001). We must understand the motives behind situational "code switching" in order to understand whether it represents flexibility and fluidity or internalized oppression. We likewise must explore whether the "color-blind" approach of the transcendent client is naïveté or a sociopolitically informed deliberate effort to transgress racialized notions of identity. Moreover, clinicians must understand their own reactions to biracial identity resolutions that make them uncomfortable and for which they may have easy, pejorative explanations.

Finally, when biracial clients do bring biracial issues to treatment, it is important to allow them to explore their ambivalence about race; suppressing it will imply that something is wrong with them for feeling the way they do (Deters, 1997). Therapists must encourage exploration of both heritages and examine the variables that might influence identity. The racial differences between therapist and client are also important to discuss. Racism is a reality, and the client needs to know that the therapist is open to all of who he or she are without conditions. As Guideline 2 underscores, cultural knowledge and sensitivity are important for mental health professionals in working with biracial individuals. Thus, such knowledge and sensitivity undoubtedly will assist them in identifying and implementing culturally appropriate skills with that population.

Guideline 5 urges psychologists to use culturally appropriate skills in their work with clients. However, clinical trials have yet to be designed that explore the most effective treatment modalities with particular racial groups in varying psychosocial circumstances. We base the following therapeutic recommendations on suggestions from clinical and empirical literature, as well as on the issues presented by biracial individuals in therapy.

Relational, Narrative, and Positive-Psychology Approaches

Rockquemore and Laszloffy (2003) suggest "relational narrative therapy" to deal with the effects of racial identity invalidation. Relational therapy, based in systems theory, presupposes that interpersonal interactions bring people into therapy. Narrative therapy is based on the social construction-ist notion that people create reality in social interactions through the stories that they tell. Through relational narrative therapy, the client learns how to "re-author" narratives that have been "warped" through invalidating interactions. Family therapists also can use this approach to explore the individual and familial narratives that give meaning to historical and episodic events that have affected interracial families (Milan & Keiley, 2000).

Some authors suggest a positive psychology, strengths-based approach rather than focusing only on invalidating experiences (Edwards & Pedrotti, 2004; Suyemoto, 2004). Therapists can explore the richness and strengths of dual heritages, racial/cultural flexibility and fluidity, open-mindedness and acceptance of differences, opportunities to educate others and facilitate social change (Thompson, 1999), and the resilience required of biraciality.

Family Therapy

Family therapy is important when working with biracial children and adolescents. Often, youngsters receive confusing messages about their racial/ethnic identity from the family. Resolution of parents' differences and acceptance of each other affect the adolescent's ability to attain a "positive and cohesive sense of identity" (Gibbs & Moskowitz-Sweet, 1991, p. 588).

Oriti, Bibb, and Mahboubi (1996) advocated taking a strengths-based approach. They suggested that clinicians need an understanding and awareness of the dynamics of privilege and oppression as they affect a particular family, emphasizing adaptability rather than pathology around these issues. They recommended helping family members articulate differing experiences around being in an interracial family, allowing them to present their perspectives on race so that they could understand one another. As an example, they presented the following case:

> The Ks' biracial son had a run-in with police. The parents took a color-blind approach that race was not important, while their son was struggling with racial identity and saw race as a factor in the altercation. The parents did not associate with anyone who considered race important and did not

emphasize race in their marriage or with their children. They were also concerned that their children would be negatively affected by the rejection they experienced from their extended families. Thus, the Ks did not fully prepare their children for racism or for the conflicts they might experience as biracial individuals.

Brown (2001) recommended against sheltering biracial children from outside attitudes about race or biracial people. Parents' sharing of their own experiences or race-related pain can help their children to feel comfortable talking about racial issues, rather than avoiding such discussions as a means of protecting their parents from their biracial realities (Root, 2001). Discussions in the home about racism can prepare family members to cope with challenges to their racial identities. However, it is important, as Oriti and colleagues (1996) indicate, not to invalidate either the parents or the children for their approaches to race. It is more important to explore both adaptive and maladaptive approaches in order to modify them for improved family functioning.

Techniques

Logan, Freeman, and McRoy (1987) suggested a number of techniques to incorporate into any psychotherapeutic modality. Therapists could use genograms to explore family's racial makeup, relationships, labels, attitudes, themes, and stressors, as well as the identified client's position and acceptance within the family. Cultural genograms can be used to make more obvious the ancestral strengths and adversities of each heritage group, helping family members understand their cultural histories and how those histories might be translated in their lives (see Hardy & Laszloffy, 1995; and Rigazio-DiGilio, Ivey, Kunkler-Peck, & Grady, 2005, for a full discussion of genograms). In particular, it can help the White parent respond to the oppression her or his child might be experiencing, but with which she or he has had no experience (Milan & Keiley, 2000). Ecomaps (see Cox, Keltner, & Hogan, 2003, for a discussion of family assessment using ecomaps) are useful to examine the social systems within which the family is embedded and to explore environmental supports, role models, and social cutoffs, helping to identify problems between the client/family and the external environment (Logan et al., 1987).

Logan and colleagues (1987) suggested using a "cultural continuum" incorporating a range of identity resolutions, from denial of the importance of race to multiculturalism, to explore how clients adapt to their cultural and racial backgrounds. This technique can provide a base from which to discuss identity process and resolution. However, this approach implies a hierarchy of identity resolutions. We believe that identity development and resolution are dynamic, fluid, sometimes situational, nonlinear, and nonhierarchical. We prefer an open exploration of the client's identity without the implied hierarchy that the cultural continuum might impose.

Therapy and Support Groups

Bemak and Chung (1997) recommended group psychotherapy for their Vietnamese Amerasian participants, thereby facilitating a sense of "shared experience" with respect to "feelings of loss, persecution, biracial identity, alienation, displacement and absent biological fathers" (p. 86). Group therapy could provide community, validation, and possibly role models (especially if the therapists are biracial) that clients are unable to find within their families.

Therapists also can refer families to support groups for interracial and intercultural families. This requires that the therapist become familiar with programs that mental health, community, church, and social groups offer. Gibbs and Moskowitz-Sweet (1991) also suggested encouraging families to participate in activities and events that might nurture racial and cultural pride. However, it is important to prepare the family for involvement, exploring the meaning of cultural activities and clarifying their appropriateness for family members.

Parent and Family Education

There are several recommendations to parents made in the literature and supported by empirical evidence. Often, parents do not know how to address the needs of their biracial children because their children's experiences are so different from their own. As a result, they rely on approaches that distance them from their children's experiences. For example, Root (2001) described four problematic family approaches:

1. The color-blind approach, most common in those living in predominantly White communities, minimizes the importance of race and the associated power dynamics.
2. The "race is everything" approach reduces everything to race and minimizes the significance of other factors in making sense of the world.
3. The "don't make race an issue" approach is espoused by parents who themselves are uncomfortable or unequipped to deal with race in spite of their likely awareness of race as an issue.
4. The "we don't understand Americans and race" approach often is found among immigrant parents who are unfamiliar with U.S. racism (p. 147).

Therapists can provide consultation and psychoeducation to parents to help address race with their children. It is important for parents to openly explore racial/ethnic heritage and racism, not minimizing or overemphasizing (at the expense of other issues) the importance of race in their children's lives.

Parents should recognize that their children's racial identity will take a different course and resolution from their own. They need to understand that identity fluctuations and experimentation are normal for all adolescents, and that racial identity experimentation is normal for biracial youngsters. Parents should provide connections to extended family and information about their heritage, but let children find the label(s) that feel comfortable to them. Parents should provide an interracial family identity and encourage their children to embrace both heritages, offering appropriate responses to those who challenge their family makeup. It is particularly important to provide positive information about the minority heritage in order to counter society's negative messages. Diverse neighborhoods and integrated schools and community events, particularly those with a number of other interracial families, may provide children with the opportunity to socialize with similar others.

School Counseling

Guideline 6 encourages psychologists to support culturally informed practices and to act as change agents in organizations, including schools (APA, 2003). In the 2000 U.S. Census, 6,368,075 individuals assigned themselves to two races and 458,153 respondents designated three or more races (U.S. Bureau of the Census, 2000). As interracial marriage increases and the "biracial baby boom" (Root, 1999) continues, biracial students will represent an increasing portion of the school-aged population. Although empirical studies have found that biracial students do not exhibit more counseling-related problems than their monoracial peers (Nishimura & Bol, 1997), counselors and psychologists should collaborate with parents, teachers, and administrators to facilitate the healthy development of biracial children. School is a constant in their lives as they move through childhood and encounter adolescence, a life phase during which some biracial identity development models predict issues of confusion and guilt. It is essential for school counselors to recognize the unique experiences and needs of their biracial students, providing support and empowerment to challenge monoracial hierarchies upheld within the school environment (Clancy, 1995).

School counselors and psychologists need to be leaders in promoting "sustained attention to diversity related objectives, and changes in policy and practices" that make schools inclusive and pluralistic (APA, 2003, p. 394). Harris (2002) noted that school counselors working in culturally competent environments were more apt to hold accurate perceptions of their biracial students' experiences. This includes recognizing that biracial children may identify with both parents, rather than just the minority parent, and that minority groups are not necessarily more accepting of biracial children than are nonminorities.

In promoting greater biracial competence in school counselors, Benedetto and Olisky (2001) identified three areas around which counselors' interventions may focus: awareness, communication, and exposure. *Awareness* refers to recognizing unique issues for biracial students, *communication* entails discussing biracial issues in order to facilitate healthy biracial identity, and *exposure* is aimed toward exploring racial/ethnic heritage in order to help students acquire "culturally linked social skills" (p. 68). Suggested interventions include classroom lessons geared toward debunking racial stereotypes, celebrating cultural diversity days and diverse cultural holidays, constructing family heritage trees, generating ideas for future action via diaries and creative-writing exercises, taking field trips to cultural centers, and creating mentoring programs with local minority and biracial role models. Exposure to varying family configurations and racial mixes within school curricula promotes the notion that differences are normal, and that different is not automatically synonymous with abnormal (Nishimura, 1995).

PROFESSIONAL DEVELOPMENT STRATEGIES

Self Awareness

First and foremost, consistent with Guideline 1, we believe that practicing clinicians and trainees should challenge themselves to be self aware by honestly assessing their biases regarding biracial individuals, including biases regarding dual-racial/ethnic heritage, interracial families and relationships, biracial identity, and the social construction of race. Peer supervision groups with professionals of varying levels of experience enable clinicians to explore attitudes, values, and biases as they come up in working with mixed race people and their families. Additionally, consistent with Guideline 3, psychology training institutions should support constructive cross-racial discussion at all levels of training (including among faculty), creating a space where students can step aside from "political correctness" and address racial issues (Baptiste, 1990; Bemak & Chung, 1997; Herring, 1995; C. B. Williams, 1999; Winn & Priest, 1993).

Trainees and professionals should be aware of feelings about their own racial and ethnic identity. Security in their own identity will allow them to manage countertransference to their mixed race clients and avoid pathologizing biracial identity resolutions (Deters, 1997). For example, C. B. Williams (1999) addressed the discomfort of White counselors in bringing up racial issues with clients of color. This discomfort often is related to the lack of awareness of the salience of race or concern about offending clients, imposing a racial agenda where there is none, or being able to handle a client's feelings about racism, including the client's distrust of the White counselor. However, one cannot assume that people of color will be any more sensitive to the needs of clients who are of a mixed or different racial heritage from their own. Regardless of whether the counselor is White, of color, or mixed, race and culture are always part of the therapeutic landscape and need to be addressed.

Knowledge and Skills

Biracial people have unique psychosocial and developmental needs that must be addressed and not subsumed under a general "minority" group umbrella. In compliance with Guideline 3, course curricula in training programs should include information about biracials, along with information about other racial and ethnic groups. We advocate a holistic approach by integrating multicultural information throughout all coursework and not just in a one-semester course. Training institutions can utilize case studies, case conferences, student discussions, and guest lecturers as instructional methods to enhance students' understanding of biracial psychology. Live or taped observation of trainees working with biracial clients will allow faculty to pick up on any countertransference issues related to biracial status of clients.

Organizers of multicultural continuing education workshops should include biracial psychology as a regular workshop offering. Also, clinicians should research information and resources in their community that may be useful to mixed race clients. Whenever possible, resources should address both cultures in the interracial/interethnic family. There are several online resources available, including the American Multiethnic Association's website (ameasite.com), which contains information about books and films, educational resources, and legal issues across the globe; interracialweb.com, which is a directory of interracial and intercultural resources on the web; and mixedfolks.com, a site dedicated to celebrating mixed racial heritage.

FUTURE DIRECTIONS

Most of the biracial research and clinical literature has emerged in the past 15 years and has utilized measures and models designed for monoracial individuals. In keeping with Guideline 4, which addresses culturally sensitive research and assessment, new biracially sensitive measures must be developed. Given the large volume of qualitative data that currently exist on this population, we need quantitative studies with large randomized samples in order to generalize to segments of the biracial population and develop treatment approaches that address their needs.

Many studies combined biracial and bicultural people into one group; other studies combined biracials with multiracial individuals; and still others used individuals whose parents were of mixed heritage. These are all distinct groups that cannot be intermixed without some confounding of the data. Doing so is similar to combining Latinos and Asians, for example, and looking for one homogeneous outcome. Research and clinical tools should be developed that will be sensitive enough to capture data for each respective group, while allowing for comparisons across groups (e.g., monoracial vs. biracial) and across different biracial combinations.

Finally, it has been suggested that data on biracial youth be analyzed to determine possible interactional effects specific to the racial status of each parent (Cooney & Radina, 2000). It also would be interesting to explore further the differences among biracials across the various identity resolutions and over the lifespan (Root, 1998).

REFERENCES

Aldarondo, F. (2001). Racial and ethnic identity models and their application: Counseling biracial individuals. *Journal of Mental Health Counseling, 23*, 238–255.

American Psychological Association. (2003). Guidelines on multicultural education, training, research, practice, and organizational change for psychologists. *American Psychologist, 58*, 377–402.

Baptiste, D. A. (1990). Therapeutic strategies with Black-Hispanic families: Identity problems of a neglected minority. *Journal of Family Psychotherapy, 1*, 15–38.

Bemak, F., & Chung, R. C.-Y. (1997). Vietnamese Amerasians: Psychosocial adjustment and psychotherapy. *Journal of Multicultural Counseling and Development, 25*, 79–88.

Benedetto, A. E., & Olisky, T. (2001). Biracial youth: The role of the school counselor in racial identity development. *Professional School Counseling, 5*, 66–69.

Bowles, D. D. (1993). Bi-racial identity: Children born to African-American and White couples. *Clinical Social Work Journal, 21*, 417–428.

Bracey, J. R., Bamaca, M. Y., & Umana-Taylor, A. J. (2004). Examining ethnic identity and self-esteem among biracial and monoracial adolescents. *Journal of Youth and Adolescence, 33*, 123–132.

Brown, U. M. (2001). *The interracial experience: Growing up Black/White racially mixed in the United States.* Westport, CT: Praeger.

Buckley, T. R., & Carter, R. T. (2004). Biracial (Black/White) women: A qualitative study of racial attitudes and beliefs and their implications for therapy. In A. R. Gillem & C. A. Thompson (Eds.), *Biracial women in therapy: Between the rock of gender and the hard place of race* (pp. 45–64). New York: Haworth Press.

Clancy, J. (1995). Multiracial identity assertion in the sociopolitical context of primary education. In N. Zack (Ed.), *American mixed race: The culture of microdiversity* (pp. 211–220). Lanham, MD: Rowman & Littlefield.

Collins, J. F. (2000). Biracial Japanese American identity: An evolving process. *Cultural Diversity and Ethnic Minority Psychology, 6*, 115–133.

Cooney, T. M., & Radina, M. E. (2000). Adjustment problems in adolescence: Are multiracial children at risk? *American Journal of Orthopsychiatry, 70*, 433–444.

Cox, R. P., Keltner, N., & Hogan, B. (2003). Family assessment tools. In R. P. Cox (Ed.), *Health related counseling with families of diverse cultures: Family, health, and cultural competencies* (pp. 145–167). Westport, CT: Greenwood Press.

Deters, K. A. (1997). Belonging nowhere and everywhere: Multiracial identity development. *Bulletin of the Menninger Clinic, 61*, 368–384.

Edwards, L. M., & Pedrotti, J. T. (2004). Utilizing the strengths of our cultures: Therapy with biracial women and girls. In A. R. Gillem & C. A. Thompson (Eds.), *Biracial women in therapy: Between the rock of gender and the hard place of race* (pp. 33–43). New York: Haworth Press.

Field, L. D. (1993). Self-concept and adjustment in biracial adolescents. *Dissertation Abstracts International, 53*, 5973.

Fukuyama, M. A. (1999). Personal narrative: Growing up biracial. *Journal of Counseling and Development, 77*, 12–14.

Gibbs, J. T. (1989). Biracial adolescents. In J. T. Gibbs & L. N. Huang (Eds.), *Children of color: Psychological interventions with minority youth* (pp. 322–350). San Francisco: Jossey-Bass.

Gibbs, J. T. (1998). Biracial adolescents. In J. T. Gibbs & L. N. Huang (Eds.), *Children of color: Psychological interventions with culturally diverse youth* (Rev. ed., pp. 305–332). San Francisco: Jossey-Bass.

Gibbs, J. T., & Moskowitz-Sweet, G. (1991). Clinical and cultural issues in the treatment of biracial and bicultural adolescents. *Families in Society, 72*, 579–592.

Gillem, A. R. (2004). Triple jeopardy in the lives of biracial Black/White women. In J. C. Chrisler, C. Golden, & P. D. Rozee (Eds.), *Lectures on the psychology of women* (3rd ed., pp. 220–235). New York: McGraw-Hill.

Gillem, A. R., Cohn, L. R., & Throne, C. (2001). Black identity in biracial Black/White people: A comparison of Jacqueline who refuses to be exclusively Black and Adolphus who wishes he were. *Cultural Diversity and Ethnic Minority Psychology, 7*, 182–196.

Grove, K. J. (1991). Identity development in interracial, Asian/White late adolescents: Must it be so problematic? *Journal of Youth and Adolescence, 20*, 617–628.

Hardy, K. V., & Laszloffy, T. A. (1995). The cultural genogram: Key to training culturally competent family therapists. *Journal of Marital and Family Therapy, 21*, 227–237.

Harris, H. L. (2002). School counselors' perceptions of biracial children: A pilot study. *Professional School Counseling, 6*, 120–129.

Harrison, P. M. (1997). Racial identification and self-concept issues in biracial girls. *Dissertation Abstracts International: Section B: The Sciences and Engineering, 58*, 2123.

Hart-Webb, D. (1999). The biracial bind: An identity dilemma. In Y. M. Jenkins (Ed.), *Diversity in college settings: Directives for helping professionals* (pp. 117–127). Florence, KY: Taylor & Francis/Routledge.

Helms, J. E., & Cook, D. A. (1999). *Using race and culture in counseling and psychotherapy: Theory and process.* Boston: Allyn and Bacon.

Henriksen, R. C., Jr. (2001). Black/white biracial identity development: A grounded theory study. *Dissertation Abstracts International: Section A: Humanities and Social Sciences, 61*, 2605.

Henriksen, R. C., Jr., & Trusty, J. (2004). Understanding and assisting Black/White biracial women in their identity development. In A. R. Gillem & C. A. Thompson (Eds.),

Biracial women in therapy: Between the rock of gender and the hard place of race (pp. 65–83). New York: Haworth Press.

Herman, M. (2004). Forced to choose: Some determinants of racial identification in multiracial adolescents. *Child Development, 75,* 730–748.

Herring, R. D. (1995). Developing biracial ethnic identity: A review of the increasing dilemma. *Journal of Multicultural Counseling and Development, 23,* 29–38.

Jacobs, J. H. (1992). Identity development in biracial children. In M. P. P. Root (Ed.), *Racially mixed people in America* (pp. 190–206). Thousand Oaks, CA: Sage.

Jaret, C., & Reitzes, D. C. (1999). The importance of racial-ethnic identity and social setting for Blacks, Whites, and multiracials. *Sociological Perspectives, 42,* 711–737.

Johnson, R. C., & Nagoshi, C. T. (1986). The adjustment of offspring of within-group and interracial/intercultural marriages: A comparison of personality factor scores. *Journal of Marriage and the Family, 48,* 279–284.

Jones, J. E. (2000). Multiethnic identity development, psychological adjustment, and parental attachment in adolescence. *Dissertation Abstracts International: Section B: The Sciences and Engineering, 60,* 5227.

Kerwin, C., & Ponterotto, J. G. (1995). Biracial identity development: Theory and research. In J. G. Ponterotto, J. M. Casas, L. A. Suzuki, & C. M. Alexander (Eds.), *Handbook of multicultural counseling* (pp. 199–217). Thousand Oaks, CA: Sage.

Kerwin, C., Ponterotto, J. G., Jackson, B. L., & Harris, A. (1993). Racial identity in biracial children: A qualitative investigation. *Journal of Counseling Psychology, 40,* 221–231.

Kich, G. K. (1992). The developmental process of asserting a biracial, bicultural identity. In M. P. P. Root (Ed.), *Racially mixed people in America* (pp. 304–317). Thousand Oaks, CA: Sage.

Logan, S. L., Freeman, E. M., & McRoy, R. G. (1987). Racial identity problems of biracial clients: Implications for social work practice. *Journal of Intergroup Relations, 15,* 11–24.

Looby, E. J. (2001). Valuing human diversity: Counseling multiracial and multiethnic children. In D. S. Sandhu (Ed.), *Elementary school counseling in the new millennium* (pp. 193–207). Alexandria, VA: American Counseling Association.

Mass, A. I. (1992). Interracial Japanese Americans: The best of both worlds or the end of the Japanese American community? In M. P. P. Root (Ed.), *Racially mixed people in America* (pp. 265–279). Thousand Oaks, CA: Sage.

McKelvey, R. S., & Webb, J. A. (1996). A comparative study of Vietnamese Amerasians, their non-Amerasian siblings, and unrelated, like-aged Vietnamese immigrants. *American Journal of Psychiatry, 153,* 561–563.

Milan, S., & Keiley, M. K. (2000). Biracial youth and families in therapy: Issues and interventions. *Journal of Marital and Family Therapy, 26,* 305–315.

Morrison, J. W. (1995). Developing identity formation and self-concept in preschool-aged biracial children. *Early Child Development and Care, 111,* 141–152.

Motoyoshi, M. M. (1990). The experience of mixed-race people: Some thoughts and theories. *Journal of Ethnic Studies, 18,* 77–94.

Nishimura, N. J. (1995). Addressing the needs of biracial children: An issue for counselors in a multicultural school environment. *School Counselor, 43,* 52–57.

Nishimura, N. J., & Bol, L. (1997). School counselors' perceptions of the counseling needs of biracial children in an urban educational setting. *Research in the Schools, 4,* 17–23.

Oriti, B., Bibb, A., & Mahboubi, J. (1996). Family-centered practice with racially/ethnically mixed families. *Families in Society, 77,* 573–582.

Phillips, L. (2004). Fitting in and feeling good: Patterns of self-evaluation and psychological stress among biracial adolescent girls. In A. R. Gillem & C. A. Thompson (Eds.), *Biracial women in therapy: Between the rock of gender and the hard place of race* (pp. 217–236). New York: Haworth Press.

Phinney, J. S., & Alipuria, L. L. (1996). At the interface of cultures: Multiethnic/multiracial high school and college students. *Journal of Social Psychology, 136*, 139–158.

Pinderhughes, E. (1995). Biracial identity—asset or handicap? In H. W. Harris, H. C. Blue, & E. E. H. Griffith (Eds.), *Racial and ethnic identity: Psychological development and creative expression* (pp. 73–93). Florence, KY: Taylor & Francis/Routledge.

Poston, W. C. (1990). The biracial identity development model: A needed addition. *Journal of Counseling and Development, 69*, 152–155.

Rigazio-DiGilio, S. A., Ivey, A. E., Kunkler-Peck, K. P., & Grady, L. T. (2005). *Community genograms: Using individual, family, and cultural narratives with clients.* New York: Teachers College Press.

Roberts-Clarke, I., Roberts, A. C., & Morokoff, P. (2004). Dating practices, racial identity, and psychotherapeutic needs of biracial women. In A. R. Gillem & C. A. Thompson (Eds.), *Biracial women in therapy: Between the rock of gender and the hard place of race* (pp. 103–117). New York: Haworth Press.

Rockquemore, K. A., & Brunsma, D. L. (2002). *Beyond Black: Biracial identity in America.* Thousand Oaks, CA: Sage.

Rockquemore, K. A., & Laszloffy, T. A. (2003). Multiple realities: A relational narrative approach in therapy with Black-White mixed-race clients. *Family Relations: Interdisciplinary Journal of Applied Family Studies, 52*, 119–128.

Root, M. P. P. (1990). Resolving "other" status: Identity development of biracial individuals. *Women and Therapy, 9*, 185–205.

Root, M. P. P. (1995). The multiracial contribution to the psychological browning of America. In N. Zack (Ed.), *American mixed race: The culture of microdiversity* (pp. 231–236). Lanham, MD: Rowman & Littlefield.

Root, M. P. P. (1997). Contemporary mixed-heritage Filipino Americans: Fighting colonized identities. In M. P. P. Root (Ed.), *Filipino Americans: Transformation and identity* (pp. 80–94). Thousand Oaks, CA: Sage.

Root, M. P. P. (1998). Multiracial Americans: Changing the face of Asian America. In L. C. Lee & N. W. S. Zane (Eds.), *Handbook of Asian American psychology* (pp. 261–287). Thousand Oaks, CA: Sage.

Root, M. P. P. (1999). The biracial baby boom: Understanding ecological constructions of racial identity in the 21st century. In R. H. Sheets & E. R. Hollins (Eds.), *Racial and ethnic identity in school practices: Aspects of human development* (pp. 67–89). Mahwah, NJ: Erlbaum.

Root, M. P. P. (2001). *Love's revolution: Interracial marriage.* Philadelphia: Temple University Press.

Stephan, W. G., & Stephan, C. W. (1991). Intermarriage: Effects on personality, adjustment, and intergroup relations in two samples of students. *Journal of Marriage and the Family, 53*, 241–250.

Storrs, D. (1999). Whiteness as stigma: Essentialist identity work by mixed-race women. *Symbolic Interaction, 22*, 187–212.

Suyemoto, K. L. (2004). Racial/ethnic identities and related attributed experiences of multiracial Japanese European Americans. *Journal of Multicultural Counseling and Development, 32*, 206–221.

Thompson, C. A. (1999). *Identity resolution in biracial Black/White individuals: The process of asserting a biracial identity.* Unpublished doctoral dissertation, California School of Professional Psychology, San Diego.

U.S. Bureau of the Census. (2000). *CensusScope: Multiracial population statistics for United States.* Retrieved on August 19, 2002, from http://www.censusscope.org/us/chart_multi.html

Williams, C. B. (1999). Claiming a biracial identity: Resisting social constructions of race and culture. *Journal of Counseling and Development, 77,* 32–35.

Williams, T. K. (1995). The theater of identity. In N. Zack (Ed.), *American mixed race: The culture of microdiversity* (pp. 79–96). Lanham, MD: Rowman & Littlefield.

Winn, N. N., & Priest, R. (1993). Counseling biracial children: A forgotten component of multicultural counseling. *Family Therapy, 20,* 29–36.

8

Immigrant and Refugee Populations

Rita Chi-Ying Chung
and Fred Bemak

As the world becomes more interconnected and globalized, there has been a growing mass movement of people worldwide. It has been estimated that there are 175 million people currently residing in a country other than where they were born. The number of migrants in the world has more than doubled since 1975, with most living in Europe (56 million), Asia (50 million), and North America (41 million) (United Nations, 2002). The past decade in the United States has seen the greatest migration in its history, with an increase of 44% since 1990 (U.S. Department of Homeland Security, 2003). The U.S. 2000 Census estimated that the foreign-born population was 28 to 31 million, with one in ten people being a refugee or immigrant, and one in five people foreign born or having at least one parent born outside the United States (U.S. Bureau of the Census, 2002). With the events of September 11, 2001, immigration to the United States has decreased slightly, although estimates predict that migration trends will continue to increase, reaching more than 34 million (Capps & Passel, 2004).

A large number of immigrants (47%) already have relatives living in the United States. Even with the decline in migration after September 11, 2001, the main emphasis of immigration continues to be on family reunification, with two-thirds of the immigrant population living in California, New York, Texas, Florida, Illinois, and New Jersey. States located in the middle of the United States (Rocky Mountain, midwest, and southeast states) have witnessed rapidly growing immigrant populations, mostly from Mexico (31%), Asia (26%), and Latin America (23%) (U.S. Department of Homeland Security, 2003).

Given these statistics, it is critical for mental health professionals working with immigrant and refugee populations to be multiculturally skilled and competent. To achieve effectiveness in working with this population, psychologists and counselors need to attain the level of multicultural competence that has been adopted by the American Psychological Association (APA, 2003; Sue et al., 1998). It has been widely acknowledged that to be effective with diverse populations, psychologists and counselors need to embrace, accept, acknowledge, and understand the Multicultural Guidelines (e.g., Helms & Cook, 1999; Pedersen, Draguns, Lonner, & Trimble, 2002; Ponterotto, Casas, Suzuki, & Alexander, 2001). However, until this book, little has been written about how to operationalize these guidelines. After a brief discussion of the pertinent Guidelines, we present an overview of the immigrant and refugee experience, followed by a discussion of the challenges of postmigration adjustment and adaptation to the United States. Then, through the use of case vignettes, we show how to effectively apply the Multicultural Guidelines for this population. It should be noted that, although this chapter focuses on immigrants and refugees in the United States, the information presented has relevance and applicability to immigrant and refugee populations in other resettlement countries. A list of additional resources is provided at the end of the chapter.

KEY ELEMENTS OF THE MULTICULTURAL GUIDELINES

Three Multicultural Guidelines are essential in working with refugee and immigrant populations. As stated in Guideline 1, it is of the utmost importance for psychologists and counselors to be aware of their own assumptions, biases, attitudes, beliefs, values, prejudices, stereotypes, and privileges that may detrimentally influence their interactions with migrant populations. For example, as pointed out in Chapter 6, there are approximately 3 million Arab Americans living in the United States (U.S. Bureau of the Census, 2002) and, similar to people worldwide, mental health professionals were directly or indirectly affected by the events of September 11, 2001. Compounding the mental health counselors' reactions and responses is the media coverage about people from Arab, Muslim, and Middle Eastern backgrounds, and their reactions and responses can lead some therapists to experience countertransference with Arab American clients. Derived from the concept of countertransference is the notion of *political countertransference,* which refers to personal reactions to sociopolitical issues (Chung, 2005), such as the ongoing concerns about terrorism and its linkage to specific migrant populations. Furthermore, many of the immigrants and refugees who migrated to the United States came from collectivistic cultures and thus have very different worldviews from those of people from predominately individualistic cultures, such as the United States. As noted in Guideline 5, U.S. mental health professionals are trained to focus on individualism and independence, whereas many immigrants and refugees value interdependence and cooperation. Problems arise if a therapist perceives and judges a client's values and worldview as negative, unhealthy, or abnormal and thinks about the therapeutic relationship only in terms of theories, skills, techniques, strategies, and interventions that are based on Western constructs.

Consistent with Guideline 2, it is also essential that multiculturally competent mental health professionals working with migrants understand their historical, sociopolitical, and cultural backgrounds, as well as the challenges this group encounters in their psychosocial adjustment and adaptation. It is also important to distinguish inter- and intragroup differences rather than categorizing and stereotyping all migrants as similar (Chung & Kagawa-Singer, 1993), as well as to recognize gender differences (Chung & Bemak, 2002; Chung, Bemak, & Kagawa-Singer, 1998). Finally, as stated in Guideline 5, not only should therapists utilize culturally sensitive interventions, but they also must acknowledge and accept that for this population, the preference is for indigenous traditional healing and community practices rather than mainstream Western services. Being respectful of valued indigenous methods is not only important, but requires reaching out into the migrant communities to form partnerships with creditable indigenous healers (Bemak et al., 2003).

REFUGEE VERSUS IMMIGRANT MIGRATION STATUS

Referring to Guideline 2, one of the important issues in understanding immigrants and refugees is the difference between immigrant and refugee status. Although both groups share similar experiences in their psychosocial adjustment and adaptation, there are also unique differences related to their migration status. The term *forced versus free* migration often is used to identify the differences between refugees and immigrants (Murphy, 1977). Immigrants typically migrate voluntarily to another country in search of a better quality of life and economic conditions. In contrast, refugees are forced to leave their home country due to war, genocide, natural disaster, or political, religious, or ethnic persecution (Bemak, Chung, & Pedersen, 2003). Their departure is usually sudden, with little or no planning, preparation, or choice. Although both immigrants and refugees migrating to a foreign country leave families, communities, and social support networks, the situation for refugees may be more difficult in that they may have lost family members, friends, and community members to war or disaster.

The Refugee Experience

The degree of premigration trauma experienced by refugees is significant (Bemak et al, 2003). Studies have found many refugees were subjected to the atrocities of war, including experiencing and/or witnessing torture and killings, being forced to commit atrocities, being incarcerated and placed in re-education camps, and being subjected to starvation, physical beatings, rape, and sexual abuse (e.g., Marsella, Bornemann, Ekblad, & Orley, 1994; Miller, Worthington, Muzurovic, Tipping, & Goldman, 2002; Weine & Henderson, 2005). Many have experienced multiple traumas during war and while escaping or residing in refugee camps. Thus, it is not surprising to find that refugees are at risk for developing serious physical and mental health problems, including depression, anxiety, and post traumatic stress disorder (PTSD), and generalized psychological difficulties (e.g., Ajdukovic & Ajdukovic, 1993; Fawzi et al., 1997; Hinton et al., 1997; Karadaghi, 1994; Mollica & Jalbert, 1989).

Findings have shown that refugees exhibit a higher incidence of psychopathology and other psychological problems compared with the general population of their resettlement country (e.g., Kinzie, 1993; Marsella, Friedman, & Spain, 1993; Mollica & Lavelle, 1988; Weisaeth & Eitinger, 1993). Due to the deep-rooted experiences during premigration, traumatic effects may linger during postmigration, making it critical that psychologists and counselors examine the interaction between premigration trauma and postmigration adjustment (Chung & Kagawa-Singer, 1993). It is also important that mental health professionals be aware of other variables that affect postmigration adjustment, such as survivor's guilt (Lin, Masuda, & Tazuma, 1982), and of higher risks for mental health disorders within the specific subgroups of older refugees, women, children, and unaccompanied minors (Bemak et al., 2003).

The Immigrant Experience

Even though immigrants migrate voluntarily and are thus psychologically prepared to leave their home countries, they still encounter challenges in resettlement countries. Issues such as culture shock and acculturation, geographic and climatic differences, and different social and cultural customs may cause significant problems in adaptation. Immigrants, similar to their refugee counterparts, may not have family, community or social supports, or financial resources to assist their adjustment. Migration to a different culture also highlights and exacerbates cultural differences in attitudes, values, beliefs, and worldviews. As already pointed out, statistics (U.S. Bureau of the Census, 2002) show a majority of immigrants come from collectivistic cultures and therefore must adapt to the individualistic and competitive cultural base of the United States, which may be extremely different from their own. Hence, the culture shock may precipitate feelings of helplessness, disorientation, hopelessness, and doubts about whether the choice to migrate was correct.

CHALLENGES IN PSYCHOSOCIAL ADJUSTMENT AND ADAPTATION

This section presents a brief overview of the types of psychosocial adjustment challenges faced by immigrants and refugees. A more detailed description of these challenges can be found elsewhere (e.g., Bemak et al., 2003).

Education, English Language Proficiency, and Employment

Immigrants and refugees may feel that they are in a "Catch-22" situation regarding employment. To obtain work and professionally advance in the United States, one needs to have English language proficiency and educa tion. In the United States, immigrants represent 22% of low-wage workers and 40% of low-skilled workers (Capps & Passel, 2004). Almost 50% of this population reported having low English proficiency (U.S. Bureau of the Census, 2002). Even immigrants with an education may find if difficult to secure a job consistent with their educational background, since degrees and qualifications from non-Western countries are not necessarily transferable to the United States and sometimes additional training or internship experiences are required for licensure or certification.

The obstacles related to employment opportunities and advancement present a number of difficulties for migrants. One challenge is to support family members. This may be particularly difficult when extended-family members and friends are dependent. A second challenge is the inability, given financial demands and expenses, to take time to acquire the additional education or training necessary to become licensed or certified in one's former profession. In many cases this results in being underemployed and working multiple low-income positions requiring minimal skills. A third challenge is the lack of English proficiency, which inhibits job access and employment options, as well as the mastery of skills to successfully adapt in mainstream society (Bemak, 1989). This results in migrants not being able to access community resources and available supports, thus inhibiting their access to social services, participation in their children's progress and performance in school, utilization of public transport, access to computers, and so forth (Bemak & Chung, 2000). Fourth, even when migrants have the time to take English language classes, the problem of "learning how to learn" presents itself, especially for those who are illiterate in their native language (Chung & Bemak, 2005). Finally, refugees, as a result of injuries caused by beatings and torture, may have impaired memory and concentration, which also may interfere with learning English, working, daily functioning, socialization skills, and problem-solving abilities (Chung & Bemak, 2005).

Changing Family Dynamics

Adjusting to the United States presents numerous challenges and changes for migrant families. Given economic demands and the challenges to find gainful employment, women often are forced to enter the workplace. For those from traditional cultures where there are prescribed gender roles, this may cause significant shifts in family dynamics whereby women are financially contributing to the family while concomitantly being exposed to U.S. women's rights issues (Chung & Okazaki, 1991). Simultaneously, children may acculturate faster and question traditional norms and roles in areas such as dating or extracurricular activities. Often, children assume the role of cultural translators for adult family members, dramatically changing traditional roles between parents and children. Furthermore, parents may be questioned by professionals regarding their traditional practices, such as discipline or healing practices that may be viewed in the United States as a form of abuse (Bemak et al., 2003). These changing family dynamics can create frustration and family tension and may lead to domestic and family violence (Chung & Okazaki, 1991).

Daily Stressors

Although the United States and other countries generally welcome immigrants and refugees, this may change according to politics and the economy. Migrants may be seen as taking available jobs, generating resentment and anger (Bemak et al., 2003). They may encounter racism and discrimination on multiple levels, from individual comments to discrimination in housing and employment (Chung & Bemak, 2005). The feeling of not belonging or being wanted can promote young migrants to join gangs where there is a sense of family, protection, and security (Chung & Bemak, 2005).

CULTURE AND MENTAL HEALTH

Culture has a major influence on the conceptualization and manifestation of mental illness, and influences help-seeking behavior and treatment expectations (e.g., Chung & Kagawa-Singer, 1995; Fabrega, 1989; Kirmayer, 1989; Kleinman, 1980). Since many migrants come from collectivistic cultures, their beliefs, attitudes, and worldviews toward mental health may differ from mainstream traditional Western treatment methods. For some migrant populations, there is an integration of mind, body, and spirit, compared with the Western views of a dichotomy between mind and body, and mental and physical (Bemak et al., 2003). Although symptoms can be viewed as similar across cultures, the actual meaning and interpretation of symptoms may be culturally construed. For example, with Asian migrants, neurasthenia is a culturally sanctioned method of expressing mental illness (Chung & Kagawa-Singer, 1995) that manifests as depression, anxiety, somatic symptoms, and psychosocial dysfunction. This is consistent with Asian nosology, yet does not fit into the Western framework of mental illness within the *Diagnostic and Statistical Manual of Mental Disorders* (DSM) or the *International Classification of Diseases* (ICD). Therefore, it is critical that psychologists and counselors understand the impact of culture on mental health, and that their assessments take into account cultural variance (Good & Good, 1981).

As previously noted, migrants' first choice for mental health treatment is traditional indigenous healing methods (Chung & Lin, 1994; Higginbotham, Trevino, & Ray, 1990), and mainstream mental health services may be their last option. Chung and Lin (1994) found that even if migrants access mainstream mental health services, there is a tendency to concurrently utilize indigenous healing methodologies. Mental health professionals therefore must be aware of cross-cultural misdiagnosis, underdiagnosis, and overdiagnosis of symptomatology and mental health problems (Draguns, 2000).

Given the brief overview of immigrants' and refugees' historical, sociopolitical, and cultural backgrounds; challenges encountered in psychosocial adjustment and adaptation; and cultural worldviews, beliefs, and attitudes toward mental health, it is clear that effective work with these populations requires that psychologists and counselors have multicultural competence and skills.

THE APPLICATION OF MULTICULTURAL
GUIDELINES WITH IMMIGRANT AND REFUGEE POPULATIONS

Just knowing the Multicultural Guidelines is not sufficient. It is critical for mental health professionals to be able to apply the Guidelines to their everyday work. Therefore, this section will present three representative case vignettes, and then describe how to operationalize the Multicultural Guidelines using these cases as a basis for considering immigrant and refugee populations.

Immigrant and Refugee Case Vignettes

Three case study vignettes are presented that represent diversity and heterogeneity within the immigrant and refugee population, but it is impossible to be all-inclusive. The situations the immigrants and refugees face in the three cases studied parallel and can be generalized to many other immigrant and refugee experiences.

Elderly Migrant: The Case of Mrs. W.

Mrs. W. is from China. She is in her mid-60s, and when her husband died 3 years ago, her eldest son Johnny convinced her to come from China to live with his family in the United States. He had come to the United States to study for a Ph.D. in engineering and is now working for a major corporation. Mrs. W. now lives with Johnny and his wife, Jennifer, who left China at the age of 3, and their 4-year-child, Christopher. Mrs. W. is having problems sleeping, is depressed and anxious, and feels isolated since she does not have anyone to talk to and misses her friends from China. Due to limited English, Mrs. W. is afraid to take local transportation to go to the Chinese cultural center and stays home all the time. She is extremely frustrated and feels useless. Food has become a point of tension in the household, with Mrs. W. upset that Jennifer does not cook proper "Chinese" food, and Jennifer complaining about her mother-in-law's cooking. Mrs. W.'s only joy in life is her son and grandson. She is upset about how Jennifer is raising Christopher, believing her parenting lacks proper discipline, and she has problems communicating with Jennifer, who does not speak Chinese.

Rebellious Adolescent: The Case of Maria

Maria is a 16-year-old refugee from El Salvador who came to the United States with her family a year ago. She speaks very broken English and recently was suspended from school for fighting with other girls from El Salvador and Nicaragua. Although Maria has been referred to the school counselor, she is resistant to counseling and rarely shares personal information during her counseling sessions. Maria remains cautious and distrustful with school authorities and is especially wary of the school counselor since her good friend was suspended for a week after she told the school counselor she had once used drugs in school. The school counselor, who is frustrated with Maria, referred her to an outside therapist to work on her behavior and problems with authority in school.

Maria is sad about her two older brothers who were killed along with her grandparents during the civil war in El Salvador. Maria's parents explained to her how her grandparents were sympathizers of the *Frente Farabundo Marti de Liberacion,* the grassroots group that fought against the U.S.-supported government during the civil war, and that one weekend her two older brothers, who were just young children, were at their grandparents' home when a group of government soldiers raided the home and killed them all.

Although Maria no longer has brothers, she has two younger sisters who are in elementary and middle school; they do not have problems at school. Maria's parents are working at menial jobs, living in subsidized housing, and having a difficult time "keeping control" over Maria. Maria angrily reports that her mother is depressed about being in *"this* country" and her father has been drinking more than usual. Her parents constantly talk about being home in El Salvador, about her deceased brothers, and about how things were so different "back then."

Maria feels a growing distance from her parents, who are highly critical of her friends, always sad and tired, and increasingly trying to restrict her social activities. This has caused a growing tension in her home and constant arguments with her mother. It is unclear whether Maria is in a gang, although she has visible tattoos on her body, and there are rumors among girls in the high school about Maria's sexual activity with other gang members.

Premigration Trauma: The Case of Deng

Deng fled the civil war in Sudan and has been in the United States for the past 2 years. He is 28 years old and spent 4 years in a refugee camp before coming to the United States. He describes fleeing burning villages outside of Darfur and seeing many people from his own family and community slaughtered, raped, and beaten. He remembers running and hiding, being near starvation, drinking muddy water, avoiding crocodiles and once a lion, and being alarmed when bombs dropped nearby. Deng describes his journey from Sudan to Ethiopia trying to find safety, then returning to Sudan, and eventually making his way to Kenya, approximately 1,000 miles away, by foot. Having experienced so much horror and brutality, he questions why the United States didn't intervene in his country as they did in Afghanistan and Iraq. He gets angry at the lack of U.S. support as well as the lack of media coverage and international assistance to the Darfur region. Sometime he flashes back to these difficult times and cannot sleep or eat. He wonders what happened to his family and friends and feels guilty for having escaped. He arrived in the United States without parents or family and with no possessions. He had to figure out how to use a toothbrush, flush a toilet, and use such things as electric appliances and the telephone. He would like to get married one day, but is concerned about how many cattle must be promised as a dowry.

Operationalization of Multicultural Guidelines

Using the case vignettes as a basis, this section will discuss applying Multicultural Guidelines 1, 2, and 5 with refugee and immigrant populations. The cases of Mrs. W., Maria, and Deng involve numerous issues that are applicable to many other immigrants and refugees and encompass the broad dimensions of the migration experience. Premigration and life prior to leaving one's home country, transitional issues in the actual departure that may involve refugee camp experience and flight, and postmigration-resettlement adjustment to a new location or country are universal experiences for all migrants. Associated with premigration, transition, and postmigration may be trauma, pain, loss, transition, and change.

Guideline 1: Personal Awareness. Effective work with migrants requires that personal reactions to people from cultural and racial backgrounds different from one's own be clearly understood. For example, if a therapist had a family member who was threatened by Latino gangs and harbored strong negative feelings about Latino gangs, this could interfere with the therapist's working effectively and openly with Maria. If that same professional lived in a neighborhood that housed a large and transient African extended family, it might have an impact on the therapist's response to Deng. Or if the therapist carried strong feelings that elders should be treated with respect, Mrs. W.'s situation would be viewed through the lens of expectations and personal values and beliefs about what is right and wrong behavior.

These cases illustrate the critical need for mental health professionals to be aware of their own racial/ethnic stereotypes. Working with migrants adds another dimension that may go beyond the typical experiences with people of color who were born and raised in the United States. For example, therapists working with Mrs. W., Maria, and Deng are not only dealing with stereotypes and preconceived notions of Asian Americans, Latina/o Americans, and African Americans, but now are faced with addressing Asians, Latina/os, and Blacks who are foreign born. The situation may raise issues about the therapists' views on migration, inclusion, and receptivity to other *different* cultures, spending tax dollars to support migrants, the competitive job market as it relates to migrants, and public policy.

Furthermore, it can be extremely painful and difficult to hear accounts of migrants' experiences of rape, torture, abuse, exploitation, or punishment; about their fear and inability to sleep; or stories about witnessing their wife or husband being murdered or raped. Reports of this nature may evoke strong reactions and countertransference by therapists, raising awareness about their capacity to work effectively with pain and trauma. For example, if Maria shared in counseling that she had sexual intercourse with several men in the gang as part of an initiation rite of passage and the therapist personally had experienced sexual abuse, it might inhibit the therapist's ability to work with Maria.

There is also a need to understand the historical, sociopolitical, and ecological context for how one's own racial and cultural identity interacts with that of migrants. For example, for Mrs. W., who is from China, to work with a Japanese American therapist may be problematic given the historical tensions and warfare between China and Japan. Similarly, the counseling relationship with Deng could be affected if the therapist were an African American who traced his or her family origins to Africa and then for the first time worked with someone born and raised in Africa, or were a European American whose family success was based on slavery. Counseling Maria may raise issues for a therapist given Maria's strong feelings about the murder of her grandparents and brothers with U.S.-made weapons in a civil war that was financed by the United States.

Guideline 2: Knowledge of a Client's Culture. Migrants similar to Mrs. W., Maria, and Deng have had profound life experiences as they moved from their home countries to the United States. Being multiculturally competent means understanding and appreciating others' worldviews. As discussed previously, the departure from one's homeland involves many life events during premigration. The premigration experiences for each of these three individuals must be clearly understood by the therapist, to recognize who they are today and how they have constructed their worlds. To gain an understanding and appreciation regarding the migrant experience, therapists must ask such questions as:

- How do such life events shape one's beliefs?
- What happens to one's values?
- What assumptions do each of the individuals have about life and people?
- How do their responses fit into the cultural context of their worldviews?

Yet, mental health professionals cannot stop with premigration. The lives of migrants are unique and complex, requiring adaptation, adjustment, and acculturation to a new culture. How does Mrs. W. adapt in the United States after spending more than 60 years in China, an environment where she had established social relationships and a well-defined place in society, and understood the social, cultural, and political elements of her life? Her values, beliefs, and expectations about how life will ebb and flow, her weekly routines, and what happens in her community, which had been clearly defined over 6 decades, are now disrupted and radically different. The same holds true for Maria, at a much younger age, who is exploring belonging to a gang, sexuality, and rebelling from her parents. Deng is trying to come to terms with his anger and resentment toward the U.S. government for not helping his country, while simultaneously experiencing survivor's guilt about the friends and family he left behind, which is underscored by flashbacks about the traumatic events he experienced in Sudan. Thus, to foster multicultural competence, therapists must clearly examine and understand the interrelationship between postmigration shifts and premigration trauma.

Becoming competent to work across cultures also requires an understanding about the context of migrant experiences. Sociopolitical and historical context may have a great impact on the therapeutic relationship. For example, Deng may be hesitant to disclose some personal things with the therapist because of his past, based on the fact that if you were "found out," you might be killed or imprisoned. It is critical that therapists familiarize themselves with the unique histories, sociopolitical context, and backgrounds of migrants in order to provide effective psychotherapy.

Finally, to better comprehend the worldview of migrants and become culturally competent, it is important to become familiar with and knowledgeable about their world outside therapy. Given the primacy of social relationships in so many migrant cultures, and expectations regarding helping relationships as more personal and intimate and less rigidly defined by professional boundaries, active participation in community events and activities is helpful. We regularly attend community events and celebrations with migrant clients similar to Mrs. W., Maria, and Deng. One recent example was the 30-year celebration of the Vietnamese refugees in the United States, in which we participated. Attending ongoing events, festivals, celebrations, and holidays that take place in all migrant communities not only is a rich experience, but also extends one's knowledge, understanding, and appreciation of different cultures, which in turn establishes therapist credibility. Seeing the therapist attend important events has significance in the community, demonstrating an interest, responsiveness, and knowledge seeking about the larger migrant culture. There are numerous ways to find out about these events, such as checking with state Offices of Refugee or Migrant Services, contacting local agencies working with diverse migrant groups, calling local religious and community organizations, and asking people within the community about various functions. The resource list at the end of the chapter may be useful in working with this population.

Guideline 5: Culturally Responsive Interventions. Guideline 5 acknowledges that most therapists have been trained using traditional Eurocentric therapeutic intervention models, which may be inappropriate when working across cultures. To work effectively, therapists must employ culture-centered interventions. To this end, we have developed a culturally responsive model of intervention with migrants called the Multilevel Model of Intervention for Psychotherapy and Social Justice (MLM) (Bemak et al., 2003). Developed as a result of extensive work with this population, this model is based on the premise that traditional assessments (e.g., the DSM; Chung & Kagawa-Singer, 1995) and interventions are not culturally responsive and may lead to misdiagnosis, inappropriate treatment, and subsequent harm to the migrant clients and their families and communities.

In the MLM we denote five interrelated levels of intervention for mental health professionals to use in a culturally sensitive framework that are consistent with Guideline 5. *Mental Health Education* is one level, involving a two-way educational process. Along with gathering vital and relevant cultural and sociopolitical premigration, migration, and postmigration information, the therapist discusses therapeutic expectations with migrant clients and their families. This may include explanations about the role of a bilingual/bicultural interpreter, the purpose of intake and consent forms, and cultural issues of confidentiality and boundaries. It is also important for the therapist to be aware, understand, and appreciate that migrant clients, based on past experiences, may be suspicious and distrustful of the therapist's questions. For example, Deng may associate being questioned by an authority figure with situations in Sudan that had the potential to lead to torture and death. Mrs. W., having lived under the Chinese Communist regime, may be wary of questioning by a stranger, while for Maria the therapist may generate distrust as an authority figure that may challenge her rebellious acts.

Another level in the MLM is *Cultural Empowerment*, which assists migrant clients in determining and overcoming individual, institutional, and/or societal barriers. We believe this is critical as a therapeutic intervention for migrants to successfully access mental health and other associated services that are conducive to positive psychological well-being. An example of this would be counseling a migrant client whose apartment rent increased, forcing the family to move. Rather than talking about the frustration of not being able to figure out how to access the public housing office or determine the best areas for relocation, incorporating phone calls during psychotherapy to offices and realtors and undertaking apartment searches through the newspapers would provide support and help the client feel empowered to more effectively master his or her environment (Bemak, 1989).

Another level in the MLM, entitled *Psychotherapy: Individual, Group, and Family,* emphasizes culturally sensitive psychotherapy based on Western training and practice. Consistent with Guideline 5, this level describes the importance of integrating a wide range of intervention techniques and strategies that are culturally applicable to migrants and gives greater attention to culturally relevant interventions that are group, family, and community based rather than individual based. Intervention strategies that incorporate dreamwork, cognitive-behavioral work, gestalt, relaxation therapy, narrative therapy, role playing, and psychodrama have all been found to be effective and extend beyond traditional "talk therapy" (Bemak et al., 2003).

Further expanding Western techniques, we also identified another level in the MLM as *Integration of Western and Indigenous Healing Methodologies,* whereby there is a respect for the migrants' cultural context and preference for indigenous healing practices. Spiritual beliefs and values about healing are developed within a framework of culture. Consistent with Guideline 2, therapists must be aware, understand, appreciate, and acknowledge migrant clients' beliefs in the conceptualizations of mental illness, help-seeking behavior, and treatment expectations and outcomes. Thus, indigenous practices within the migrant community may be the treatment of choice that mental health professionals must not only respect but actually encourage. Consistent with Guideline 5, this results in combining Western mental health interventions with indigenous healing practices and a need for consultation and collaboration with a broad range of healers. It is also appropriate in many cultures for elders to assume the role of the healer, so that Mrs. W., Maria, or Deng might benefit greatly from talking to a respected elder in the community. To locate traditional healers who are reliable, authentic, and reputable, therapists must contact community leaders, elders, and business owners.

The final level in the MLM is *Social Justice and Human Rights,* targeting issues of fairness and equity in terms of rights, opportunities, and access to resources. Traditionally, psychotherapy has disregarded these issues, focusing instead on intrapsychic dynamics and psychopathology. The MLM, in line with Guideline 5, dynamically changes traditional practice and requires the therapist to attend to and accentuate human rights and social justice, thus addressing a broader context than individual issues. Consequently, with Mrs. W., Maria, and Deng, it is important not to discount the impact of their sociopolitical and historical realities in China, El Salvador, or Sudan, where they may have been threatened or hurt, directly or indirectly, by U.S. foreign policy. Their reactions to the United States during premigration may affect their outlook and psychological well-being during postmigration, and have an influence on their work with a therapist. Simultaneously, we would suggest that therapists working with other migrant clients whose human rights have been or are being violated or who are facing injustices, must work in collaboration with their clients to challenge those issues, whether unfair housing practices, racial discrimination at the workplace, wage inequities, unequal access to educational opportunities, denial of medical care, social services or benefits, and so forth. This is consistent with Guideline 5, which advocates basic human rights.

In addition, it is important to respect and honor the native language of the migrant. Speaking in one's own vernacular allows clearer and more expressive communication, and in many instances will require the use of bilingual and bicultural translators. Mrs. W., Maria, and Deng may well have difficulties sharing their deeper feelings and thoughts in English, and be much more comfortable speaking in their native dialect. Bilingual translators must be neutral persons from the community who will not prejudge the client or discuss the client's situation in the larger community. As stated in Guideline 5, it is important that therapists respect clients' boundaries by not using family members, authorities in the community, or unskilled and untrained interpreters. Therefore, it is also critical when using interpreters that they do not just translate verbatim, but also convey the cultural idioms/nuances that go beyond word-for-word translation. Variations and irregularities in sentence structure and words must be translated and reported, as well as cultural nuances and disrespectful comments made to the therapist. Clarity regarding the interpreter's role provides a more accurate picture about who the client really is, rather than a filtered version by a well intentioned bilingual interpreter.

Consistent with Guideline 2, when developing appropriate culturally sensitive interventions, it is also important that the mental health professional have a clear sense about clashing values. For example, Maria comes from a *machismo* culture where her father has a certain role within the family that must be honored by the therapist. Mrs. W. is the elder in the family so her clash with her daughter-in-law is fraught with cultural nuances and meaning about respect, piety, and deference to an elder. In other instances, there may be community hierarchies that must be honored. Similarly, before working with Deng it may be necessary to receive a "blessing" from the leader in the Sudanese community, whose approval will both honor age-old traditions about sanctioning social relationships and facilitate openness in Deng to work with the therapist. In these and numerous other situations, the culturally skilled therapist must not only respect and honor the client's values, but be careful not to impose his or her own values and beliefs on the client.

CONCLUSION

Working with immigrants and refugees requires unique multicultural skills and understanding. Premigration; transitions to a new country; postmigration; the subsequent histories of trauma, disruption, losses of family and community; and problems with language, school, and employment all contribute to special circumstances that are underscored by moving to a new culture. Therapists must be prepared by understanding themselves and their clients' worlds, and developing culturally sensitive and responsive interventions to work with these complex populations.

RESOURCES

Books

Bemak, F., Chung, R.C-Y., & Pedersen, P. (2003). *Counseling refugees: A psychosocial approach to innovative multicultural interventions.* Westport, CT: Greenwood Press.
Cole, E., Espin, O. M., & Rothblum, E. D. (1992). *Refugee women and their mental health: Shattered societies, shattered lives.* Binghamton, NY: Harrington Park Press.
Fadiman, A. (1997). *The spirit catches you and you fall down.* New York: Noonday Press.

Video Companies (with videos about migrants)

Filmakers Library (www.filmaker.com)
Insight Media (www.insight-media.com)
National Asian American Telecommunication Association (www/naatanet.org/distri)

Websites

Oxford University, Refugee Studies Center (www.rsc.ox.ac.uk)
Survivors International (http://www.survivorsintl.org/)
The Center for Victims of Torture (www.cvt.org)
Harvard Program in Refugee Trauma (www.hprt-cambridge.org)
Center for Refugee Studies (http://www.yorku.ca/crs/)
The Center for Refugee and Disaster Response (http://www.jhsph.edu/Refugee/)

REFERENCES

Ajdukovic M., & Ajdukovic D. (1993). Psychological well-being of refugee children. *Child Abuse and Neglect, 17,* 843-854.
American Psychological Association. (2003). Guidelines on multicultural education, training, research, practice, and organizational change for psychologists. *American Psychologist, 58,* 377-402.
Bemak, F. (1989). Cross-cultural family therapy with Southeast Asian refugees. *Journal of Strategic and Systemic Therapies, 8,* 22-27.
Bemak, F., & Chung, R. C-Y. (2000). Psychological intervention with immigrants and refugees. In J. F. Aponte & J. Wohl (Eds.), *Psychological intervention and cultural diversity* (2nd ed., pp. 200–214). Needham Heights, MA: Allyn & Bacon.
Bemak, F., Chung, R. C-Y., & Pedersen, P. B. (2003). *Counseling refugees: A psychosocial approach to innovative multicultural interventions.* Westport, CT: Greenwood Press.
Capps, R., & Passel, J. S. (2004). *Describing immigrant communities..* Washington, DC: Urban Institute.
Chung, R. C-Y., (2005). Women, human rights, and counseling: Crossing international boundaries. *Journal of Counseling and Development, 83,* 262–268.
Chung R., C-Y., & Bemak, F. (2002). Revisiting the California Southeast Asian mental health needs assessment data: An examination of refugee ethnic and gender differences. *Journal of Counseling and Development, 80,* 111–119.

Chung, R. C-Y., & Bemak, F. (2006). Counseling Americans of Southeast Asian descent: The impact of the refugee experience. In C. C. Lee (Ed.), *Multicultural issues in counseling* (3rd ed., pp. 151–170). Alexandria, VA: American Counseling Association.

Chung, R. C-Y., Bemak, F., & Kagawa-Singer, M. (1998). Gender differences in psychological distress among Southeast Asian refugees. *Journal of Nervous and Mental Disease, 186*, 112–119.

Chung, R. C-Y., & Kagawa-Singer, M. (1993). Predictors of psychological distress among Southeast Asian refugees. *Social Science and Medicine, 36*, 631–639.

Chung, R. C-Y., & Kagawa-Singer, M. (1995). Interpretation of symptom presentation and distress: A Southeast Asian refugee example. *Journal of Nervous and Mental Disease, 183*, 639–648.

Chung, R. C-Y., & Lin, K. M. (1994). Help-seeking behavior among Southeast Asian refugees. *Journal of Community Psychology, 22*, 109–120.

Chung, R. C-Y., & Okazaki, S. (1991). Counseling Americans of Southeast Asian descent: The impact of the refugee experience. In C. C. Lee & B. L. Richardson (Eds.), *Multicultural issues in counseling: New approaches to diversity* (pp. 107–126). Alexandria, VA: American Association for Counseling and Development.

Draguns, J. (2000). Psychopathology and ethnicity. In J. F. Aponte & J. Wohl (Eds.), *Psychological Intervention and Cultural Diversity* (2nd ed., pp. 40–58). Needham Heights, MA: Allyn & Bacon.

Fabrega, H. (1989). Cultural relativism and psychiatric illness. *Journal of Nervous and Mental Disease, 177*, 415–425.

Fawzi, M. C. S., Pham, T., Lin, L., Nguyen, T. V., Ngo, D., Murphy, E., & Mollica, R. F. (1997). The validity of posttraumatic stress disorder among Vietnamese refugees. *International Society for Traumatic Stress Studies, 10*, 101–108.

Good, B. J., & Good, M. J. D. (1981). The meaning of symptoms: A cultural hermeneutic model of clinical practice. In L. Eisenberg & A. Kleinman (Eds.), *The relevance of social science for medicine* (pp.165–196). Dordrecht, Holland: Reidel.

Helms, J. E., & Cook, D. A. (1999). *Using race and culture in counseling and psychotherapy: Theory and process*. Needham Heights, MA: Allyn & Bacon.

Higginbotham, J. C., Trevino, F. M., & Ray, L. A. (1990). Utilization of curanderos by Mexican Americans: Prevalence and predictors findings from HHANES 1982–1984. *American Journal of Public Health, 80*(Suppl.), 32–35.

Hinton, W. L., Tiet, Q., Tran, C. G., & Chesney, M. (1997). Predictors of depression among refugees from Vietnam: A longitudinal study of new arrivals. *Journal of Nervous and Mental Disease, 185*, 39–45.

Karadaghi, P. (1994). The Kurds: Refugees in their own land. In A. J. Marsella, T. Bornemann, S. Ekblad, & J. Orley (Eds.), *Amidst peril and pain: The mental health and well-being of the world's refugees* (pp. 115–124). Washington, DC: American Psychological Association.

Kinzie, J. D. (1993). Posttraumatic effects and their treatment among Southeast Asian refugees. In J. Wilson & B. Raphael (Eds.), *International handbook of traumatic stress syndromes* (pp. 311–320). New York: Plenum Press.

Kirmayer, L. J. (1989). Cultural variation in the response to psychiatric disorders and emotional distress. *Social Science and Medicine, 28*, 327–339.

Kleinman, A. (1980). *Patients and healers in the context of culture*. Berkeley: University of California Press.

Lin, K. M., Masuda M., & Tazuma, L. (1982). Adaptational problems of Vietnamese refugees: Part III. Case studies in clinic and field: Adaptive and maladaptive. *Psychiatric Journal of University of Ottawa, 7*, 173–183.

Marsella, A. J., Bornemann, T., Ekblad, S., & Orley, J. (Eds.). (1994). *Amidst peril and pain: The mental health and well-being of the world's refugees.* Washington, DC: American Psychological Association.

Marsella, A. J., Friedman, M., & Spain, H. (1993). Ethnocultural aspects of PTSD. In J. Oldham, M. Riba, & A. Tasman (Eds.), *Review of psychiatry* (pp. 157–181). Washington, DC: American Psychiatric Press.

Miller, K., Worthington, G. J., Muzurovic, J., Tipping, S., & Goldman, A. (2002). Bosnian refugees and the stressors of exile: A narrative study. *American Journal of Orthopsychiatry, 72,* 341–354.

Mollica, R. F., & Jalbert, R. R. (1989). *Community of confinement: The mental health crisis on Site Two: Displaced persons' camps on the Thai–Kampuchean border.* Boston: Committee on World Federation for Mental Health.

Mollica, R. F., & Lavelle, J. (1988). Southeast Asian refugees. In L. Comas-Diaz & E. H. Griffith (Eds.), *Clinical guidelines in cross-cultural mental health* (pp. 262–303). New York: Wiley.

Murphy, H. B. (1977). Migration, culture and mental health. *Psychological Medicine, 7,* 677–684.

Pedersen, P. B., Draguns, J. G., Lonner, W. J., & Trimble, J. E. (Eds.). (2002). *Counseling across cultures* (5th ed.). Thousand Oaks, CA: Sage.

Ponterotto, J. G., Casas, J. M., Suzuki, L. A., & Alexander, C. M. (Eds.). (2001). *Handbook of multicultural counseling* (2nd ed.). Thousand Oaks, CA: Sage.

Sue, D. W., Carter, R. T., Casas, J. M., Fouad, N. A., Ivey, A. E., Jensen, M., et al. (1998). *Multicultural counseling competencies.* Thousand Oaks, CA: Sage.

United Nations. (2002). *International migration 2002.* Geneva: United Nations Population Division.

U.S. Bureau of the Census. (2002, July). *United States Census 2000.* Washington, DC: U.S. Department of Commerce, Economics and Statistics Administration.

U. S. Department of Homeland Security. (2003). *2002 yearbook of immigration statistics.* Retrieved November 9, 2003, from http://uscis.gov/graphics/shared/aboutus/statistics/IMM02yrbk/IMM2003list.htm

Weine, S., & Henderson, S. W. (2005). Rethinking the role of posttraumatic stress disorder in refugee mental health services. In T. A. Corales (Ed.), *Trends in posttraumatic stress disorder research* (pp. 157–183). Hauppauge, NY: Nova.

Weisaeth, L., & Eitinger, L. (1993). Posttraumatic stress phenomena: Common themes across wars, disasters, and traumatic events. In J. Wilson & B. Raphael (Eds.), *International handbook of traumatic stress syndromes* (pp. 69–78). New York: Plenum Press.

9

Lesbian, Gay, and Bisexual People of Color

Y. Barry Chung

The multicultural movement in psychology has evolved in the past few decades from a predominant focus on race and ethnicity to a more inclusive approach that attends to other cultural dimensions (e.g., age, gender identity, sexual orientation, disability, religion/spirituality, social class) and most recently to the recognition of individuals' multiple cultural identities. This trend is evident in the collaborations in the American Psychological Association (APA) Divisions 44 (lesbian, gay, and bisexual issues) and 45 (ethnic minority issues). Furthermore, the National Multicultural Conference and Summit (NMCS) has shown increased attention to various cultural and multiple identity issues through more active sponsorships by APA divisions that have a multicultural focus (e.g., Divisions 17, 35, 44, and 45). On the other hand, critical incidents and difficult dialogues at the NMCS continue to reveal challenges facing this more inclusive multicultural movement. Issues for lesbian, gay, and bisexual (LGB) people of color remained largely absent from the psychology literature, until the past decade, when some notable publications on these populations emerged.

The limited amount of literature available on LGB people of color leaves psychologists ill equipped to work effectively with these populations (Greene, 1997b). Both racial/ethnic minorities and sexual minorities (i.e., LGB persons) have to deal with social oppression and identity development issues (Israel & Selvidge, 2003). With a dual minority status, LGB people of color may experience multiple layers of oppression; some may feel the stress of having to choose between their racial/ethnic and sexual identities (Diaz, Ayala, & Bein, 2004; Harper, Jernewall, & Zea, 2004). Guidelines for psychological practice with LGB people of color are sorely needed.

A large number of multicultural scholars have contributed to the "Guidelines on Multicultural Education, Training, Research, Practice, and Organizational Change for Psychologists" (APA, 2003) over the past 2 decades. Although these Guidelines focus on racial and ethnic minority groups as well as multiracial and multiethnic persons in the United States (collectively referred to as "people of color" in this chapter), the Guidelines also address multiple-identity or cultural issues beyond race and ethnicity. However, the Multicultural Guidelines were not intended to address these multiple-identity issues in great detail. The purpose of this chapter is to discuss the application of the Multicultural Guidelines to LGB people of color in the United States. In doing so, I incorporate the Guidelines for Psychotherapy with Lesbian, Gay, and Bisexual Clients (Division 44/Committee on Lesbian, Gay, and Bisexual Concerns Joint Task Force, 2000). I briefly state how each Multicultural Guideline applies to LGB people of color, then elaborate on strategies for developing competence, followed by a case vignette for each Guideline. While other scholars have addressed how multicultural competence can be applied to LGB clients (e.g., Israel & Selvidge, 2003; Kocarek & Pelling, 2003) and issues related to counseling LGB people of color (e.g., Fukuyama & Ferguson, 2000), this chapter focuses specifically on the APA Multicultural Guidelines' application to LGB people of color. Readers also may consult three notable publications on this topic: (1) Greene's (1997a) *Ethnic and Cultural Diversity Among Lesbians and Gay Men*; (2) Fassinger's (2003) special issue on "Multicultural Counseling with Gay, Lesbian, and Bisexual Clients"; and (3) Zea and Harper's (2004) special issue on "Lesbian, Gay, and Bisexual Racial and Ethnic Minority Individuals: Empirical Explorations."

The Multicultural Guidelines have six items, which can be grouped under five topics: (1) awareness and knowledge, (2) education, (3) research, (4) practice, and (5) organizational change and policy development. The LGB Guidelines have 16 items organized under four sections: (1) attitudes, (2) relationships and families, (3) diversity, and (4) education. Both sets of guidelines address attitudes, knowledge, practice, and education. However, the LGB Guidelines have a more explicit focus on diversity, whereas the Multicultural Guidelines have a broader scope to include research as well as organizational change and policy development, with the topic of diversity infused in various sections. I have organized my discussion of cultural competence with LGB people of color according to the five topics of the Multicultural Guidelines. The LGB Guidelines are incorporated when relevant.

GUIDELINES 1 AND 2: AWARENESS AND KNOWLEDGE

Two Multicultural Guidelines are the focus of this section. Guideline 1 emphasizes psychologists' awareness of how their attitudes and beliefs may detrimentally influence their perceptions of and interactions with people who are culturally different. Guideline 2 highlights the importance of multicultural sensitivity, responsiveness, knowledge, and understanding. Similarly, LGB Guidelines 1–4 address psychologists' attitudes and knowledge regarding LGB persons. First, psychologists should understand that homosexuality and bisexuality are not indicative of mental illness. Second, psychologists need to be aware of their biases and the need for consultation or referrals when appropriate. Third, psychologists should try to understand how social stigmatization poses risks to the well-being of LGB clients. Finally, it is important to recognize how inaccurate or prejudicial views of homosexuality or bisexuality may influence clients' behavior in treatment and the therapeutic process. LGB Guidelines 9–13 further point to the importance of understanding unique challenges facing five diverse groups within the LGB community: (1) racial and ethnic minorities, (2) bisexual persons, (3) youth, (4) older adults, and (5) persons with disabilities.

The aforementioned guidelines can be integrated to further address multicultural competence with LGB people of color. The first implication is that psychologists are encouraged to examine their attitudes, assumptions, biases, and prejudices with regard to LGB people of color, and how such attitudes and values may be related to the cultural context of their racial/ethnic and sexual-orientation backgrounds. Psychologists inevitably are influenced by racism and heterosexism in mainstream U.S. culture and may, to various degrees, consider LGB people of color as racially deficient and sexually deviant. Herek (1995) defined heterosexism as "the ideological system that denies, denigrates, and stigmatizes any nonheterosexual form of behavior, identity, relationship, or community" (p. 321). The awareness of such attitudes and beliefs requires commitment to self reflection and examination. Psychologists also strive to understand how their attitudes and values may adversely influence their work with LGB people of color and to determine when consultations are necessary or referrals are appropriate.

The second implication is that psychologists are encouraged to obtain more knowledge and understanding of LGB people of color and become more sensitive and responsive to the needs of these populations. LGB people of color often face severe discrimination because of their dual minority status. Impairment of psychological functioning among LGB people of color is often a result of such stigmatization and discrimination, rather than of their race/ethnicity or sexual orientation per se. It is also important to recognize how their experience with oppression may affect the behavior and treatment goals of LGB people of color. Some clients may feel ashamed of themselves due to internalized racial oppression or heterosexism, and may desire to change their homosexual or bisexual orientation or become more mainstream (i.e., White-identified). Psychologists are careful not to allow their personal bias to perpetuate such oppressions. Instead, psychologists can help

LGB people of color understand how their struggles result from oppression rather than internal deficits. Finally, special attention should be given to understanding cultural diversity among LGB people of color, such as females, youth, older adults, or disabled individuals. Other chapters in this volume address some of these cultural dimensions.

Strategies for Developing Competence

The Multicultural Guidelines identify several strategies from research literature for reducing stereotypic attitudes and biases:

- Being aware of these attitudes and values
- Changing the automatically favorable perceptions of "in-group" (one's own cultural group) and negative perceptions of "out-group" (other cultural groups)
- Recategorizing the out-group as members of the in-group
- Increasing contact with other groups, especially when individuals are of equal status
- Actively seeing persons as individuals rather than members of a group
- Increasing tolerance and trust of the out-group

The LGB Guidelines also can be applied here to suggest methods of self-exploration and self-education (e.g., consultation, study, and continuing education) in order to identify and deal with biases about LGB people of color and to gain better understanding of these populations.

One critical area for knowledge development is familiarity with racial/ethnic identity development models (e.g., Atkinson, Morten, & Sue, 1998; Cross, 1995; Helms, 1995; Kim, 1981; LaFromboise & Jackson, 1996; Ruiz, 1990), homosexual and bisexual identity development models (e.g., Cass, 1979; Troiden, 1989), as well as theories and research about the interaction between racial/ethnic and sexual identities (e.g., Chung, 2002; Chung & Katayama, 1998). Chan's (1997) review of literature indicates that LGB Asians and Hispanics often are seen more as sexual minorities than as racial/ethnic minorities, even though they desire both identities to be acknowledged. According to Greene (1997b), some research shows that LGB African Americans report more experience with racism than with heterosexism, and are more likely to consider their racial identity as primary. LGB Asian Americans, on the other hand, report more experience with heterosexism than with racism, and are likely to consider their sexual identity as more salient.

There seem to be more negative attitudes toward LGB identities among people of color than among White Americans (Espin, 1984; Morales, 1992;

Rosario, Schrimshaw, & Hunter, 2004). LGB people of color often face the difficult dilemma of coming out, in fear of being rejected by their own family and ethnic community. Furthermore, LGB people of color have reported experience with racism in the predominately White LGB community (Chan, 1989; Diaz et al., 2004; Greene, 1997b; Harper et al., 2004). Therefore, some LGB people of color may feel marginalized from all worlds, without any community to anchor their identity. Some may develop coping strategies to manage their sexual identity in different contexts, such as social circles, work, family, and cultural community (Zea, Reisen, & Diaz, 2003). However, it is important to recognize the conceptual difference between same-sex behavior and LGB identities. Collectively, people of color seem to be more accepting of same-sex emotional and physical closeness without labeling it as LGB (Chan, 1992; Espin, 1984; Greene, 1997b; Smith, 1997). On the other hand, the acknowledgment and disclosure of an LGB identity would engender severe negative reactions in racial/ethnic minority communities. LGB identities seem to be a Western ideology among these cultural groups. Greene (1997b) stated that families of LGB people of color often respond to their LGB family member's coming out by quiet toleration or denial, believing that LGB orientation is something acquired through assimilation into the White culture.

I present a theoretical model of the interaction between racial and sexual identities among Asian American gay men, with empirical support from quantitative and qualitative research (Chung, 2002). I operationalized racial identity attitudes using Berry's (1980) two-dimensional model of acculturation (i.e., attitudes toward one's own culture and toward the dominant culture). Integrationists and Marginalists are those who have positive or negative attitudes toward both cultures, respectively. Separationists have positive attitudes toward their own culture and negative attitudes toward the dominant culture, while the reverse is true for Assimilationists. Based on a framework of parallel and interactive processes between racial and sexual identity development (Chung & Katayama, 1998), I described the pattern of increasingly affirmative sexual-identity attitudes that follow the order of Assimilationists, Marginalists, Separationists, and Integrationists. Asian gay persons who are beginning to come out have the least affirmative attitudes about their sexual identity. They tend to distance themselves from their Asian community and attempt to acculturate into the mainstream White gay community (Assimilationists). However, experience with racism in the gay community results in withdrawal from the predominately White gay community (Marginalists). Those who continue to strengthen their gay identity may have sufficient ego strength to reconnect with the Asian community, especially Asian gay peers (Separationists). With continued development of an integrated Asian gay identity and understanding of racism and heterosexism, Asian gay persons finally are able to feel positive about both Asian and White cultures (Integrationists). More research on this theoretical model and its application to other racial/ethnic groups is needed. Recently, other researchers have begun to examine hypotheses about the relation between racial and sexual identities. For example, Crawford, Allison, Zamboni, and Soto (2002) found that African American gay and bisexual men who achieved positive racial and sexual identities reported higher levels of self-esteem, social support, and life satisfaction, and lower levels of psychosocial distress, than men with other identity attitudes.

Finally, it is helpful to understand special attitudes and behaviors associated with different racial/ethnic groups. Among Latinos, an active or masculine role in same-sex behavior seems to be more acceptable than a passive or feminine role (Espin, 1984). For Native Americans, an androgynous gender role, or the Two Spirit, is traditionally desirable for men and women (Garrett & Barret, 2003; Weinrich & Williams, 1991). However, colonization may have changed this value, especially among those living on reservations, resulting in more pressure to conform to rigid gender roles and remain closeted on reservations (Balsam, Huang, Fieland, Simoni, & Walters, 2004). Fukuyama and Ferguson (2000) summarized additional culture-specific perspectives for the four racial/ethnic minority groups of LGB persons.

Case Vignette: Gay Racial Identity Attitudes

> Some time ago I was supervising a White male heterosexual student doing a counseling practicum. He was counseling a young Vietnamese immigrant gay male client who was in the process of coming out. My student thought that the client could benefit from joining a social group for Asian gay men in the community. When he made the suggestion, the client became noticeably uncomfortable and inquired whether Asians or Whites were leading the social group. My student brought this to my attention during supervision. I conveyed that the client's anxiety was understandable, and I shared with the student the research I had done regarding racial and sexual identities of Asian gay men. When my student learned that Asian gay men may have Assimilationist attitudes when they begin their coming out, the client's reaction began to make sense to him. The client was not comfortable being with other Asians at that time because of the association of Asian culture with homonegativity. He felt more drawn to the mainstream predominately White gay community because it seemed to provide a safer space for him to explore his sexuality without the shadow of Asian censorship.

This case vignette illustrates the importance of gaining awareness and knowledge of the racial/ethnic and sexual-identity development of LGB people of color.

GUIDELINE 3: EDUCATION

Multicultural Guideline 3 encourages psychology educators to embrace multiculturalism and diversity in education and training. LGB Guidelines 14–16 further address educational issues related to LGB clients. First, psychologists support the provision of education and training on LGB issues. Second, psychologists are encouraged to increase their knowledge of LGB issues through continuing education, training, supervision, and consultation. Finally, it is important to be familiar with mental health, educational, and community resources for LGB persons.

The above Guidelines are applied here for psychology education related to LGB people of color. The first implication is that psychology educators are urged to value and infuse multicultural issues in education and training, with specific emphasis on the inclusion of various cultural dimensions (e.g., race/ethnicity and sexual orientation) and the intersection of multiple identities (e.g., LGB people of color). In addition to addressing issues pertaining to LGB people of color, attention may be given to the provision of an affirmative learning atmosphere for LGB people of color. The second implication is that training programs may promote self-education about LGB people of color through continuing education, training, supervision, and consultation. Obtaining knowledge about resources for LGB people of color can be part of continuous self-education. Psychology educators can be role models for their students by actively engaging in self-education.

Strategies for Developing Competence

Chung and Brack (2005) proposed several strategies for enhancing sexual-orientation equity in academic and clinical training. These strategies are modified here for the purpose of addressing education and training issues related to LGB people of color. First, multicultural counseling or LGB courses may be offered that explicitly address the topics of LGB people of color and the intersecting identities of race/ethnicity and sexual orientation. According to the LGB Guidelines, the following areas of training are relevant: human sexuality, LGB identity development, effects of stigmatization, racial/ethnic and cultural factors, and career development and workplace issues. Second, multicultural issues can be infused in all courses whenever appropriate. In doing so, attention may be given to LGB people of color in course content and case examples. Third, recruitment and retention efforts may value faculty, students, and staff who are LGB people of color. Such efforts should be sensitive to the needs of these populations. The presence of LGB people of color on the faculty allows for role modeling and mentoring that empower individuals with multiple minority identities. Fourth, training environments can be affirmative to LGB people of color. The Multicultural Guidelines urge faculty, advisors, and supervisors to provide a safe and responsive learning environment when addressing multicultural issues in course content and clinical training. The creation of such environments can be facilitated by routine climate assessments, mentoring, and the establishment of organizations for LGB people of color. Fifth, clinical supervision may employ appropriate approaches that correspond to trainees' level of functioning with regard to racial/ethnic and LGB issues. Readers are referred to Chung and Brack's (2005) discussion of three training levels: (1) didactic learning, (2) encouragement of trainee independence, and (3) learning to use self as an instrument.

To facilitate self-education, educators may actively seek out opportunities for continuing education, training, supervision, consultation, and resources that are relevant for working with LGB people of color. Educators routinely may forward information about these opportunities to students and encourage students to seek out opportunities on their own and exchange such information among themselves. Educators can act as role models by taking on self-education opportunities and sharing their learning when teaching and mentoring students. Community resources for LGB people of color can be included in student recruitment brochures and websites, and be available in clinical training facilities.

Case Vignette: A Multicultural Affirmation Plan

My academic department is very committed to the creation of a multiculturally affirmative atmosphere for faculty, students, and staff. We have a strategic plan for the recruitment and retention of underrepresented students and faculty that is tailored to the representation of faculty and students along various cultural dimensions, such as race/ethnicity and sexual orientation. There are 24 recommendations in this document, addressing issues such as:

- Proactive recruitment of underrepresented faculty and students
- Provision of scholarships and financial aid
- Applying strategic plans for mentoring faculty and students
- Protection from work overload due to service activities
- Support for scholarly work through teaching-load reduction, research resources, and conference travel money
- Periodical feedback to facilitate retention
- Encouraging connection to relevant student and professional organizations and the local community for underrepresented groups
- Consultation and training to enhance multicultural sensitivity and competence

Three student organizations were founded in our department during the past few years for people of color, international students, and LGB persons, respectively. These organizations actively engage in social functions, colloquia, and education in the department to increase awareness of issues pertaining to people of color and LGB persons. I, an Asian gay man, serve as faculty advisor to some of these organizations, and I am glad to see some LGB students of color serve as officers and leaders. The visibility of LGB people of color helps create a supportive atmosphere. Students and faculty who are not LGB people of color also participate in these organizations.

GUIDELINE 4: RESEARCH

Guideline 4 emphasizes the importance of conducting culture-centered and ethical research. Three elements of research are specifically addressed: (1) research generation and design, (2) assessment, and (3) analysis and interpretation. The implication of this Guideline is that research involving LGB people of color should consider the cultures and contextual factors related to participants' racial/ethnic and sexual identities, and should be conducted in a manner that is ethical and sensitive to these populations. More specifically, generation of research questions should be closely tied to the cultural experiences of LGB people of color, focusing on both strengths and challenges facing these populations rather than taking on a pathological model. Researchers are urged to be knowledgeable about unique research design issues related to LGB people of color. Assessments should be appropriate to participants' languages, cultures, and sexual identities. Data analysis and interpretation can be aided by soliciting the involvement of LGB people of color.

Strategies for Developing Competence

To conduct culture-centered and ethical research with LGB people of color, a researcher must consider the fundamental question as to whether LGB people of color can benefit from the research. To answer this question, the researcher may evaluate the design, process, and outcome of the study.

- Does the research question matter to LGB people of color?
- Is it informed by literature and cultural experiences of these populations?
- Is it based on assumptions of deficits because of participants' ethnic and sexual minority backgrounds?
- Can the design be enhanced by consultation with LGB people of color?

Regarding research process, assessment is often a critical element. Scholars have raised concerns about traditional assessments for people of color (e.g., Helms, 1992; Spengler, 1998) and LGB persons (e.g., Chernin, Holden, & Chandler 1997; Pope, 1992; Prince, 1997). Researchers need to consider how a measure was developed and normed, whether it is culturally biased, whether the language and reading level are appropriate, whether special norming groups are warranted, and whether the assessment contributes to feelings of invalidation and marginalization. An assessment may assume that some cultural behaviors are undesirable, abnormal, or pathological (e.g., African Americans who speak loudly or expressively are interpreted as aggressive or histrionic; an Asian American's interdependent career-decision-making style is considered immature). Some test contents or languages can be culturally exclusive (e.g., assumption of heterosexuality among respondents). Also, some respondents may require assessments in their native language.

In terms of outcome, data analysis and interpretation should be performed in ways that not only evaluate how the data correspond to culture-centered theories and hypotheses, but also allow the discovery of cultural phenomena. Researchers may report rich data about the cultural and demographic information of participants, as well as the limits of the study, in order to enhance knowledge of the generalizability of the study. LGB people of color may be invited to participate in the data-interpretation process, and research findings can be reported to communities of LGB people of color in ways that facilitate the advancement of these populations.

Finally, Chung and Brack's (2005) recommendations are also applicable to research and publications related to LGB people of color. Academic administrators, promotion and tenure committees, and journal editorial boards are encouraged to value research on LGB people of color and understand the unique methods and difficulties in such research. Professional organizations such as the APA and the American Counseling Association are encouraged to educate their editors and editorial consultants on these matters.

Case Vignette: Bias in the Research Community

A gay psychologist of color conducted a study about gay men of color. The research was grounded in a culture-centered theory and produced supporting results. Although the sample size was small by conventional standards, it was larger than previous research on the same kind of population. The response rate was also better than in most LGB studies published in prominent journals as well as other survey studies in general. The psychologist felt that his study was a significant contribution, but had a difficult time deciding on a publication outlet. Most of the LGB journals available were not geared specifically toward a psychological perspective. Journals focusing on multicultural or racial/ethnic issues were perceived to be unwelcoming of LGB articles. The psychologist decided to submit the article to a psychological journal about race and ethnicity. Review of the study was unreasonably harsh, focusing on the small sample size and low response rate, among other criticisms that seemed to be uninformed by LGB research methodology. The psychologist wrote to the editor to explain how the study compared well with other studies on LGB people of color, but never received any response from the editor. This incident was very discouraging to the psychologist, who felt that the review involved attitudinal bias and ignorance of LGB research methods.

This case speaks to the existence of heterosexism in the profession, the need for support of researchers conducting studies about LGB people of color, and the need for educating the research community about biases and research methodology related to LGB people of color.

GUIDELINE 5: PRACTICE

Guideline 5 addresses the application of culturally appropriate skills in clinical and other applied practices. The implication of this Guideline for LGB people of color is that any psychological practice with LGB people of color should utilize culturally appropriate skills that are responsive to the racial/ethnic and sexual identities of the client. Such practice builds on the foundations of Multicultural Guidelines 1–4, which address awareness, knowledge, education, and research, respectively. Guideline 5 further elaborates on three aspects in practice: client in context, assessment, and interventions.

Strategies for Developing Competence

To develop culturally appropriate skills for practice with LGB people of color, psychologists need to continuously develop their awareness and knowledge regarding LGB people of color, actively engage in self-education, and keep themselves up-to-date with research and literature on these populations. Below I discuss developing competence in the three areas specified in Guideline 5.

Client in Context. When conceptualizing cases, it is important to put clients' presenting problems in context (e.g., generational history, citizenship or residency status, fluency in standard English and other languages, family and cultural community's attitudes toward homosexuality and bisexuality, family structure and support, availability of community resources, level of education, social status, work history and experience with discrimination, and acculturative stress). LGB Guidelines 5–8 seem particularly helpful for understanding LGB people of color in their contextual environment. These Guidelines address relationship and family issues:

- Knowledge about and respect for LGB couple relationships
- Challenges faced by LGB parents
- Families of LGB persons who may include people who are not legally or biologically related
- The impact of LGB persons' sexual orientation on their family of origin and their relationship to that family

Psychologists should realize the complexity of couple and family relationships among LGB people of color. As discussed previously, LGB people of color may have more difficulties than White LGB persons coming out to their families. The linear assumption of traditional LGB identity development models may not apply to the identity development of LGB people of color. Rather than urging clients to come out totally, psychologists should realize that healthy, functioning LGB persons of color can be differentially out in different parts of their lives. To establish their own community and support system, LGB people of color may include persons who are not legally or biologically related as their family members, such as other LGB people of color.

Psychologists should not only value and respect couple relationships among LGB people of color, but should also attempt to understand how they establish and maintain such relationships. LGB people of color often are either categorically considered unattractive or romanticized as exotic sexual objects in the larger LGB community (Harper et al., 2004). These dichotomous treatments may be due to racial stereotypes and discrimination. There are also speculations that Asian and Hispanic American LGB persons may tend to desire White Americans as romantic partners (Chung, 2002). Psychologists may explore whether such desires are results of internalized racial oppression. Regarding the experience of being parents, it is particularly difficult for LGB people of color to adopt children because of discrimination based on race/ethnicity and sexual orientation. Such discrimination can be covert (e.g., denial of right to adopt due to racial background, but framed in terms of being unfit parents) or overt (e.g., legal prohibition against adoption by LGB persons in certain states). There are additional barriers when an LGB person of color is partnered with a person of another race. Such couples may face discrimination from both racial-group communities, and their children may endure multiple layers of oppression. An understanding of the aforementioned contextual factors is important for conceptualizing issues facing LGB clients of color.

Assessment. Psychologists are urged to be knowledgeable about assessment issues related to racial/ethnic and sexual minorities when working with LGB people of color. In addition to the aforementioned assessment issues related to research, two broad recommendations are discussed here.

First, psychologists may become familiar with various tools for assessing multicultural constructs such as racial/ethnic identity, acculturation, acculturative stress, sexual identity, internalized homophobia, and sexual-identity management. Readers may refer to Part IV (Psychological Measurement of Multicultural Constructs) of the *Handbook of Multicultural Counseling* (Ponterotto, Casas, Suzuki, & Alexander, 2001).

Second, psychologists should note the appropriate application of various assessment instruments for LGB people of color in their selection of instrument, assessment procedure, data interpretation, and use of assessment results. Psychologists should become familiar with assessment issues such as test development and norming, test bias, and client responsiveness to assessment results. Selection of assessment instruments for individual cases should be based on the client's cultural identities and backgrounds, the psychometric quality and cultural appropriateness of the instrument, and the client's receptiveness to assessment. Interpretation and utilization of assessment results should be suitable for the client's readiness and response style. Active participation on the part of the client is strongly encouraged.

Interventions. Interventions for LGB people of color should be sensitive to the culture and individual needs of the client. Two elements of intervention are highlighted here: goal and process. Psychologists should ensure that therapeutic goals are not determined based on therapist bias or the client's internalized oppression. For example, one therapist bias is to direct LGB people of color to become totally open about their sexual orientation and immerse themselves in their own culture and racial/ethnic community. This bias fails to recognize the complexity of identity issues for LGB people of color by assuming a White LGB perspective (Smith, 1997). On the other hand, complying with a client's request to convert to a heterosexual orientation or to behave according to the White cultural norm, without addressing discrimination and internalized oppression, is also harmful to LGB people of color.

In terms of treatment process, the applicability of traditional and nontraditional practices should be carefully evaluated for the purpose of selecting interventions. Psychologists should consider the appropriate inclusion of consultants, interpreters, other healers, religious leaders, family, or significant others in their interventions with LGB people of color.

Case Vignette: Culturally Sensitive Counseling

Mario, a 27-year-old Hispanic gay man, was referred to counseling at a community service center because he tested HIV positive. He was depressed, angry, and hopeless, but was not suicidal.

Mario was born in Mexico and immigrated to America after marrying a Mexican woman who was a good friend and had U.S. citizenship. She was aware of his sexual orientation and was only helping him to gain legal status through marriage. After immigration, Mario became co-owner of a small house-cleaning business. He enjoyed hanging out with the female workers, who spoke little English. At night, Mario frequented gay clubs and had a close circle of Hispanic gay friends. He admitted that he played a receptive role sexually and engaged in unprotected sex. Mario remained married to his female friend, but they never had a sexual relationship.

The counselor, a White female psychologist, provided psychoeducation about HIV and AIDS, safer sex, treatment options, and lifestyles for healthy living. She also treated his depression, anger, and anxiety, using a cognitive-behavioral approach. She attempted to understand his social network and family, which seemed nontraditional to her. After some discussion, they decided to invite his wife and some of his female co-workers and Hispanic gay friends to a few counseling sessions, which sometimes were conducted at the client's home. These sessions were helpful because Mario was able to work through his reaction to his HIV status in the context of social support, and his significant others also were able to process their own reactions because of their emotional attachment to Mario. The counselor respected Mario's wish not to disclose his sexual identity and HIV status to his family of origin in Mexico. They discussed how to manage such information when he planned to visit his family.

In this case, the counselor utilized both traditional and nontraditional interventions with the client, after attempting to understand the cultural background and dynamics surrounding the client's presenting problem.

GUIDELINE 6:
ORGANIZATIONAL CHANGE AND POLICY DEVELOPMENT

Guideline 6 addresses the utilization of organizational change processes to facilitate culturally informed organizational/policy development and practices. The implication of this Guideline for LGB people of color is that psychologists are encouraged to support organizational changes that ensure equity and an affirmative climate for LGB people of color, and to engage in social justice advocacy in policy development and legislation.

Strategies for Developing Competence

The increased emphasis on social justice and advocacy in organizational change and policy development could become the fifth force in psychology and counseling, after the psychodynamic, behavioral, humanistic, and multicultural movements (Chung & Brack, 2005). This trend may be a result of three major factors. First, American society is rapidly becoming more culturally diverse. Second, social injustice, discrimination, and oppression cannot be deconstructed merely through psychological interventions with the oppressed. Third, everyone suffers from oppression, including the oppressors (Sue & Sue, 2003). Therefore, psychologists are urged to step beyond their traditional roles (as educators, researchers, or practitioners) and actively become social justice agents through organizational change and policy development. This means applying psychological knowledge to enhance social justice in (1) organizations (e.g., place of employment, social groups, professional associations) and communities (e.g., housing community, city, county, state, and country) to which a psychologist belongs, and (2) organizations and governments for which the psychologist is a consultant.

Relevant to LGB people of color, a fundamental strategy for organizational change and policy development is the deconstruction of racism and heterosexism. Consistent with the Multicultural Guidelines, psychologists may keep up with knowledge about federal, state, and local legislation such as the Civil Rights Act and laws relating to affirmative action, equal employment opportunity, sodomy, civil unions, and same-sex marriage. Here are some examples of advocacy for LGB people of color:

- Advocate for nondiscrimination policies and domestic-partner benefits
- Encourage more representation of LGB people of color in the organization's membership and governing bodies
- Help create an affirmative climate for LGB people of color
- Lobby and vote for civil unions, same-sex marriages, and same-sex couples' eligibility for immigration applications
- Increase awareness of LGB people of color through professional presentations and publications
- Recognize and honor achievements and contributions of LGB people of color.

One particularly powerful strategy for advocacy is the use of narrative voices. People may not change because of an intellectual argument, but may be emotionally touched by a personal story, resulting in attitudinal and behavioral change. Two notable publications utilized personal stories to facilitate the deconstruction of racism (Robinson & Ginter, 1999) and heterosexism in the counseling professions (Croteau, Lark, Lidderdale, & Chung, 2005). These stories can be effective in touching readers' hearts, resulting in empathy and empowerment. Movies and music can have similar effects, and I use all three methods in my teaching of multicultural counseling. Some of the media I have used include:

- HBO's production "Out at Work," a documentary movie about three persons' experiences with work discrimination due to their LGB identities
- The music about racism "Let Them Hear You," sung by the Three Mo' Tenors
- Reading the narrative voices of LGB persons of color in Croteau and colleagues' (2005) book

Case Vignette: Governmental Barriers to Same-Sex Couples

Tina, an African American lesbian, met Mimi, an Asian female international student, who was coming out while attending graduate school in America. They fell in love and moved in together. This relationship played a significant role in Mimi's coming-out process, although she remained closeted to her family and friends in Asia. Unfortunately, when Mimi graduated she was unable to find a job in America. Due to the U.S. immigration laws, which do not recognize same-sex relationships, Mimi felt that there was no option but to return to Asia. The couple could not entertain the idea of faking a heterosexual marriage in order for Mimi to apply for immigration. On the other hand, Tina did not feel that she could leave everything behind and move to Asia, where she did not speak the language and had no family connection. Discussion of their future became tense and quite emotional. Tina and Mimi envied the progress made in Canada where same-sex couples can legally marry and file for immigration applications. Mimi eventually moved back alone to her home country, and her relationship with Tina faded over the next 2 years despite their efforts to stay connected.

In contrast to Canada and some other countries, 11 states in the United States passed amendments to their state constitutions in the 2004 election to define marriage as only between a man and a woman. Many LGB people of color are forced to be separated from their partners in the United States because of how marriage is defined and because same-sex relationships are not a legitimate basis for immigration applications. Psychologists are encouraged to take actions in correcting this social injustice by educating others on these issues, voting for same-sex rights, and working together in professional organizations to provide position statements and research evidence to support same-sex relationships.

CONCLUSION

In this chapter I discussed how the Multicultural Guidelines can be applied to the advancement of LGB people of color through awareness and knowledge, education, research, practice, and organizational change and policy development. The deconstruction of racism and heterosexism requires a lifelong personal and professional commitment. Every psychologist can play an important role in this process in his or her own way. No effort is too small or insignificant.

Every step someone takes contributes to a collective movement for liberation.

REFERENCES

American Psychological Association. (2003). Guidelines on multicultural education, training, research, practice, and organizational change for psychologists. *American Psychologist, 58,* 377–402.

Atkinson, D. R., Morten, G., & Sue, D. W. (Eds.). (1998). *Counseling American minorities* (5th ed.). Boston: McGraw-Hill.

Balsam, K. F., Huang, B., Fieland, K. C., Simoni, J. M., & Walters, K. L. (2004). Culture, trauma, and wellness: A comparison of heterosexual and lesbian, gay, bisexual, and two-spirit Native Americans. *Cultural Diversity and Ethnic Minority Psychology, 10,* 287–301.

Berry, J. W. (1980). Acculturation as varieties of adaptation. In A. M. Padilla (Ed.), *Acculturation: Theory, models and some new findings* (pp. 9-25). Boulder, CO: Westview Press.

Cass, V. C. (1979). Homosexuality identity formation: A theoretical model. *Journal of Homosexuality, 4,* 219–235.

Chan, C. S. (1989). Issues of identity development among Asian-American lesbians and gay men. *Journal of Counseling and Development, 68,* 16–20.

Chan, C. S. (1992). Cultural considerations in counseling Asian American lesbians and gay men. In S. H. Dworkin & F. J. Gutierrez (Eds.), *Counseling gay men and lesbians: Journey to the end of the rainbow* (pp. 115–124). Alexandria, VA: American Association for Counseling and Development.

Chan, C. S. (1997). Don't ask, don't tell, don't know: The formation of a homosexual identity and sexual expression among Asian American lesbians. In B. Greene (Ed.), *Ethnic and cultural diversity among lesbians and gay men* (pp. 240–248). Thousand Oaks, CA: Sage.

Chernin, J., Holden, J. M., & Chandler, C. (1997). Bias in psychological assessment: Heterosexism. *Measurement and Evaluation in Counseling and Development, 30,* 68–76.

Chung, Y. B. (2002, August). *Theory and research on Asian American sexual minorities.* Paper presented at the annual convention of the American Psychological Association, Chicago.

Chung, Y. B., & Brack, C. J. (2005). Those who care, teach: Toward sexual orientation equity in academic and clinical training. In J. M. Croteau, J. S. Lark, M. A. Lidderdale, & Y. B. Chung (Eds.), *Deconstructing heterosexism in the counseling professions: A narrative approach* (pp. 211–228). Thousand Oaks, CA: Sage.

Chung, Y. B., & Katayama, M. (1998). Ethnic and sexual identity development of Asian-American lesbian and gay adolescents. *Professional School Counseling, 1*(3), 21–25.

Crawford, I., Allison, K. W., Zamboni, B. D., & Soto, T. (2002). The influence of dual-identity development on the psychosocial functioning of African American gay and bisexual men. *Journal of Sex Research, 39,* 179–189.

Cross, W. E. (1995). The psychology of Nigrescence: Revising the Cross model. In J. G. Ponterotto, J. M. Casas, L. A. Suzuki, & C. M. Alexander (Eds.), *Handbook of multicultural counseling* (pp. 93–122). Thousand Oaks, CA: Sage.

Croteau, J. M., Lark, J. S., Lidderdale, M. A., & Chung, Y. B. (Eds.). (2005). *Deconstructing heterosexism in the counseling professions: A narrative approach.* Thousand Oaks, CA: Sage.

Diaz, R. M., Ayala, G., & Bein, E. (2004). Sexual risk as an outcome of social oppression: Data for a probability sample of Latino gay men in three U.S. cities. *Cultural Diversity and Ethnic Minority Psychology, 10,* 255–267.

Division 44/Committee on Lesbian, Gay, and Bisexual Concerns Joint Task Force. (2000). Guidelines for psychotherapy with lesbian, gay, and bisexual clients. *American Psychologist, 55,* 1440–1451.

Espin, O. (1984). Cultural and historical influences on sexuality in Hispanic/Latina women: Implications for psychotherapy. In C. Vance (Ed.), *Pleasure and danger: Exploring female sexuality* (pp. 149–163). London: Routledge & Kegan Paul.

Fassinger, R. E. (Ed.). (2003). Multicultural counseling with gay, lesbian, and bisexual clients [Special issue]. *Journal of Multicultural Counseling and Development, 31*(2).

Fukuyama, M. A., & Ferguson, A. D. (2000). Lesbian, gay, and bisexual people of color: Understanding cultural complexity and managing multiple oppressions. In R. M. Perez, K. A. DeBord, & K. J. Bieschke (Eds.), *Handbook of counseling and psychotherapy with lesbian, gay, and bisexual clients* (pp. 81–105). Washington, DC: American Psychological Association.

Garrett, M. T., & Barret, B. (2003). Two spirit: Counseling Native American gay, lesbian, and bisexual people. *Journal of Multicultural Counseling and Development, 31,* 131–142.

Greene, B. (Ed.). (1997a). *Ethnic and cultural diversity among lesbians and gay men.* Thousand Oaks, CA: Sage.

Greene, B. (1997b). Ethnic minority lesbians and gay men: Mental health and treatment issues. In B. Greene (Ed.), *Ethnic and cultural diversity among lesbians and gay men* (pp. 216–239). Thousand Oaks, CA: Sage.

Harper, G. W., Jernewall, N., & Zea, M. C. (2004). Giving voice to emerging science and theory for lesbian, gay, and bisexual people of color. *Cultural Diversity and Ethnic Minority Psychology, 10,* 187–199.

Helms, J. E. (1992). Why is there no study of cultural equivalence in standardized cognitive ability testing? *American Psychologist, 47,* 1083–1101.

Helms, J. E. (1995). An update of Helms's White and people of color racial identity models. In J. G. Ponterotto, J. M. Casas, L. A. Suzuki, & C. M. Alexander (Eds.), *Handbook of multicultural counseling* (pp. 181–191). Thousand Oaks, CA: Sage.

Herek, G. (1995). Psychological heterosexism in the United States: In A. D'Augelli & C. Patterson (Eds.), *Lesbian, gay, and bisexual identities over the life span: Psychological perspectives* (pp. 321–346). New York: Oxford University Press.

Israel, T., & Selvidge, M. M. D. (2003). Contributions of multicultural counseling to counselor competence with lesbian, gay, and bisexual clients. *Journal of Multicultural Counseling and Development, 31,* 84–98.

Kim, J. (1981). The process of Asian American identity development: A study of Japanese-American women's perceptions of their struggle to achieve personal identities as Americans of Asian ancestry. *Dissertation Abstracts International, 42,* 155 1A. (University Microfilms No. 81-18080)

Kocarek, C. E., & Pelling, N. J. (2003). Beyond knowledge and awareness: Enhancing counselor skills for work with gay, lesbian, and bisexual clients. *Journal of Multicultural Counseling and Development, 31,* 99–112.

LaFromboise, T. D., & Jackson, M. (1996). MCT theory and Native-American populations. In D. W. Sue, A. E. Ivey, & P. B. Pedersen (Eds.), *A theory of multicultural counseling and therapy* (pp. 192–203). Pacific Grove, CA: Brooks/Cole.

Morales, E. (1992). Latino gays and Latina lesbians. In S. H. Dworkin & F. J. Gutierrez (Eds.), *Counseling gay men and lesbians: Journey to the end of the rainbow* (pp. 125–139). Alexandria, VA: American Association for Counseling and Development.

Ponterotto, J. G., Casas, J. M., Suzuki, L. A., & Alexander, C. M. (Eds.). (2001). *Handbook of multicultural counseling* (2nd ed.). Thousand Oaks, CA: Sage.

Pope, M. (1992). Bias in the interpretation of psychological tests. In S. H. Dworkin & F. J. Gutierrez (Eds.), *Counseling gay men and lesbians: Journey to the end of the rainbow* (pp. 277–292). Alexandria, VA: American Association for Counseling and Development.

Prince, J. P. (1997). Career assessment with lesbian, gay, and bisexual individuals. *Journal of Career Assessment, 5,* 225–238.

Robinson, T. L., & Ginter, E. J. (Eds.). (1999). Racism healing its effects [Special issue]. *Journal of Counseling and Development, 77*(1).

Rosario, M., Schrimshaw, E. W., & Hunter, J. (2004). Ethnic/racial differences in the coming-out process of lesbian, gay, and bisexual youths: A comparison of sexual identity development over time. *Cultural Diversity and Ethnic Minority Psychology, 10,* 215–228.

Ruiz, A. S. (1990). Ethnic identity: Crisis and resolution. *Journal of Multicultural Counseling and Development, 18,* 29–40.

Smith, A. (1997). Cultural diversity and the coming-out process: Implications for clinical practice. In B. Greene (Ed.), *Ethnic and cultural diversity among lesbians and gay men* (pp. 279–300). Thousand Oaks, CA: Sage.

Spengler, P. M. (1998). Multicultural assessment and a scientist-practitioner model of psychological assessment. *The Counseling Psychologist, 6,* 930–938.

Sue, D. W., & Sue, D. (2003). *Counseling the culturally diverse: Theory and practice* (4th ed.). Hoboken, NJ: Wiley.

Troiden, R. (1989). The formation of homosexual identities. *Journal of Homosexuality, 17*(1/2), 43–73.

Weinrich, J., & Williams, W. L. (1991). Strange customs, familiar lives: Homosexuality in other cultures. In J. C. Gonsiorek & J. D. Weinrich (Eds.), *Homosexuality: Research implications for public policy* (pp. 44–59). Newbury Park, CA: Sage.

Zea, M. C., & Harper, G. W. (Eds.). (2004). Lesbian, gay, and bisexual racial and ethnic minority individuals: Empirical explorations [Special issue]. *Cultural Diversity and Ethnic Minority Psychology, 10*(3).

Zea, M. C., Reisen, C. A., & Diaz, R. M. (2003). Methodological issues in research with Latino gay and bisexual men. *American Journal of Community Psychology, 31,* 281–291.

10

Persons of Color
with Disabilities

Rhoda Olkin

How is it possible to write about disability and ethnicity, each a broad term denoting myriad categories and characteristics? Disability can be described by categories (e.g., hearing, visual, learning, cognitive, physical, systemic, and developmental), or by function (e.g., uses wheelchair or scooter). In turn, ethnicity ranges from Hmong to African American to Brazilian to Egyptian and beyond. Should we construct a giant grid, one that has every conceivable ethnicity across the top, and all possible disabilities down the side? Is this the only way to fairly consider the intersection of these two characteristics?

The answer is both yes and no. *Yes*, we must speak with greater precision, because there is such conflation of characteristics that important distinctions are ignored. For example, just as grouping Laotian, Cambodian, Mainland Chinese, Hong Kong Chinese, and Vietnamese into the rubric Asian blurs important cultural differences, grouping hearing loss but uses speech with Deaf and uses sign language, or multiple sclerosis (nonfatal) and amyotrophic lateral sclerosis (ALS; usually fatal within 5 years), is almost nonsensical. *No*, because if we reduce the discussion to the grid posed above, we obscure important commonalities and hamper the quest for knowledge of the confluence of ethnicity and disability.

This chapter explores the nascent study of disability and ethnicity. First is a review of some research findings as they relate to the American Psychological Associations's Multicultural Guidelines (APA, 2003). This review is followed by a discussion of critical conceptual issues related to disability. Several examples are given to illustrate some points about disability and ethnicity, followed by suggestions for mental health professionals.

RELATING THE APA MULTICULTURAL GUIDELINES TO DISABILITY

Guideline 1: Polarization of Psychology and Disability

Scores of studies have demonstrated the predominately negative view Americans hold toward disability and people with disabilities (Olkin, 1999; Yuker, 1994). Although it might seem that psychologists would hold more positive attitudes toward disability than does the general public, it is unclear whether this is the case. This may be because the psychologist is in the superior role of helper, and the person with the disability is in the inferior role of client or consumer.

Undergraduate training in psychology introduces disability through a chapter on abnormal psychology. Disability is labeled as deviant or special, and viewed through a pathologizing lens. Not only is disability generally invisible in graduate training, but it also is devoid of positive role models of psychologists with disabilities. Further, the culture of psychology is entrenched in the need for standardization (e.g., in assessment), whereas laws related to disability codify individualization (e.g., in reasonable accommodations). These conflicting cultures further polarize psychology and disability (Olkin & Pledger, 2003).

Guideline 2: Disability in Context

It is hard to imagine the serious study of multicultural issues without concomitant attention to disability, because disability is disproportionately found among certain populations of color (Sotnik & Jezewski, 2005). It is lamentable that psychology is prone to taking diversity characteristics out of context. Status as a person of color, or a person who is gay, lesbian, or bisexual, or who has a disability or in other ways is seen as a minority, is made so salient that it precludes consideration of other features. But disability cannot be considered outside context.

Guideline 3: Education Through Multiple Modalities

The concept of universal design (a design that maximizes usability for most, such as ramps as opposed to stairs) works well in education for both students with disabilities and students of color. Many learners may benefit from the flexibility and variability of teaching from multiple modalities. For example, sending PowerPoint slides to students in advance of a lecture might enhance sighted students' learning as well as blind students' learning. Using pictures and graphs as well as words can help a student with a learning disability but also may address the visual learning style of other students. Thus educators should not think in terms of doing something extra or special for one or two or even a few students, but rather about how they can become better teachers for all students by employing multiple modalities and methods. Diversity tends to be seen as an add-on, rather than embraced as a way of enhancing learning for all.

Guideline 4: Inclusive Research

Research must incorporate issues of cultural diversity not as an afterthought but as part of the development of the research design. Yet there is much research that is designed in ways that can ignore or alienate certain groups. Elsewhere I have discussed making research accessible to people (both as researchers and those researched) with a variety of disabilities (Olkin, 2004b) in terms of eight key research activities:

1. Input from consumers
2. Outreach specific to various disability populations
3. The use of language acceptable to different disability populations
4. The process and content of informed consent
5. The content of measures
6. The process of data collection
7. The interpretation of data
8. The dissemination of results

Without attention to the first five items, researchers may wonder at step 6, data collection, why they are not attracting more participants of color or with disabilities. Again, diversity must be integral, not auxiliary.

Guideline 5: Disability-Affirmative Therapy

Early research on cultures, whether based on ethnicity or disability, seems to follow a certain pattern. The first question addressed is what can we learn *about* these people; only much later comes the question of what we can learn *from* these people. The results from these questions are not always translated into practical information about therapy and treatment. Disability and people of color are not always included (or specified) in evidence-based research, and such research may not adequately address cultural differences (Olkin & Taliaferro, 2005). Some groups have responded by developing affirmative therapies specific to their group (e.g., gay-affirmative therapy). Borrowing from this idea, I developed disability-affirmative therapy (DAT) (Olkin, 1999, 2001). Yet information on the convergence and divergence of disability-affirmative and other affirmative therapies is lacking. It is possible that the very aspects that are affirming for one group may not be appropriate for or may be harmful to another group. This possibility is one of the drawbacks to consideration of only one characteristic at a time.

Guideline 6: Social-Change Agents

It is not possible to work with persons with disabilities without an awareness of the sociopolitical realities of disability in the United States. But "psychology primarily trains practitioners to intervene on the personal level rather than to alter the environment" (Linton, 1998, p. 6). To intervene only on the personal level is countertherapeutic. Almost 20 years ago Biklen (1988) noted that "it serves the interests of neither professionals nor their clients—indeed it perpetuates a myth—to ignore people's need for political and economic changes while offering them only clinical treatment" (p. 137). Whether trained for it or not, psychologists are social-change agents, and failure to responsibly embrace this duty makes us part of the status quo (i.e., part of the perpetuation of oppression).

EMPIRICAL AND CONCEPTUAL INFORMATION

There are four essential conceptual issues that mental health professionals should understand about disability. The first is how disability is conceptualized according to three main models of disability—moral, medical, and social. The second is the ways that disability is like and unlike other minorities. The third is disability culture, which is virtually invisible to those outside the group. And fourth is the critical interplay of disability and ethnicity. Because I have described the first two issues in some detail elsewhere (Olkin, 1999; see Chapter 2), the discussion here will be limited to major points.

Models of Disability

There are many ways to conceptualize disability, but three models are widely discussed: the moral, medical, and social models. These are described and contrasted in Olkin (1999; see chapter 2). In brief, the *moral model* views disability as a manifestation of a past life, of sin, or of misbehavior of ancestors or parents, especially the mother (e.g., coming in contact with a person with a disability during pregnancy). The disability resides in an individual but is a reflection of the entire family. The *medical model,* which prevails in the United States and underlies the rehabilitation delivery service system, views disability as a defect in or failure of a bodily system that resides in the individual and is inherently abnormal. The *social model* construes disability as a social construct, in which the disability resides not in the individual but rather in the mismatch between society and the needs of its citizenry

The responses or solutions to the disability reflect these models: in spiritual or community realms for the moral model; in science, medicine, and technology for the medical model; and in society, economics, politics, education, and law for the social model. In the moral model, intervention might be done by the community or a respected person or healer, and might involve the family. In the medical model, intervention is by professionals who practice their services on the person with the disability, who is expected to be the consumer of these services. In the social model, the intervention is in the social, political, and economic arenas, often instigated by as well as for people with disabilities.

Disability as a Minority Group

Persons with disabilities constitute approximately 19% of the U.S. population (Sotnik & Jezewski, 2005), making them the largest single minority group. What does it mean to refer to persons with disabilities as constituting a minority group? There are many similarities of experience across different minority groups, whether based on race or ethnicity, sexual orientation, or disability. Most notable is the core triad of minority experience: prejudice, stigma, and discrimination. The minority status is viewed as outside the norm or deviant, and there is pressure to assimilate to the majority culture. Role models, particularly positive role models, are lacking in politics, movies, television, and newspapers, and there is underrepresentation in many professions, including teaching and mental health. For example, people of color collectively constitute 25–30% of the U.S. population but less than 8% of health and rehabilitation professionals (Leavitt, 1999). There is a confusion of sociological aspects of the minority group (e.g., high unemployment) with assumed inherent group traits. Some minority groups share a higher risk for high school dropout, substance abuse, living below the poverty level, unemployment, and being victims of crime.

But there are important differences between disability and other minority groups. One key difference is related to the Supreme Court doctrine of separate is not equal. For persons with disabilities, separate is not viewed as inherently unequal. There are separate drinking fountains, restaurant entrances, seating areas in movie theaters, access days at museums, classrooms, buses, transportation systems, bathroom stalls, and so forth. It is now unthinkable to label one door for everyone except one group, but the wheelchair sign often points to special entrances and procedures for people with disabilities.

A related issue is that disadvantage occurs in almost every major life activity (e.g., phones, stairs, shopping, employment, movies, restaurants, bathrooms, water fountains, sidewalks). Certainly this is reflected in employment figures. Employment data for people with moderate to severe disabilities are abysmal and virtually unchanged since passage of the Americans with Disabilities Act of 1990 (Kaye, 1998; McNeil, 1997). The situation is even worse for women with disabilities (Danek, 1992) and people of color with disabilities (Fujiura, Yamaki, & Czechowicz, 1998).

Another key difference is that although most minorities are in a family of a like minority (although this is not necessarily the case for biracial individuals and gays and lesbians), this may not be true for persons with disabilities. For most minorities, the family may represent a place of refuge and a transmitter of their own culture, and may provide instruction on how to cope with oppression. In contrast, people with disabilities may experience prejudice within their own family, are not taught to associate with other people with disabilities or about disability culture, and do not receive training in how to survive daily assaults of discrimination or how to embrace and celebrate minority status.

Disability Culture

Culture encompasses many aspects, not only including sociopolitical, economic, legal, and educational experiences, but also music, art, history, humor, media images, food, and social connection. Culture is both learned and shared, and imparts values about what is normal, proper, desirable, and right (Sotnik & Jezewski, 2005). There is a disability culture (Makelprang & Salsgiver, 1999), although it is not well known by those outside the disability community. Elements of this culture reflect mainstream White values in the United States, and thus the culture is at odds with the cultures of some ethnic groups.

The elements of disability culture have only begun to be articulated (Longmore, 2003; Mackelprang & Salsgiver, 1999; Olkin, 2005a). They might include the following 13 elements, as discussed by Olkin (2005a).

1. *A definition of the in- and out-groups.* The in-group is people with disabilities and those close to them, and the out-group is everyone else. Importantly, the in-group tries to be inclusive of all types of disabilities, especially those which are highly stigmatized (e.g., intellectual impairments), so as not to duplicate the prejudice and discrimination experienced in the larger society.
2. *Pride in the identity, advocacy, activism, struggles and survival of people with disabilities, and the valuing of what they have learned.* Values include comfort around diverse disabilities; openness about disability; knowledge of disability history, rights, and needs; advocacy on behalf of oneself and the community; and ability to effect societal change.

3. *The shared model of disability (the social model).* In the social model, disability is a social construct resulting from the mismatch between needs of persons with disabilities and their familial, social, educational, economic, political, and legal options. The locus for change is no longer intrapsychic or interpersonal but sociopolitical.

4. *A shared personal and social history* (Longmore & Umansky, 2001). Persons with disabilities share membership in a protected class under most state laws and under federal law. Their history includes a collective coming of age in the 1970s, at the beginning of the disability rights movement. And they have similarities in their personal histories as well, such as history of hospitalizations, medical traumas, separation from parents, cruelty by other children, and so forth.

5. *Art, music, literature, and humor, which are emerging areas for the disability community.* Some artists are little known outside the disability community, and others are very well known (e.g., writer Ved Mehta, violinist Itzak Perlman). Inclusion in this group means that the person has a disability and that the disability is embraced in the art, whether it's Perlman's activism to make concert halls of the world accessible, or Cheryl Wades's poetry about bodies with disabilities.

6. *Language.* Similar to other minority groups, the disability community wants to be in charge of the words that are used to describe it. With rejection of crippled, handicapped, differently abled, special needs, and the disabled, *persons with disabilities* is the currently preferred term (subject to change at any time). Important distinctions are made in language, such as deaf (loss of hearing) versus Deaf (culturally and linguistically deaf), blind versus low vision, chair user versus scooter user, and able-bodied (AB) versus temporarily able-bodied (TAB).

7. *Disability norms that are different from nondisabled norms.* For example, a person using crutches may carry items in her teeth. Leaving spaces without chairs at a table is a polite way to indicate that wheelchairs are welcome. Not closing a door makes it easier for Deaf people to find their destination and not have to knock and wait for an answer they cannot hear.

8. *Role models.* Although children with disabilities often are not exposed to many role models of adults with disabilities, there are public role models. Just as with icons of disability culture, some are well known to all, and others are well known mostly in the disability community. The disability community generally rejects having its role models foisted upon it. Christopher Reeve is an example of a role model selected by the AB community to speak for the disability community, and was received with some antipathy in the disability community as he promoted finding a cure for spinal cord injury (a disability community slogan is *care not cure*).

9. *A commonality of concerns.* Some examples are physical access, attitudinal barriers to equity, civil rights for persons with disabilities, problems with chronic un- and underemployment. There are positions on issues directly relevant to disability, such as prenatal testing and the right to die (Olkin, 2005b). Regardless of personal beliefs, there is a united political stance that upholds the dignity of the disability community.

10. *Disability expertise.* Unlike persons of color or of specific religious groups, persons with disabilities have been so devalued that they rarely are assumed to be experts on disability. Instead, the field is dominated by able-bodied persons, and this domination is rarely questioned. But, of course, people with disabilities have out of necessity developed expertise about their own disability and related research, about accessibility, and about the legal rights of people with disabilities.

11. *Assistive technology as parts of the body image of persons with disabilities.* People are expected to respect the body boundaries of others. For people with disabilities, these boundaries include their assistive devices (e.g., a scooter) as part of their personal space. Leaning on a wheelchair arm is like leaning on a person's arm; scooters, crutches, canes, wheelchairs, and communication devices are considered body parts, functioning as extensions of the self.

12. *Emotions.* This element and the next one are imposed on persons with disabilities rather than emanating from the disability community. There is a sublime paradox about disability: Disability is assumed to be a loss, and therefore the person with the disability and the family are expected to mourn the loss. The stage model of response to loss (denial, depression, anger, acceptance) is imposed on this loss. However, depression is not a modal response to disability onset (only about 30% will be depressed at some point in the first year). Depression in the first year is best predicted by previous depression, and is the best predictor of future depression (Olkin, 2004a). Defining depression as normative results in accepting a condition that can and should be treated as aggressively as one would for persons without disabilities. Further, so strong is the presumption of mourning that persons with disabilities who are not depressed often are labeled as being in denial. The paradox is this: Persons with disabilities are relentlessly portrayed as brave, courageous, inspirational, plucky, and miraculously able to get up each morning, eat breakfast, and go about their day, always with a smile, despite the disability. Thus there is an affective prescription to be both in mourning and eternally plucky. This is combined with the prohibition against anger, which is interpreted as denoting maladjustment to the disability. In spite of the pervasive stigma, discrimination, and oppression of people with disabilities, anger is seen decontextually from its social roots and is attributed to

personal characteristics. This combination—mourn, be plucky, do not be angry—is a potent destructive force.

13. *Group definition.* In the United States extremely disparate impairments and conditions are grouped under the label *disability.* People with disabilities are seen as a group, much the way people of color are combined, despite tremendous inter- and intragroup differences. The media uses the term *the disabled* without modification or more explicit explanation, and presumes shared attributes. Negative terms are used to describe the group, such as *suffering from, afflicted with,* or *persistent vegetative state.* Some individuals may conflate many disabilities with illness, then generalize to all people with disabilities.

Disability and Ethnicity

Virtually every society views individuals with disabilities as distinct from the general population. However, that distinction is not always pejorative, and the view held of the impairment is socially determined. For example, a White woman with polio living in the United States may still work, marry, have children, and thus be viewed as having only a relatively minor disability. But a similar woman in India may be deemed unmarriageable, and hence the disability is profound. Clinicians need to recognize ways in which ethnicity and culture interplay with disability. As Groce (1999) states, "Understanding sociocultural models of disability is more than an academic interest. Unless programs for individuals with disabilities are designed in a culturally appropriate way, the opportunity to make real and effective change is lost" (p. 38). What could be more self-evident? Yet the literature on disability and on people of color or of various cultures is scant. The two literatures often use very different language and come from disparate assumptions or worldviews, and mostly the emphasis is on teaching about ethnicity/culture to rehabilitation professionals rather than truly on the confluence of these two characteristics.

However, some important voices are starting to emerge (Balcazar, Keys, & Suarez-Balcazar, 2001; Choi & Wynne, 2000; Marshall, Leung, Johnson, & Busby, 2003; National Institute of Disability & Rehabilitation Research, 2001). Still, this area is in its infancy, and there is much that is unknown about the confluence of disability and people of color in the United States, both theoretically or empirically (Groce, 2005).

For example, in trying to ascertain the number of parents with disabilities raising teens in the United States, using data from the National Health Interview Survey (NHIS), we found that how the question of whether the respondent had a disability was posed made a critical difference in the number of Hispanics responding affirmatively (Olkin, Abrams, Preston, & Kirshbaum,

2006). Hispanics were less likely to respond to a general question (Are you limited in your ability to perform major life activities . . . due to a physical, mental, or emotional health problem?) than they were to respond that they had a specific medical condition (e.g., asthma, diabetes) or impairment. Thus, studies that emulate the government's wording on the NHIS in the pursuit of standardization of language are likely to underestimate the number of Hispanics with disabilities. Ethnic differences in how respondents interpret questions on disabilities underscore that disability is a social construct and therefore, not surprisingly, varies with culture.

Important aspects of cultural views on disability are the culture's beliefs about the causality of disability, what attributes are valued and devalued in that culture, and what roles the person with a disability is expected to play in the family and the community (Groce, 2005). Causal attributions are fundamental to how the person with a disability is viewed and hence treated in the family and community. Belief in reincarnation can lead to the belief that disability has been earned by a past life, and that lessening the suffering in the present life reduces the probability of future birth at a higher level (Groce, 2005). Contrast this with the belief that disability is a random accident of infection, or a genetic anomaly, in which the person and the family are blameless. However, laying blame for the causes of disability is fairly widespread, but in different guises. Although one ethnic group may place the blame on social contagion when the mother was pregnant and encountered a person with a disability, Western medicine looks for other but equally blaming causes, such as behavioral factors (smoking, drinking, drugs, carelessness).

Valued and devalued attributes are another perspective on how disability will be viewed. Needing assistance with or not performing valued attributes may devalue the person. For example, in some cultures one is not to draw attention to oneself, and disability tends to stand out, going against the social norms. A third critical element is the role of the person with the disability. If work and productivity are expected, then return to employment is a key goal of rehabilitation. But if the person is expected to be able to marry and contribute to the family welfare through marriage, then the stigma of the disability is critical. The role of the professional is another element of the role the person with the disability takes on. In mainstream U.S. culture, persons with disabilities are expected to be clients and to avail themselves of services provided to them. They should be assertive in asking for needed services, but grateful and compliant with those services. In contrast, some groups of persons of color may be unaware of what services are available, especially if such services were not available in their country of origin, or the purpose of the services. They may view the professional as someone of a higher social class and politely agree with everything the professional says and recommends, without any intention of following the recommendations. Or they may view any agencies, especially those associated with government, with suspicion and even alarm and fear of deportation, abuse, imprisonment, harassment for themselves and their family, or other detrimental incursions, based on such histories in other countries.

The rehabilitation system has its own set of values, and is not culture free, yet falsely may assume that "the ethnic or minority community studies are variables, necessitating deviations from the 'right approach' to programs or services that are professionally agreed upon as culture-free 'norms' or 'standards'" (Groce, 2005, p. 3). The rehabilitation services system is driven by rules and regulations, and has a preferred methodology of rapid assessment, intervention, and desired outcomes that may be in conflict with many cultures. For example, rehabilitation interacts mostly with individuals, not families; it is geared toward maximal independence and use of assistive technology to achieve that independence; its key outcome measure is employment; it encourages self-confident disclosure of disability status; it grants confidentiality to individuals and upholds privacy; and it values change, progress, informality, achievement, materialism, and assertiveness (Sotnik & Jezewski, 2005). In contrast, many cultures value functioning in the family and community over employment, may feel that the family should provide care for the member with a disability and that it would be shameful to expect that person to work, may believe thatthat disability represents dishonor and should not be freely disclosed, and may desire the use of technology but for different ends (e.g., to function in the family rather than for work). These are only a few examples of the ways that rehabilitation services are likely to encounter a culture clash in working with many clients of color.

The worldview of service providers and their clients may be discrepant. There are at least three key elements of worldview, namely, the individual's place in nature (human life is more important than nature versus humans are part of nature and nature cannot be modified), science and technology (explanations of and solutions to problems are found through scientific method versus problems are predetermined by fate and cannot be solved by human intervention), and materialism (acquisition of material goods is important versus the valuing of self-sacrifice) (Sotnik & Jezewski, 2005). The rehabilitation system embraces the former views, while many cultures embrace the latter perspectives. Further, rehabilitation and the surrounding services evidence the mainstream White U.S. value of individualism, in contrast to the views of collectivism found in many cultures.

These profound discrepancies will translate into practical differences on questions such as whether a family member or paid employee should act as interpreter, willingness to accept work outside one's community, feeling free (or not) to disagree with the service provider, bringing in extended-family members to rehabilitation sessions, and eschewing assistive technology so that a family member can continue to provide support. These discrepancies are very much in evidence with regard to activities of daily living (ADL) and instrumental activities of daily living (IADL). There are over 50 versions of the ADL used by different agencies, but they share many similarities and all are about levels of individual functioning. ADL and IADL are routinely used to determine eligibility for a variety of services. ADL includes items related to individual self-care, such as hygiene, safety, bathing, dressing, eating, household chores, and cooking. IADL are similar but somewhat broader, such as shopping, financial management, laundry, and gardening. There are several questions that might be asked about these lists:

- How universal are the items, and are they the items various cultures would endorse as critical to determining disability?
- How do people from various cultures perform these tasks (e.g., do persons from a particular ethnic group engage in ceremonial hand washing before meals, do people eat sitting in chairs or on the floor, with forks or with chopsticks)?
- What is the perception of receiving help for these tasks (e.g., gardening versus bathing), and from whom do people feel most comfortable receiving assistance (paid employee or family member, person of same gender only)?
- What activities do people engage in due solely to their disability (e.g., accessing special transportation, filling out specific forms)?
- What is the stance toward assistive technology (AT) in general, and what if the AT replaces the need for help from a family member?

As seen in these questions, ADL and IADL reflect certain cultural assumptions that probably do not hold for many people of color.

If the ADL and IADL are used to determine eligibility, they are based on the assumption that inability to do certain tasks constitutes a disability. But the concept of disability itself is not universal. In the United States, laws and regulations group together disparate types of impairments under the rubric *disability* that other cultures may not see as related. Distinction among these disabilities may determine how the person is treated in his or her own ethnic group (Groce, 2005). Blindness may be perceived very differently from epilepsy or cerebral palsy or intellectual impairments. The legal and service delivery systems gather all of these under one umbrella, and the disability community has banded these disparate conditions together for political and social clout, but that does not make them truly related.

CRITICAL INCIDENTS

Several examples serve to illustrate the aforementioned points. The first example demonstrates the narrow definition of disability embodied in the rules and regulations that govern procurement of assistive technology.

> When I had my first child, my disability (aftermath of polio as an infant) worsened, and I needed to augment my use of crutches with the use of a scooter to carry my baby. Without this I could not do child care without assistance. My health insurance company sent a nurse to evaluate me. She asked me what ADL I did independently; she asked no questions about my functioning as a family member, especially as a mother. My request for the scooter was denied because I could do most of the designated activities independently, and child care is not an ADL as defined by my health insurance and the rehabilitation service delivery system.

In many cultures ability to function within the family and community is seen as more paramount than individual independence, and this woman's difficulties with child care would be seen as a legitimate need.

The next example shows the way in which the culture of disability of the White majority is at odds with Chinese American culture.

> I was attending a function at my child's high school and chatted briefly with a Chinese parent. When she later saw me in the parking lot putting my scooter into the car, she asked if I needed help. I politely said no thank you, but felt annoyed. Didn't she see I could do it myself? Didn't she know it's impolitic to assume I am dependent on others? Several weeks later I saw this woman again at a music recital. At the end of the recital we found ourselves standing together, and again she asked if I needed help. I again said no thank you, but this time my internal response was different. The audience was largely Hong Kong Chinese. Several audience members were elderly, and a few had impairments of one kind or another. I suddenly saw this woman's offer of help for what it was in her context—the politeness one extends to those older or less able. Disability culture—doing things independently—was contrary to Chinese culture, in which extending offers of assistance was a sign of respect.

This third example again shows a conflict of cultures, related to models of disability. Recall the discussion of disability models (moral, medical, and social) and note that the moral model is quite vilified in the disability community. However, such a view is a value judgment that may oppress certain people of color with disabilities who ascribe to the moral model, as shown in this example:

> I was riding in a taxi, and the driver, a man in his 50s from the Middle East, commented on my disability. He then told me about his leg. I paraphrase, but the sentiment was his: "I stepped on a land mine when I was 10. I spent over 2 months in the hospital far away from my family. The doctors did many surgeries on my leg, and now I have pain in my leg and hip. Every day I wake up and notice the pain, and I remember to thank Allah for saving my life, and to be glad that I am here on this earth and still alive to feel this pain.

From this man I understood that each disability model has benefits and drawbacks. From the social model perspective, the moral model, with its conflation of physical impairment with moral impairment, is the antithesis of disability pride. But this incident shows how each model can bestow meaning on its believers. If the disability community continues to denigrate the moral model, it will alienate some people of color whose religious teachings are more in keeping with that model. Therefore, the goal should not be to change people's models, but to help them realize the benefits of their model and minimize its drawbacks. This was for me a revelation with profound clinical implications for working respectfully with clients with disabilities from many cultures.

There are many times when I am suddenly made aware of my status as a minority person in kinship with people of color. Nowhere was this more powerful than at a symposium on physician-assisted suicide, in which the straight White participants kept talking about the right to die, and the sole African American in attendance voiced the fear of being killed (Olkin, 2005b). This African American woman and I perhaps shared a history, both personal and from our respective communities, of negative interactions with the medical profession. Rather than viewing medical professionals as saviors, we viewed them with caution and even distrust. These feelings became more evident in our opposition to the majority on many issues (e.g., should the second opinion of informed consent be another medical doctor or a different professional? Should the family have rights to know of a patient's intent of assisted suicide?). From our two different minority backgrounds we came together in our opposition to the way in which physician-assisted suicide might be implemented. Yet, in other contexts, disability is pitted against issues of ethnicity: We vie for limited training time for our students, funding for minority scholarships, air time at professional conferences allotted to diversity—all the scarce resources of attention and funding. This careening between identification and bonding on one hand, and cultures in conflict on the other, is dizzying.

STRATEGIES FOR MENTAL HEALTH PROFESSIONALS
TO DEVELOP COMPETENCE IN DISABILITY ISSUES

Clinicians often want to know what to do: What do I say when . . . ? How do I handle . . . ? Should I offer to . . . ? But to know what to *do* clinicians need to know what to *think*. Thus the conceptual parts of this chapter are important because they translate into assessment, formulation, treatment, and evaluation in real ways. Clinicians' actions can be guided by their understanding of (1) similarities and differences between disability as a minority group and minority status based on being a person of color; (2) the disability models and their relative strengths and weaknesses; and (3) disability culture. My book *What Psychotherapists Should Know About Disability* (Olkin, 1999) was designed to help clinicians less familiar with disability issues understand these features and to introduce the practice of disability-affirmative therapy. DAT is not a theory of therapy but rather is meant to be integrated into the clinician's own theoretical approach to treatment. Its main contribution is to explicate how disability can be integrated into the case formulation without either over- or underestimating the role of disability in the client's history, presenting problems, social interactions, and current functioning.

One aspect of DAT is understanding how to work within the client's and family's model of disability. The clinician is encouraged to hold the social model of disability, but it is not necessary for the client to subscribe to the same model. As Miles (1999) elucidates:

> It is hardly the therapist's job to try to change a client's fundamental beliefs–to do so might be seen as unprofessional conduct. . . . To listen attentively and with understanding requires the competent therapist to have some broad awareness of the range of human beliefs in the disability area, and at least an outward tolerance of some that may seem personally repugnant. (p. 55)

Models help clinicians know what disability language to use. For example, those clinicians espousing the medical model might talk about special needs and medical diagnoses. Those using the moral model might talk of sin, defects or dishonor, or being chosen to have a disability. The social model promotes making distinctions among impairment (polio), handicap (mobility limitations), and disability (a social construct encountered in an inaccessible environment). Using the wrong language tends to alienate clients. For example, drug companies that manufacture pain relievers mostly like to use a scale of 1–10 to describe pain, and to know that their drugs reduce pain on this scale to 4 or below. But most people do not think of pain in this way. Instead they make important distinctions in their description of pain and in the level of pain as it impinges on functioning (Zelman et al., 2004).

Understanding conceptually about disability is a solid beginning, but that is not enough. The interface of disability and culture is critical to providing appropriate services. Thus, the familial, social, and cultural context of the disability must be incorporated into the treatment of people of color with disabilities.

It is hard to talk about disabilities without thinking about countertransference issues. If it is normative for people in general to distance themselves from disability by blaming, and to hold negative or devaluing attitudes toward disability, then we should expect that clinicians will have incorporated many of these aspects into their own responses. Just as racism is rampant, so too is ableism. Exposure to clients with disabilities is not sufficient to overcome this learning, because therapy involves an unequal relationship. In my book I give specific suggestions for increasing exposure to and developing awareness of and knowledge about persons with disabilities, in an effort to reduce negative countertransference (Olkin, 1999). For example, clinicians need to understand how to make therapy itself accessible to, and make adaptations for, different kinds of disabilities. They should become more comfortable asking about clients' disabilities. They should be versed in problems inherent in bicultural therapy (able-bodied therapist and client with a disability) and be prepared to demonstrate their familiarity and comfort with a disability and its attendant issues. Assessment tools and processes may require alteration, and results may call for contextual interpretation. Resources outside the therapy office (e.g., resource room teachers, occupational therapists) are not just useful but critical in treatment, especially for children with disabilities. The range of emotions engendered by stigma and discrimination must be handled empathically. And countertransference must be understood and managed effectively, without putting the responsibility on clients to teach us about disability.

Clinicians are encouraged to think beyond treatment of individuals and families to larger entities (i.e., to be agents of social change). "The relationship of laws and court rulings to the everyday lives of minorities is tangible. For minorities, issues of oppression, discrimination, stigma, poverty, immigration, stereotyping, and powerlessness are not abstract concepts or only distally meaningful laws but quotidian events, protections, and civil rights" (Olkin, 1999, pp. 299–300). If clients' problems are both psychological and sociological, do we not have a responsibility to respond to both levels, and is it not injustice to attend only to the former?

CONCLUSION

If we revisit the original question of this chapter about how to understand the intersection of disability and people of color (as well as gender, sexual orientation, class, age, religion), and whether we need to construct a giant grid of disability by ethnicity, again we are left with the answer both yes and no. There are core aspects to master, both about disability and about specific ethnic groups. But all of the permutations and combinations can never be fully mastered. However, it is important that we not throw up our hands in dismissal and state that all clients are individuals and we will learn about them individually. This abdicates our responsibility to be proactive in our learning and to start the journey of understanding each client from a higher plane.

REFERENCES

American Psychological Association. (2003). Guidelines on multicultural education, train-ing, research, practice, and organizational change for psychologists. *American Psycholo-gist, 58*, 377–402.

Americans with Disabilities Act of 1990, Public Law 101-336, 42 U.S.C. 12111, 12112.

Balcazar, F. E., Keys, C. B., & Suarez-Balcazar, Y. (2001). Empowering Latinos with dis-abilities to address issues of independent living and disability rights: A capacity-build-ing approach. *Journal of Prevention and Intervention in the Community, 21*, 53–70.

Biklen, B. (1988). The myth of clinical judgment. *Journal of Social Issues, 44*, 127–140.

Choi, K., & Wynne, M. (2000). Providing services to Asian Americans with developmental disabilities and their families: Mainstream service providers' perspective. *Community Mental Health Journal, 36*, 589–595.

Danek, M. (1992). The status of women with disabilities revisited. *Journal of Applied Reha-bilitation Counseling, 23*, 7–23.

Fujiura, G. T., Yamaki, K., & Czechowicz, S. (1998). Disability among ethnic and racial minorities in the US: A summary of economic status and family structure. *Journal of Disability Policy Studies, 9*, 111–130.

Groce, N. (1999). Health beliefs and behavior towards individuals with disability cross-culturally. In R. Leavitt (Ed.), *Cross-cultural rehabilitation: An international perspective* (pp. 37–47). London: W. B. Saunders.

Groce, N. (2005). Immigrants, disability, and rehabilitation. In J. H. Stone (Ed.), *Culture and disability: Providing culturally competent services* (pp. 1–13). Thousand Oaks, CA: Sage.

Kaye, S. (1998). *Is the status of people with disabilities improving?* (Disability Statistics Ab-stract No. 21). Washington, DC: National Institute on Disability and Rehabilitation Research.

Leavitt, R. (1999). Introduction. In R. Leavitt (Ed.), *Cross-cultural rehabilitation: An interna-tional perspective* (pp. 1–7). London: W. B. Saunders.

Linton, S. (1998). *Claiming disability: Knowledge and identity.* New York: New York Univer-sity Press.

Longmore, P. K. (2003). *Why I burned my book and other essays on disability.* Philadelphia: Temple University Press.

Longmore, P. K., & Umansky, L. (Eds.). (2001). *The new disability history: American perspec-tives.* New York: New York University Press.

Mackelprang, R., & Salsgiver, R. (1999). *Disability: A diversity model approach in human service practice.* Belmont, CA: Brooks/Cole.

Marshall, C. A., Leung, P., Johnson, S. R., & Busby, H. (2003). Ethical practice and cultural factors in rehabilitation. *Rehabilitation Education, 17*, 55–65.

McNeil, J. M. (1997). *Americans with disabilities: 1994–95* (Current Population Reports P70-61). Washington, DC: U.S. Bureau of the Census.

Miles, M. (1999). Some influences of religions on attitudes towards disability and people with disabilities. In R. Leavitt (Ed.), *Cross-cultural rehabilitation: An international perspective* (pp. 49–57). London: W. B. Saunders.

National Institute of Disability & Rehabilitation Research. (2001). Disability among ethnic minorities. *Research Exchange, 6*, 2–20.

Olkin, R. (1999). *What psychotherapists should know about disability*. New York: Guilford Press.

Olkin, R. (2001). Disability-affirmative therapy. *Spinal Cord Injury Psychosocial Process, 14*, 12–23.

Olkin, R. (2004a). Disability and depression. In S. L. Welner & F. Haseltineb (Eds.), *Welner's guide to the care of women with disabilities*. Philadelphia: Lippincott, Williams & Wilkins.

Olkin, R. (2004b). Making research accessible to participants with disabilities. *Journal of Multicultural Counseling and Development, 32*(extra), 332–343.

Olkin, R. (2005a). Disability culture for the clinician: A baker's dozen. *Newsletter of the Contra Costa County Psychological Association*.

Olkin, R. (2005b). Why I changed my mind about physician-assisted suicide: How Stanford University made a radical out of me. *Journal of Disability Policy Studies, 16*, 68–71.

Olkin, R., Abrams, K., Preston, P., & Kirshbaum, M. (2006). Comparison of parents with and without disabilities raising teens: Information from the NHIS and two national surveys. *Rehabilitation Psychology, 51*, 43–49.

Olkin, R., & Pledger, C. (2003). Can disability studies and psychology join hands? *American Psychologist, 58*, 296–304.

Olkin, R., & Taliaferro, G. (2005). Evidence-based practices have ignored people with disabilities: Dialogue. In J. Norcross, L. Beutler, & R. Levant (Eds.), *Evidence based practice*. Washington, DC: American Psychological Association.

Sotnik, P., & Jezewski, M. A. (2005). In J. H. Stone (Ed.), *Culture and disability: Providing culturally competent services* (pp. 15–36). Thousand Oaks, CA: Sage.

Yuker, H. E. (1994). Variables that influence attitudes toward persons with disabilities: Conclusions from the data. Psychosocial perspectives on disability [special issue]. *Journal of Social Behavior and Personality, 9*, 3–22.

Zelman, D., Smith, M. Y., Hoffman, D., Edwards, L., Reed, P., Levine, E., Siefeldin, R., & Dukes, E. (2004). Acceptable, manageable, and tolerable days: Patient daily goals for medication management of persistent pain. *Journal of Pain and Symptom Management, 28*, 474–487.

Part II

CONSIDERATIONS IN APPLYING THE GUIDELINES TO PEOPLE OF COLOR

Part II of this book comprises four chapters that present salient considerations in applying the Multicultural Guidelines. In Chapter 11, Sanchez-Hucles and Jones discuss the concept of gender through racial/cultural lenses, detailing differences in gender roles, beliefs, and practices among various racial and ethnic groups. Further, this chapter emphasizes the intersection of gender with race and ethnicity, and uses the Multicultural Guidelines to offer suggestions for gender-competent practice in conjunction with racial/ethnic competence. Through a review of extant literature and relevant theories, Ali, Fridman, Hall, and Leathers (Chapter 12) focus on the unique contribution of social class dynamics to a comprehensive understanding of culturally competent practice. In this chapter, theoretical models of social class are presented and future research directions with social class as a cultural variable are discussed. In Chapter 13, Fukuyama, Hernandez, and Robinson explore differences in religion and spirituality among specific populations of color. The chapter also examines current religious trends as well as their implications for mental health practice, and integrated throughout the chapter are strategies for developing religious and spiritual competence. The book concludes with Chapter 14, in which Warren and Constantine provide final thoughts on the social justice implications of applying the Multicultural Guidelines to specific populations of color. Through a discussion of the multidimensional nature of social justice, this chapter highlights the current state of education, training, research, practice, and policy with regard to social justice and provides future directions in each of these areas. Social justice implications for mental health practitioners on the individual, societal, and systemic levels are integrated throughout their discussion.

11

Gender Issues

*Janis Sanchez-Hucles
and Nneka Jones*

The approval of the "Guidelines on Multicultural Education, Training, Research, Practice, and Organizational Change for Psychologists" (American Psychological Association, 2003) reflects a growing awareness that professional psychologists must become more culturally competent when providing services to the increasing percentages of people of color in the United States. Race and ethnicity alone, however, do not go far enough in increasing our cultural competence with individuals. A complete multicultural perspective requires that professionals examine and understand the intersections of race and ethnicity with other salient identity dimensions such as age, sexual orientation, disability, gender, socioeconomic status, educational background, and religious/spiritual preference. This chapter highlights the significance of gender issues for people of color as they intersect with other identity dimensions in the context of the Guidelines. The chapter will discuss the relevance of gender issues to each of the Guidelines, present empirical and conceptual information on gender, and offer illustrative vignettes and practical strategies for implementing the Guidelines.

THE MULTICULTURAL GUIDELINES
AS APPLIED TO RACE AND GENDER

Guideline 1: Awareness of Personal Beliefs

Guideline 1 addresses the reality that psychologists, like all other individuals, operate with a cultural lens that shapes how they view themselves and how they perceive others. Therefore, psychologists are not immune to assumptions and prejudices about people who are culturally different from themselves, although these biases may not be consciously recognized (American Psychological Association, 2003). Further, although many individuals have learned to be sensitive to racial or gender dynamics, the interaction of race and gender all too often is overlooked.

Increasingly, scholars are becoming more aware of the fact that gender and race are not independent dimensions that can be combined. Because race is "gendered" and gender is "racialized," these two aspects of identity come together to create unique experiences that render disentangling one identity from the other impossible (Browne & Misra, 2003). Both race and gender are social constructions that produce and maintain social hierarchy. When other dimensions such as class, sexual orientation, and ability status are added, individuals can simultaneously experience different levels of privilege or disadvantage based on these combined identities (Baca Zinn & Thornton Dill, 1996).

Mental health professionals' lack of awareness of how these cultural variables intersect can lead to unconscious internalization of stereotypes, which can have profound effects on their work with clients of color. Whereas some attitudes are explicit and conscious, implicit attitudes and stereotypes can be activated automatically in unintentional and unconscious ways (Dovidio, Gaertner, Kawakami, & Hodson, 2002). A therapist may have internalized implicit stereotypes that, if unexplored and unchecked, may negatively influence his or her work with clients of color. In particular, the lack of awareness about people of color with respect to gender can be significant. For example, what issues do White therapists bring to their work with women of color when their primary interactions with members of this group have been as service providers? What are the issues when therapists think of men of color only in terms of media images that portray these men as hypersexual, aggressive, and athletic, or as passive, self-effacing, and asexual? How are conflicting gender-role expectations between therapist and client manifested in counseling sessions? For example, what happens if a therapist's values reflect traditional gender-role expectations (e.g., that men should be breadwinners and women should prioritize care of children and home) that are neither viable for nor desired by clients? In this instance, therapists potentially can impose their personal gender-role expectations onto clients, allowing their work together to be influenced by what men or women "should" be and how they "should" behave. Therapists should reflect upon not only their interactions with individuals in different racial and gender groups, but also their own beliefs about gender roles, and explore how these may have shaped their expectations and perceptions.

Guideline 2: Knowledge of Gendered Perceptions of Therapy

The intersection of gender and race creates unique challenges in the provision of culturally appropriate interventions for clients who are racially and culturally different from the therapist. It is important for psychologists to understand how men and women of color may perceive traditional counseling and therapy. Men of color tend to view mental and psychological problems as signs of personal weakness and failure. As a result, they are less willing to seek help on a voluntary basis and are more likely to be referred to or man dated for services by external agencies such as the legal system, school settings, or employers (Chow, Jaffee, & Snowden, 2003). Men of color may view mandated therapy as another assault on their threatened sense of masculinity and may minimize and deny problems or resort to abusing substances in an attempt to self medicate (Boyd-Franklin, 1989).

Women of color struggle with the psychological stress of chronic and episodic difficulties relating to issues of gender, race, poverty, acculturation pressures, and family and environmental tensions (Myers et al., 2002). Culturally sensitive mental health assistance can help them attain a greater coherence within both the White culture and their own communities of color (Arredondo, 1991; Comas-Diaz, 1994). Some women of color also may be fearful that failure to comply with therapy will lead to the loss of custody of their children. Both men and women of color may fear that failure to progress in therapy will have a negative impact on their work, school, or legal status, or their interpersonal relationships (Coridan & O'Connell, 2002; Ro & Takeuchi, 2003).

Guideline 3: Examination of Race and Gender

Just as there have been barriers to increasing individuals' racial self-awareness in clinical contexts, there have been historical impediments to incorporating multiculturalism into educational environments. There has been a reluctance to depart from what are believed to be more objective, biological, and scientific antecedents of behaviors linked to race and gender in favor of including historical and sociopolitical dynamics that are seen as more subjective and less rigorous academically (Bronstein & Quina, 1988; Hall, 2001). Quina and Bronstein (2003) asserted that faculty need to move beyond their concerns that they will trigger defensiveness and biases in students and themselves when discussing issues related to race and gender. A willingness to discuss complex issues such as the interaction of race and gender, and to explore possible areas of bias and ignorance, can lead to powerful role modeling for students.

Part of the impetus to make psychology more attentive to multicultural-ism in general, and gender specifically, is the changing demographics of students. Quina and Bronstein (2003) reported that since 1992, the percentage of individuals of color receiving baccalaureate degrees in psychology has increased by 58%, and 60% of all psychology degrees are awarded to women. In graduate-level doctoral programs, 70% of entering students are female, and almost 20% are women of color.

Another step that educators can take to be more inclusive of the relationships of men and women of color is to use the gender-neutral term *partner*, rather than using spousal terms. This term may allow clients to feel safer and more comfortable about disclosing or clarifying their sexual orientation in therapy. Course and practicum experiences also need to provide training in helping students listen to whether a client is focusing on a general life concern or an area that requires closer examination of additional identities and their interaction, such as gender, race, ability, sexual orientation, or class.

Both faculty and students can be resistant to exploring the intersection of race and gender. Workshops, courses, and practica should be designed to provide learning experiences that build proficiency in working with men and women of color. Leslie Jackson (1999) offers some practical suggestions for dealing with possible resistance. She suggests the following: providing support and structure to decrease anxiety, encouraging but not forcing participation, keeping the focus away from socially desirable responses in favor of candor, and offering multiple safe opportunities for students and faculty to communicate.

Guideline 4: Research Focus on Multiple Dimensions

Simply put, most psychological research has been conducted on White male college sophomores from North America, who represent less than 5% of the world's population, and therefore the research findings ignore racial, gender, and cultural diversity (Sue, 2003). Research also has focused too frequently on one unit of analysis, such as race or gender. In order to best meet the needs of men and women of color, research must include multiple dimensions. Reid (2002) noted that gender issues have been largely excluded from ethnic and racial research, even when such basic issues as acculturation, racism, and cultural diversity are explicitly explored. Not only have gender issues been excluded in much of the literature on race, but there is a dearth of information on women and girls of color as well. These women have been shut out, silenced, and symbolically erased, as the focus of gender has been on White women and the focus of race has been on men of color (Ohye & Daniel, 1999; Reid, 1993). When women of color are studied, their experiences often are globalized rather than examined within and between race or ethnicity (Reid, 1993). This research practice has created a void of knowledge with respect to identifying the particular mental health needs and issues of specific groups of women of color.

With regard to matching therapist and client by gender, empirical examinations have yielded inconsistent findings, but historically such examinations have focused primarily on White individuals. Findings have suggested that both males and females prefer female therapists and also have shown greater satisfaction and symptom reduction with female than with male therapists (Jones, Krupnick, & Kerig, 1987). In a review of the few studies that examined gender and ethnicity, Flaherty and Adams (1998) found that ethnic matching seemed to improve the retention of Asian Americans and African Americans, lead to less attrition for Asian males, and benefit females more than males.

It would be useful to collect data from clients about their race and gender preferences and therapy satisfaction in real counseling situations. Questions could ask clients specifically to prioritize how important it is to have a counselor who is similar or different on multiple identity dimensions. Eventually, client surveys like this may be used to match clients with counselors who have the skills and competencies that will meet their needs.

Guideline 5: Sensitivity to Interaction of Race and Gender

Scher, Stevens, Good, and Eichenfield (1987) argued that providing clinical services to men of color differs in content and process from providing services to White men. They identified five areas to which service providers must be sensitive for men and women of color:

1. Differences in gender role socialization
2. The reality that issues of locus of control and responsibility are different for people of color
3. The unique cognitions, emotions, and values that people of color bring to therapy
4. The different valences assigned to issues such as competition, power, autonomy, expression of feelings, family roles, sexuality, attitudes toward the opposite sex, and spirituality
5. The differential impact of socioeconomic status

It also must be noted that women of color have different life experiences than White women, which can have implications for clinical practice. These differences include a longer history of working both within and outside of the home, the challenge of balancing multiple roles within their nuclear families as well as caring for extended-family members, extensive involvement in community activities, and contending with the stereotypes that force them to assess which dimension of their identity may be most salient in a particular instance of discrimination (Al-Mateen, Christian, Mishra, Cofield, & Tildon, 2002). Understanding the complex interaction of race and gender can allow counselors to help women of color clarify their multiple roles with respect to their own, cultural, and community expectations (Gloria, 2001).

Guideline 6: Involvement of the Community

Men and women of color face institutionalized racism and sexism. Although the ways in which a specific individual deals with these oppressions can be the focus of individual therapy, it is important to acknowledge the need for community-wide efforts to recognize and minimize discrimination, including drawing on community resources such as spiritual centers, lodges, sororities, and social services.

Several therapists have suggested developing community centered support groups and psychoeducational approaches that will allow men of color to thoughtfully critique the challenges that they face by analyzing movies and rap videos and by developing effective coping skills to handle racism and discrimination (Elligan & Utsey, 1999; Watts, Abdul-Adil, & Pratt, 2002). Cognitive-behavioral and interpersonal therapies have been integrated to develop an age-sensitive therapy for depressed Puerto Rican males (Rossell & Bernal, 1996). This approach includes the use of culturally sensitive treatment manuals in Spanish, the use of metaphors and values, and the involvement of parents, after-school programs, employment services, and health resources. Arredondo (1991) developed psychoeducational support groups for Latina immigrants who must deal with multiple areas of transition and change, different social contexts, and different roles such as partner, mother, and daughter. Similarly, because of the unique stressors that African American women encounter in their families, a mother–daughter relational group therapy experience has been developed to build higher quality relationships and to enhance coping skills (Adams & LaFromboise, 2001). Community-based rites of passage programs also can be used to help young men and women gain positive role models who reflect their gender and ethnicity and, at the same time, strengthen their sense of identity, culture, and service.

CONCEPTUAL AND EMPIRICAL INFORMATION

Gender Similarities and Differences

It first must be recognized that men and women of color share common bonds: Their minority status is generally visible by virtue of skin color and physical appearance, and they are exposed to racial and ethnic discrimination. Shared experiences of oppression can lead to bonding and mutual commitment to safety and survival. Despite shared experiences, there are significant gender differences among men and women of color. For example, by virtue of being male, men of color are expected to fulfill the narrow societal gender-role stereotypes of being providers and "heads of the household," although sociopolitical pressures make this difficult for many (Wade, 1996). Women of color are confronted not only with sexism, but also with racialized sexism, that is, not adhering to the physical and psychological cultural ideals of the "feminist mystique" that idealizes White females (Greene, 1994). Men of color may face pressure to adhere to limited and inflexible expressions of emotions and to demonstrate behaviors consistent with being competitive, successful, and in control (Robinson, 1999). Counselors who are unaware of the differing gender-role realities for men and women of color inappropriately may pathologize these clients.

In addition to having to deal with racism and racialized sexism, women of color also must deal with sexism from within their own communities. Too often, many women of color feel that their bond to men of color and their unified fight against racism leave them isolated and vulnerable to sexism and violence (Sanchez-Hucles & Dutton, 1999). When women of color fight against sexism expressed as violence and abuse by men of color, they risk the alienation of these men and of women of color who believe that this sexism should not be challenged. Yet, if a woman of color emphasizes only racism, she is negating one level of her oppression. As a consequence, women of color often find themselves choosing which oppression to acknowledge (Gloria, 2001). Women of color are often reluctant to seek help when they experience violence from men of color because they know that these men also fight discrimination. They may feel that by seeking protection through police and the courts, they imperil these men who already have difficulties with racism in the legal system (Sanchez-Hucles & Dutton, 1999). These complex dynamics require therapists to be knowledgeable about the individual problems that women and men of color face, as well as the cultural and institutional forces that shape their realities.

Becoming aware of the sociopolitical realities for their clients of color is one important step therapists need to take, but they also must understand how reactions to stress, feelings of anxiety, and depression may manifest in different populations of color. For example, therapists must be aware not only that depression statistics often underrepresent men of color, but also that depression manifests itself differently in men and women of color. Research suggests that statistics on depression in men of color are underrepresented because these individuals are distrustful of participating in governmental data surveys. Also, whereas women of color may show depression through their feelings, men of color may reveal depression through self-injurious, antisocial, high-risk behaviors, and somatic complaints (U.S. Department of Health and Human Services, 2001). These manifestations of depression may be misunderstood and misdiagnosed, as they do not represent the "traditional" symptoms of depression.

Men of color also are at risk for misdiagnosis and inappropriate treatment when providers do not collect enough information and when they fail to consider the cultural contexts of symptoms. Research has shown that symptoms of agitatation, somatization, hostility, and impulsivity lead to diagnoses of schizophrenia and paranoid personality disorders for men of color, although affective disorders are underdiagnosed (Fabrega, Mezzich, & Ulrich, 1988; Williams & Fenton, 1994). The consequences of misdiagnoses include increased medication and referral to more restrictive treatment facilities. Therefore, it is critical for practitioners to utilize structured interviews and rating scales in evaluations and to clarify any areas of suspicion, paranoia, or hallucination.

Clients of color whose presenting concerns and issues are misunderstood or pathologized by therapists are unlikely to return for services. Further, for men of color, the stigma of obtaining help also may lead to premature termination. In addition, therapists sensitive to the effects of stigma may be reluctant to apply the appropriate diagnoses or treatment to these individuals. Other barriers to treatment for men of color include a lack of or inadequate mental health insurance, the paucity of culturally competent counselors, language barriers, and inadequate coordination of services among providers (Ro & Takeuchi, 2003).

Although men of color may seek assistance for mental health problems first from clergy or primary care physicians, research cited by Ro and Takeuchi (2003) indicated that a lack of adequate training and sensitivity leads to less mental health assistance and fewer referrals rather than more. These men may find it especially difficult to open up and thereby appear weak to male authority figures. Ro and Takeuchi (2003) further argue that the accumulation of social stressors that men of color face, in addition to barriers to treatment, is a significant factor in the disproportionate numbers of these individuals who are relegated to long-term health facilities and prisons.

Women of color tend to be at greater risk than men of having combined mental health and substance-abuse problems, which is associated with the following factors: early initiation to substance abuse, sexual and domestic abuse, unplanned pregnancies, low educational and occupational attainment, and the trading of sex for drugs and money (National Institute on Drug Abuse, 1998; Rach-Beisel, Scott, & Dixon, 1999). Social service workers, schools, and religious leaders need to help educate and prevent the abuse of these young women and work to provide safe housing, counseling, and information about abuse and reproductive issues.

Gender and Sexual Orientation

Male and female people of color who are lesbian, gay, or bisexual (LGB) are placed in a situation where to claim their sexual identity puts them at risk for losing the support of their communities, as well as the societal benefits of heterosexist privilege. The loss of heterosexist privilege can be a more significant issue for men and women of color than for White LGB individuals, and therapists need to be attuned to this issue. In addition, gender mediates the experience of being LGB across racial groups (Greene, 1997; see also Chapter 9, this volume).

For Latina/o individuals, there are clear gender-role expectations. The cultural acceptance of *machismo* as heightened virility and sexuality can allow for same-sex contact for Latinos without stigma (Zamora-Hernadez & Patterson, 1996). In contrast, the cultural standard that women should show *marianismo*, which involves emulating the Virgin Mary and being chaste, pure, and devoted to sex only as a form of procreation, leads to definite prohibitions against same-sex relationships for Latinas (Greene, 1997).

In American Indian communities, historically there has been mixed acceptance of cross-gender-role behaviors. Individuals who demonstrated these behaviors sometimes were viewed as having special powers and were termed "two spirited," for embodying both the masculine and the feminine. American Indian culture and spirituality often view phenomena on a continuum or circle (Cross, 2003). As a result, gender roles and sexuality are not limited to dualistic categories. A reality for Indian individuals, however, is that the genocidal activities of the past propel the view that women should have children. Thus, LGB individuals may feel deeply ambivalent in identifying more with their sexual orientation than their own supportive and collectivistic culture (Fukuyama & Ferguson, 2000).

Although Asian Americans represent a highly diverse population, there are strict gender roles that place men in a position of dominance relative to women. Strong allegiance to the family hierarchy dictates that men and women should marry and have children. Chan (1997) notes that LGB individuals of Asian descent are often invisible due to cultural mores surrounding the privacy of sexuality and intimacy. Becoming lesbian, gay, or bisexual would entail a rejection of family duties and gender-role obligations. In addition, gender stereotypes can be integrated with racial stereotypes so that gay Asian men may be associated with positions of lower power and status in these relationships (Sanitioso, 1999).

Greene (1994) has noted that, due to the problems of racism, sexism, and classism, many African Americans who are LGB have been reluctant to assert their sexual identity lest they forfeit their families, churches, and community sources of support and lose assumed heterosexist privilege. Pressures that

African American men feel to prove themselves as men may lead them to deny their sexuality and hide same-sex contacts through "down low" behavior.

CASE VIGNETTES

Insensitive Counseling: The Case of Mrs. Parks

Mrs. Parks is an African American elementary school teacher and a divorced mother. She lives with her 8-year-old daughter and her mother, who is retired. Mrs. Parks sought treatment for her daughter Nicole because she felt that Nicole might have some learning disabilities. This family of three went together to the first session. Mrs. Parks explained the situation, and her mother offered additional information. Nicole was quiet and answered by saying "yes ma'am" or "no ma'am." At the end of the first session, the White therapist explained that she felt that the major problem in this family was that it was too enmeshed and female dominant, and that Nicole was suffering from a lack of male role models. She believed that Mrs. Parks was too dependent on her mother by continuing to live with her and have her operate as an authority figure, and that Nicole was "confused" by having her mother and grandmother function as parent figures, as evidenced by her minimal verbalizations. The therapist indicated that these issues were likely related to Nicole's learning problems.

Mrs. Parks was hurt and upset by the therapist's assessment and refused to return for additional sessions. She felt that the therapist had not explored the reasons why she and her mother shared a home, which involved the pooling of economic resources, the provision of safety and child care for her daughter, and the fact that she was pessimistic about remarrying. Mrs. Parks also felt that the therapist did not understand that her daughter's minimal responses related to gender-role expectations that she should be lady-like, polite, respectful to older adults, and show extra care when relating to White authority figures.

The therapist in this scenario is not adhering to Guideline 1, as she is unaware of her own gender and racial bias and implicitly was comparing this family with those of White individuals. The therapist appeared to be unfamiliar with the practice of valuing the wisdom and experience of the grandmother, and as a result she pathologized the family as being "too enmeshed." In addition, she failed to show an appreciation of Guideline 2 by her lack of sensitivity to the different gender and cultural norms found in this family. Finally, the therapist failed to demonstrate gender and racially competent practice strategies, as set forth in Guideline 5. She pathologized, rather than affirmed, Mrs. Parks and her mother as authority figures, and she did not explore the possibility that there might be male role models in the extended circle of family and friends. She also minimized Mrs. Parks's presenting concerns about Nicole's learning problems and never addressed this area as a vital focus for intervention.

Conflicted Gay Physician: The Case of George

George is a second-generation Chinese medical resident who is due to graduate in a few months. His parents, grandparents, aunts, and uncles have all contributed to his education and look forward to his returning to his home area to set up practice. They are very proud of his accomplishments as they see him as now able to marry and help take care of aging relatives. George presents to the University Counseling Center with feelings of panic, anxiety, and gastrointestinal distress. He has been involved with a male partner for almost 2 years but is ashamed to tell his family, who will be devastated by this revelation. He feels that he is not fulfilling his family obligation to marry and have children. George has enjoyed the deference that he receives as a physician and has finally begun to enjoy a sense of camaraderie and respect among his peers. He is concerned that his stature and authority as a male physician will be diminished if he reveals his sexual orientation.

George's therapist first will have to examine any possible gender stereotypes he or she has about Asian males and homosexuality (Guideline 1). Because societal stereotypes tend to portray Asian men as asexual and passive, it will be critical for the therapist to affirm George's sense of masculine identity and help him clarify his conflicting allegiances so he can decide what he is willing to share with others. George's therapist must show sensitivity (Guideline 2) to the patriarchal and restrictive male gender roles that George has been exposed to within his family and in White culture. Therapy will need to address George's feelings of internalized homophobia, how to maintain a sense of power as a gay Chinese male in a patriarchal profession, the potential loss of heterosexist privilege, and the possibility that he will be devalued by his family, friends, and religion for his sexual orientation. Only a therapist who is well grounded in understanding the intersections of race, gender, and culture will be able to exercise appropriate skill in helping George sort out his multiple identities and conflicting feelings.

STRATEGIES FOR IMPLEMENTING THE GUIDELINES

There are several strategies that counselors can use to improve clinical outcomes with men and women of color. Paniagua (2005) suggested that therapists may need to work immediately on rapport, setting clear boundaries, and being active and authoritative to increase the expectation that therapy can help. In addition, therapy requests often are tied to the need for assistance with very concrete and pragmatic goals rather than self-growth. Men and women of color, due to their specific gender roles, often need to learn concrete problem-solving skills. Therapeutic interventions should reinforce a sense of control and empowerment in contrast to the oppression and discrimination that these individuals have faced for so long (Wade, 1996).

Constantine, Greer, and Kindaichi (2003) suggested that counselors remain mindful of the collectivistic orientation of many women of color. As such, holistic approaches that incorporate family, friends, spirituality, and community resources should be considered rather than focusing exclusively on more individualistic and introspective approaches.

Because of the systematic racism, sexism, and oppression that men and women of color have experienced, trust for authority figures can be very tenuous. As a result, it is important to build rapport by listening, limiting questions, not writing down a lot of information, avoiding the immediate recommendation for medication when possible, and not pushing for private information prematurely (Paniagua, 1998).

In order to respond to the difficulties that men of color face in overcoming their fear of and resistance to requesting mental health assistance, Ro and Takeuchi (2003) outlined a series of strategies that may facilitate treatment for men and women of color. First, stigma can be reduced by developing ads and programs that use credible men and women of color who, having sought and benefited from therapy, can serve as role models. A second approach encourages early detection and prevention efforts by training community leaders, such as clergy and other health providers, to be more effective in screening problems and making referrals. Finally, having culturally competent providers and ethnically similar therapists who match clients linguistically and culturally can encourage men and women of color to initiate and remain in treatment.

CONCLUSION

Individuals are shaped by multiple levels of identity due to the interactions of race, gender, culture, sexual orientation, class, and ability. We no longer can try to understand others from a singular perspective. Cross (2003) argued that we should not view these complex cultural interactions as problems. Instead, we should embrace these encounters as potential learning opportunities for meeting basic human needs, for developing more expansive theories of human behavior, and for implementing more effective strategies for support, problem solving, health, and well-being. As we strive to implement the Guidelines and focus on becoming more responsive to how gender issues are manifested in the lives of people of color, we will have the opportunity to offer a higher level of service, one that is attuned to multiple identities, to all of our clients. We as therapists also stand to benefit from becoming continually more culturally competent.

REFERENCES

Adams, V. L., & LaFromboise, T. D. (2001). Self-in relation theory and African American female development. In D. B. Pope-Davis & H. L. K. Coleman (Eds.), *The intersection of race, class, and gender in multicultural counseling* (pp. 25–48). Thousand Oaks, CA: Sage.

Al-Mateen, C. S., Christian, F. M., Mishra, A., Cofield, M., & Tildon, T. (2002). Women of color. In S. G. Kornstein & A. H. Clayton (Eds.), *Women's mental health* (pp. 568–583). New York: Guilford Press.

American Psychological Association. (2003). Guidelines on multicultural education, training, research, practice, and organizational change for psychologists. *American Psychologist, 58,* 377–402.

Arredondo, P. (1991). Counseling Latinas. In C. C. Lee & B. L. Richardson (Eds.), *Multicultural issues in counseling: New approaches to diversity* (pp. 143–156). Alexandria, VA: American Association for Counseling and Development.

Baca Zinn, M., & Thornton Dill, B. (1996). Theorizing difference from multiracial feminism. *Feminist Studies, 22,* 321–333.

Boyd-Franklin, N. (1989). *Black families in therapy: A multisystems approach.* New York: Guilford Press.

Browne, I., & Misra, J. (2003). The intersection of gender and race in the labor market. *Annual Review of Sociology, 29,* 487–513.

Bronstein, P., & Quina, K. (Eds.). (1988). *Teaching a psychology of people.* Washington, DC: American Psychological Association.

Chan, C. (1997). Don't ask, don't tell, don't know. In B. Greene (Ed.), *Ethnic and cultural diversity among lesbians and gay men* (pp. 240–248). Newbury Park, CA: Sage.

Chow, J. C., Jaffee, K., & Snowden, L. (2003). Racial/ethnic disparities in the use of mental health services in poverty areas. *American Journal of Public Health, 93,* 792–797.

Comas-Diaz, L. (1994). An integrative approach. In L. Comas-Diaz & B. Greene (Eds.), *Women of color: Integrating ethnic and gender identities in psychotherapy* (pp. 287–318). New York: Guilford Press.

Constantine, M. G., Greer, T. M., & Kindaichi, M. M. (2003). Theoretical and cultural considerations in counseling women of color. In M. Kopala & M. A. Keitel (Eds.), *Handbook of counseling women* (pp. 40–52). Thousand Oaks, CA: Sage.

Coridan, C., & O'Connell, C. (2002). *Meeting the challenge: Ending treatment disparities for women of color.* Alexandria, VA: National Mental Health Association.

Cross, T. (2003). Culture as a resource for mental health. *Cultural Diversity and Ethnic Minority Psychology, 9,* 354–359.

Dovidio, J., Gaertner, S., Kawakami, K., & Hudson, G. (2002). Why can't we just get along? Interpersonal biases and interracial distrust. *Cultural Diversity and Ethnic Minority Psychology, 8,* 88–102.

Elligan, D., & Utsey, S. (1999). Utility of an African-centered support group for African American men confronting societal racism and oppression. *Cultural Diversity and Ethnic Minority Psychology, 5,* 156–165.

Fabrega, H., Jr., Mezzich, J., & Ulrich, R. F. (1988). Black–White differences in psychopathology in an urban psychiatric population. *Comprehensive Psychiatry 29,* 285–297.

Flaherty, J. A., & Adams, S. (1998). Therapist–patient race and sex matching: Predictors of treatment duration. *Psychiatric Times, XV,* 41.

Fukuyama, M. A., & Ferguson, A. D. (2000). Lesbian, gay, and bisexual people of color: Understanding cultural complexity and managing multiple oppressions. In R. Perez, K. De Bord, & K. Bieschke (Eds.), *Handbook of counseling and psychotherapy with lesbian, gay, and bisexual clients* (pp. 81–106). Washington, DC: American Psychological Association.

Gloria, A. M. (2001). The cultural construction of Latinas: Practice implications of multiple realities and identities. In D. B. Pope-Davis & H. L. K. Coleman (Eds.), *The intersection of race, class, and gender in multicultural counseling* (pp. 3–24). Thousand Oaks, CA: Sage.

Greene, B. (1994). African American women. In L. Comas-Diaz & B. Greene (Eds.), *Women of color: Integrating ethnic and gender identities in psychotherapy* (pp. 10–29). New York: Guilford Press.

Greene, B. (1997). Ethnic minority lesbians and gay men: Mental health and treatment issues. In B. Greene (Ed.), *Ethnic and cultural diversity among lesbians and gay men* (pp. 216–239). Newbury Park, CA: Sage.

Hall, G. C. N. (2001). Psychotherapy research with ethnic minorities: Empirical, ethical, and conceptual issues. *Journal of Consulting and Clinical Psychology, 69,* 502–510.

Jackson, L. (1999). Ethnocultural resistance to multicultural training: Students and faculty. *Cultural Diversity and Ethnic Minority Psychology, 5,* 27–36.

Jones E. J., Krupnick, J. L., & Kerig, P. K. (1987). Some gender effects in a brief psychotherapy. *Psychotherapy, 24,* 336–352.

Myers, H. P., Lesser, I., Rodriguez, N., Mira, C. B., Hwang, W., Camp, C., Anderson, D., Erickson, L., & Wohl, M. (2002). Ethnic differences in clinical presentation of depression in adult women. *Cultural Diversity and Ethnic Minority Psychology, 8,* 138–156.

National Institute on Drug Abuse. (1998). *Drug addiction research and the health of women.* Rockville, MD: Author.

Ohye, B., & Daniel, J. (1999). The "other" adolescent girls: Who are they? In N. Johnson, M. Roberts & J. Worell (Eds.), *Beyond appearance: A new look at adolescent girls* (pp.115–128). Washington, DC: American Psychological Association.

Paniagua, F. A. (1998). *Assessing and treating culturally diverse clients: A practical guide* (2nd Ed.). Thousand Oaks, CA: Sage.

Paniagua, F. A. (2005). *Assessing and treating culturally diverse clients: A practical guide* (3rd Ed.). Thousand Oaks, CA: Sage.

Quina, K., & Bronstein, P. (2003). Gender and multiculturalism in psychology: Transformation and new directions. In P. Bronstein & K. Quina (Eds.), *Teaching gender and multicultural awareness: Resources for the psychology classroom* (pp. 3–11). Washington, DC: American Psychological Association.

Rach-Beisel, J., Scott, J., & Dixon, L. (1999). Co-occurring severe mental illness and substance abuse disorders: A review of recent research. *Psychiatric Services, 50,* 1427–1434.

Reid, P. (1993). Poor women in psychological research: Shut up and shut out. *Psychology of Women Quarterly, 17,* 133–150.

Reid, P. (2002). Multicultural psychology: Bringing together gender and ethnicity. *Cultural Diversity and Ethnic Minority Psychology, 8,* 103–114.

Ro, M. J., & Takeuchi, D. T. (2003). *Showing strength, overcoming silence: Improving the mental health of men of color.* Battle Creek, MI: W. K. Kellogg Foundation.

Robinson, T. L. (1999). The intersections of dominant discourses across race, gender, and other identities. *Journal of Counseling Development, 77,* 73–79.

Rossell, J., & Bernal, G. (1996). Adapting cognitive–behavioral and interpersonal treatments for depressed Puerto Rican adolescents. In E. D. Hibbs & P. S. Jensen (Eds.), *Psychosocial treatments for child and adolescent disorders: Empirically based strategies for clinical practice* (pp. 157–185). Washington, DC: American Psychological Association.

Sanchez-Hucles, J., & Dutton, M. (1999). The interaction between societal violence and domestic violence: Racial and cultural factors for men and women of color. In J. O'Neil & M. Harway (Eds.), *Why do men batter: New perspectives on men's violence against women* (pp. 183–203). Newbury Park, CA: Sage.

Sanitioso, R. (1999). A social psychological perspective on HIV/AIDS and gay or homosexually active Asian men. *Journal of Homosexuality, 36,* 69–85.

Scher, M., Stevens, M., Good, G., & Eichenfield, G. (Eds.). (1987). *Handbook of counseling and psychotherapy with men.* Newbury Park, CA: Sage.

Sue, S. (2003). The richness of human realities. In P. Bronstein & K. Quina (Eds.), *Teaching gender and multicultural awareness: Resources for the psychology classroom* (pp. xvii–xix). Washington, DC: American Psychological Association.

U.S. Department of Health and Human Services. (2001). *Mental health: Culture, race, and ethnicity—A supplement to Mental health: A report of the Surgeon General.* Rockville, MD: U.S. Department of Health and Human Services, Public Health Office, Office of the Surgeon General.

Wade, J. C. (1996). African American men's gender role conflict: The significance of racial identity. *Sex Roles, 34,* 17–33.

Watts, R. J., Abdul-Adil, J. K., & Pratt, T. (2002). Enhancing critical consciousness in young African American men: A psycho-educational approach. *Psychology of Men and Masculinity, 3,* 41–50.

Williams. D. R., & Fenton, B. T. (1994). The mental health of African Americans: Findings, questions, and directions. In I. Livingston (Ed.), *Handbook of Black American health: The mosaic of conditions, issues, policies, and prospects* (pp. 253–268). Westport, CT: Greenwood Press.

Zamora-Hernandez, C. E., & Patterson, D. G. (1996). Homosexually active Latino men: Issues for social practice. In J. F. Longres (Ed.), *Men of color: A context for service to homosexually active men* (pp. 69–91). Binghamton, NY: Harrington Park Press.

12

Social Class Considerations

Saba Rasheed Ali, Alice Fridman, Thomasin Hall, and Leslie Leathers

Recently, the professional psychology community has demonstrated theoretical and research-based commitments to multicultural issues and social justice and has begun to challenge the tendency to reinforce, rather than confront, societal practices and institutions that propagate inequality (Fox, 2003). However, the process of redefining psychology to include social justice is ongoing and needs constant attention. For example, within counseling psychology, the growing interest in advancing a social justice agenda has been sparked in part by two important movements within the field: (1) a focus on prevention, and (2) the need to expand the definition of multicultural competence to include social advocacy and other interventions appropriate for more diverse groups (Vera & Speight, 2003). With the expanding definition of multiculturalism, some attempts have been made to include social class as a cultural consideration that needs to be addressed. However, attention paid to clients' multiple identities, including the intersections of social class with race, gender, ethnicity, and other contextual variables, has been limited (Constantine, 2002).

Social class diversity, as with racial and ethnic diversity, contributes uniquely to the identity, values system, and worldview of every client (APA, 2003; Liu, Ali, Soleck, Hopps, Dunston, & Pickett, 2004). In order to affirm this diversity, counselors and educators first must acknowledge their preconceptions, stereotypic attitudes, and automatic biases with regard to social class. Such automatic tendencies often stem from the individual backgrounds and experiences of counselors and, in turn, may interact with other counselor–client variables to affect the integrity and effectiveness of mental health services provided to diverse populations.

In this chapter, we will utilize the "Guidelines on Multicultural Education, Training, Research, Practice, and Organizational Change for Psychologists"

(APA, 2003) in addressing the unique contribution of social-class to cultural-group membership. The chapter will first discuss relevant social class theory. Next, we will present recent literature on social class as a cultural variable, highlighting the paucity of research in this area. Third, we will explicitly apply each of the Guidelines to practical situations through case vignettes. Finally, we will integrate current theory, literature, and practical applications to provide suggestions for future directions.

SOCIAL CLASS THEORY

Incorporating social class issues into therapy, as well as acknowledging classist views, is an important yet often arduous task. Liu, Soleck, Hopps, Dunston, and Pickett (2004) assert that social class and classism are inextricably linked. They distinguish between social class as an economic system and classism as the prejudicial and discriminatory attitudes resulting from social class (Liu, Soleck, et al., 2004). Thus, in order to recognize classist beliefs, one first must have an understanding of the concept of social class and its underlying meanings.

Social class is much more complicated than is expressed through the linear variables used in most psychological research (e.g., socioeconomic status). Socioeconomic measures traditionally have supposed a linear relationship between increased attainment and increased status. Certainly, social class includes objective criteria such as social stations, lifestyles, and individuals' opportunities pertaining to education, income, and occupation. These criteria typically are aligned with classifications of under, working, middle, and upper classes (Leathers, 2004). However, such class demarcations do not necessarily imply homogeneity within classes. Individuals' subjective experiences and perceptions create their definitions of what it means to belong to a particular class. Liu, Soleck, and colleagues (2004) proposed the Social Class Worldview Model (SCWM) as a way of conceptualizing the meaning and importance of individuals' phenomenological experiences of social class. Their model assists mental health professionals in understanding how past and present social class experiences inform their own and their clients' perceptions of life events.

Liu, Soleck, and colleagues (2004) developed the SCWM to capture the variability that potentially exists in social class perceptions and experiences. The SCWM divides social class into three basic concepts that will be described briefly. The first important concept of the SCWM is the idea that people live in economic cultures that demand them to maintain their perceived position within that particular social class group (i.e., homeostasis). Hence, people attempt to live up to expectations placed upon them by their economic culture. Meeting these expectations ensures that homeostasis is maintained, but failure to meet the economic culture's expectations may lead to feelings of depression and anxiety, which Liu and colleagues term "internalized classism."

The second key concept of the SCWM is the notion that everyone possesses a social class worldview that serves as a lens through which people make sense of the expectations of their economic culture and turn them into meaningful actions to meet the goals of that culture. Individuals' social class worldviews consist of their relationships to property (e.g., materialism), social class behaviors (e.g., manners and etiquette), lifestyle choices (e.g., vacation time), referent groups (e.g., family, peers, and a group of aspiration), and consciousness about social class. People act out and experience classism in ways that are salient to them and contextually related to their economic culture. For example, individuals who live in an economic culture that values "upper-class manners and etiquette" may value those manners and behaviors because they recognize them as essential to maintain cultural connections with their social class group. Consequently, these individuals may be likely to experience and interpret classism around what is considered appropriate or inappropriate etiquette (Liu, Soleck, et al., 2004).

Third, the definition of classism is key to the SCWM. Within the SCWM, classism is defined as prejudice and discrimination directed at people engaged in behaviors incongruent with the values and expectations of one's economic culture. The four types of classism described in the SCWM are: upward (negative feelings toward those perceived as "snobs" and "elitists"), downward (negative feelings toward those perceived as "worse off"), lateral (negative feelings directed at people perceived as similar, derived from the need to "keep up with the Joneses" or from falling behind the demands of the social class group), and internalized classism. Internalized classism is the negative emotional and cognitive difficulties experienced by individuals when they fail to meet the demands of their economic culture. Low levels of internalized classism motivate people to meet the demands of their economic culture, but high levels can be experienced as problematic (Liu, 2002). Thus, the SCWM has been developed for both counselors and researchers to better understand social class and classism in the lives of the individuals with whom they work.

RESEARCH ON SOCIAL CLASS

Liu, Ali, and colleagues (2004) noted that, even though social class is an important variable associated with the effectiveness of therapy, little psychological research has been devoted to social class. Some of the extant psychological literature investigating the role(s) of social class reveals that generally social class is an important subjective variable for people. More specifically, social class research has demonstrated that people in lower social classes tend to experience significantly more stress than do people in middle and upper social classes (Liu, Ali, et al., 2004). Other findings suggest that clients from lower classes may manifest their symptoms differently than clients from more affluent classes, and that counselors may interact differently with clients from lower and upper classes (Liu, Ali, et al., 2004).

Constantine (2002) asserted that social class should not be studied in isolation. Instead, social class should be studied in conjunction with other cultural variables, such as race. She further noted that, although research on social class alone is sparse, research on the intersection of social class and race is even less prevalent. This issue is problematic because stressors with which people of color have to contend may be exacerbated by membership in a lower class group. Little research examining the nexus between social class and race translates to little knowledge about which interventions are best suited to assist clients of color from varying social class backgrounds (Constantine, 2002). Nonetheless, Harley, Jolivette, McCormick, and Tice (2002) offered some practical recommendations for approaching clients' multiple identities.

Harley and colleagues (2002) suggested that multiculturally competent practitioners should be able to work from various theories/interventions and choose the most appropriate theory/intervention for work with a given client. Moreover, they suggested that therapists acknowledge their clients' environments and the systemic societal barriers that clients may face. They also recommended that mental health providers appreciate cultural differences rather than pathologize them. Harley and colleagues (2002) further advised practitioners to recognize and value the bicultural negotiation that clients of color may experience. More specifically, mental health care providers should appreciate that some of their clients routinely function in and maneuver between at least two different cultural environments. They advocated a call to action, asking counseling professionals to challenge traditional counseling models that may contain inherent bias.

MULTICULTURAL GUIDELINES AND CASE VIGNETTES

The extant theory and research indicate that social class is a topic beginning to receive attention within psychology as an important cultural construct. However, at present, it is still largely unclear how this construct can be incorporated into practical initiatives in order to integrate multicultural awareness into psychological education, research, and practice. The following section discusses how social class is relevant to each of the Multicultural Guidelines

(APA, 2003) and provides case vignettes to illustrate the practical application of these Guidelines.

Guideline 1: Awareness of One's Own Social Class Bias

Although a lot of multicultural training emphasizes the importance of being knowledgeable about clients' cultural backgrounds, beliefs, and values, it is equally important that psychologists be familiar with their own cultural identity and the beliefs and assumptions that they hold (APA, 2003). Implicit within this Guideline is the notion that it is important that culturally competent psychologists devote conscious thought to their social class as part of their cultural background. Their own social class standing shapes their views of the world and their perceptions of and assumptions about individuals from social classes other than their own. They also should consider the intersection of their class and race and how the two together influence their views of others. As the following case vignette will demonstrate, psychologists who are not conscious of themselves as members of particular ethnic groups or social classes may make unwarranted assumptions or form unfavorable perceptions of the clients with whom they interact.

Assumption About a Client's Social Class: The Case of Bob

Bob, a 28-year-old White male, spent his childhood and college years in a predominately White, middle-class suburb in the northeastern United States. He went to graduate school in a demographically similar neighborhood and was excited about a change of pace at his internship site, a college counseling center in the midwest. After spending the first few weeks working with homesick freshmen, Bob met Kevin, a 25-year-old African American junior who was having trouble choosing a career. Right away, Bob found himself wondering why Kevin had been in college for so long. "Man," he thought, "just because he can't pick a career doesn't mean he has to hang out in college for 7 years! How can this guy afford to pay that much tuition?" When Kevin talked about his dissatisfaction with the long hours he put in at his factory job, Bob found himself changing his thinking: "He must go to school part-time and work to support himself through college; that's why he's been here so long." But when Bob mentioned available need-based financial aid, Kevin looked confused. "No," Kevin said, "I'm not looking for money, I'm trying to find work that I like!" Bob responded by listing places that offered enjoyable temporary work: the golf course, the local restaurants, and the campus shuttle service. Kevin became exasperated, "Man, what is this, career counseling or a temp job agency? Can I talk to someone else who might be able to help me out with this?" Puzzled, Bob referred Kevin to a senior staff psychologist at the counseling center.

Later, when Bob consulted with the senior psychologist, she explained that Kevin had taken a few years off to work for a drug company before starting college and that his parents were paying his tuition and living expenses. He had volunteered to work testing medicine samples at a factory to gain experience for his intended career as a chemist. However, he became bored at work and began to wonder whether he should change his major and pursue a different line of work. In session, he had become frustrated by Bob's assumptions about his situation.

Upon learning what had happened, Bob realized he had made assumptions about Kevin's social class that affected their client–counselor relationship. As a result, Bob used supervision to reflect on his class biases and how they may have impeded his ability to work effectively with Kevin.

Guideline 2: Knowledge of Social Class Identity

In addition to developing an awareness of their own ethnic and social class backgrounds, culturally competent psychologists are responsible for developing an awareness of the backgrounds of their clients (APA, 2003). Because ethnicity and social class both play large roles in shaping individuals' identities and influencing their behaviors, beliefs, and attitudes, they likely play a role in shaping counselors' and clients' reactions to each other. Understanding the values and ideas that clients adhere to as a result of their particular background is important in establishing rapport with clients and using therapeutic strategies that are suitable to their needs. However, in applying this principle, psychologists should be careful not to assume their clients' membership in a particular social class or ethnic group and not to stereotype clients based on common characteristics of a group. Rather, psychologists should listen for cues from clients that provide information about their ethnic and social class identity. Further, they should become educated about their clients' cultural background through literature or consultation with professionals knowledgeable about particular group identities.

The following vignette will illustrate how the process of understanding cultural background is important in practicing effective therapy, especially when clients look similar to the therapist. In these cases, counselors may assume familiarity with their clients' culture and overlook underlying class and ethnic differences.

Similar Yet Different: The Case of Juanita

Juanita obtained her graduate degree in community psychology with the intent of returning to her home neighborhood in Atlanta and providing mental health services there. Like Juanita, many of the neighborhood's residents were African Americans who had come from lower to middle-working-class backgrounds and struggled with many of the same issues that her own family had to contend with when she was growing up. Because of her interest in working with individuals culturally similar to herself, Juanita did not see a need to develop her cultural competence and made few efforts to become knowledgeable about the behaviors and worldviews of other ethnic and social class groups. This approach met her needs for a number of years as she worked at the community mental health center and became increasingly more knowledgeable and skilled at addressing the particular needs of the neighborhood's residents. When Priscilla, a 42-year-old Black Muslim immigrant from Mali, arrived at her office seeking help to adjust to her new surroundings, Juanita applied the same interventions that worked so well in the past. After all, she had counseled many people in the neighborhood who had taken jobs in unfamiliar communities or who had gone to college outside the neighborhood and had difficulty getting used to such changes.

Unfortunately, these tools did not apply well to Juanita's work with Priscilla. Although Priscilla had come to counseling voluntarily and was willing to talk about her difficulties adjusting to her new setting, she refused to discuss the effects that the move had on her family members and their relationships with one another. She also grew defensive and angry when Juanita tried to probe the topic. For Juanita, this resistance was a shock; not only was she used to being a trusted member of the community and encountering little secrecy from her clients, but she also relied heavily on knowledge of family relationships in devising coping strategies for her clients. Another difficulty for Juanita was that Priscilla is Muslim, and thus Juanita's suggestions for Priscilla to join churches and faith groups in the largely Southern Baptist neighborhood were not necessarily helpful or appropriate.

Juanita felt at a loss. Her client was clearly distressed, but the strategies she had so heavily relied on to solidify her other clients' support networks and integrate them into the community did not apply in this case. Moreover, Priscilla appeared dissatisfied with Juanita's suggestions to get to know other women at her job and to attend neighborhood events, such as block parties. Unsure of how to proceed, Juanita began to research Priscilla's country and culture of origin, first by reading books on the topic and, later, by emailing other mental health professionals who had more experience working with immigrant populations or were of diverse national origins themselves. One of these professionals, whose family also had immigrated to Atlanta from Mali, told Juanita about a Malian community center in a different part of the city. Juantia began to use this center both as a resource to help herself learn about Malian culture and as a place for Priscilla to meet culturally similar people who could serve as a source of support.

Eventually, as Juanita began to gain a greater understanding of her client's culture and use more appropriate intervention strategies, Priscilla also began to open up more and explain the reasons for some of her behaviors. Juanita discovered that many of Priscilla's issues stemmed from her family of origin, a prominent, wealthy family living in Mali, where it was considered inappropriate to engage in recreational activities with casual acquaintances or to mingle in large groups with people with whom the family was not familiar. Furthermore, because revealing problems to others could portray the family in a negative light, these problems were discussed only with close family members. Because Juanita was not able to identify Priscilla's social class based on her appearance, it had not even occurred to her that this might be a contributing factor to some of Priscilla's presenting issues and behaviors in therapy. As Juanita began to realize the inappropriateness of some of her early counseling techniques with Priscilla, she resolved to make a more conscious effort in the future to learn about diverse factors in her clients' backgrounds, prior to beginning therapy.

Guideline 3: Education for Increased Competence

Guideline 3 refers to the multicultural education of undergraduate and graduate students, as well as clinical and research supervision, advisement, mentoring, and postgraduate education (APA, 2003). The Guidelines state that multicultural education effectively enhances students' therapeutic competence and also may help reduce stereotyping and prejudice against people of color (APA, 2003). Because many clients do not view their racial and social class memberships as separate, it is important that educators emphasize the importance of considering clients' multiple identities. The following case of Mitchell is an example of how a supervisor helped a supervisee to understand how multiple cultural identities can greatly affect a client and his or her presenting concerns.

Effective Supervision: The Case of Mitchell

Mitchell, a counselor in a college counseling center located on the west coast, is currently supervising Angela, a beginning practicum student. Until recently, all of Angela's clients were White and middle to upper class. During her last supervision session, Angela described her newest client, K.G., to Mitchell. K.G. is an African American male freshman with no prior counseling history. He presented with heightened anxiety that began approximately 2 months into his first year of attendance at the university. Angela reported that K.G. came to the counseling center upon the recommendation of his physician, who explained that K.G.'s symptoms likely represented panic attacks. Angela conceptualized that her client's anxiety was likely due to his racial minority status at the university. After reviewing the tape of Angela's first session with K.G., as well as his intake information, Mitchell agreed that minority status was probably a contributing factor to K.G.'s anxiety.

However, Mitchell also wondered about K.G.'s past social class experiences. More specifically, Mitchell wondered how much emphasis K.G. placed on human, social, and cultural capital, as well as how much value K.G. placed on material items and his ability to acquire them. He wondered if part of K.G.'s anxiety was related to an inability to meet the demands of his social class group. While delivering feedback to Angela regarding her session with K.G., Mitchell noted that Angela did not inquire about K.G.'s social class status. Thus, he stressed the importance of considering a client's multiple identities and explained that focusing on only one cultural variable could make a client feel misunderstood. Angela admitted that she had not considered factors of social class in her work with K.G. Mitchell also helped Angela explore her own social class background via the Social Class Worldview Model (Liu, Soleck, et al., 2004) so that she could understand her own economic culture and how this culture frames her worldview. In this way, he modeled for Angela how she could incorporate this issues of social class and classism into therapy sessions with her clients.

Guideline 4: More Diverse Research Samples

One goal of conducting culturally relevant research is to expand psychologists' knowledge bases regarding various cultures so that they do not wrongly pathologize their clients' behaviors. For example, without research illuminating the collectivistic norms of Eastern cultures (such as some Chinese cultures), individuals could be considered overly dependent, instead of merely adhering to cultural norms. Despite the repeated call for more diverse research samples, many research studies continue to employ White middle-class participants, often because these are the easiest samples to access (APA, 2003). Such homogeneous sampling is problematic when findings from studies with predominately White middle-class participants are generalized to members of other racial and social class groups. Psychologists cannot assume that interventions empirically validated with middle-class samples are suitable for use with people from lower social classes. The following vignette illustrates that, although it may be hard to locate diverse samples, it is imperative that researchers study many segments of the population and reach these populations in a culturally sensitive manner.

Community Involvement: The Case of Amira

Amira has been out of graduate school for 3 years, and currently is working as an associate professor at a small 4-year university in the midwest. Combining her two research interests (the psychological well-being of Muslim Americans and career and vocational issues related to immigrant Muslim Americans), Amira began working on a research project studying career-transition issues among recent Sudanese refugees to the United States. The small midwestern town in which she lives is a relocation site for refugees from Sudan. Thinking that she would be able to form a strong connection to this community because of her own Muslim affiliation and background, Amira visited the local mosque. The Imam of the mosque facilitated contact between Amira and Mona, the relocation caseworker for the local Sudanese community. Mona introduced Amira to the informal leader of the community, Mr. Hamed. Mr. Hamed, a well-respected teacher in Sudan, now works as a janitor as a result of his relocation. When Amira met with Mr. Hamed, she immediately launched into an explanation of her study and its benefits to his community. Mr. Hamed rejected Amira's idea and seemed insulted by her invitation to participate in her study.

Amira was shocked by Mr. Hamed's decision, especially since she was convinced that her study was important and potentially could benefit the Sudanese refugee community. Amira consulted with Mona about her conversation with Mr. Hamed. Mona realized that Amira had insulted Mr. Hamed by asking him to discuss issues that were very difficult for him and his community. Mr. Hamed and many other refugees from Sudan were forced to leave highly prestigious careers when they fled their country. Their departure was a painful process and difficult to share with others, especially those like Amira who held a higher status job. After consulting with Mona, Amira realized that her drive to complete her research project had overshadowed the real experiences of the people she was trying to understand. As a result, Amira immediately began volunteering within the Sudanese community. She participated in an effort to send much-needed food and clothing to Sudan. Through her volunteer work, she interacted heavily with the community and began to understand their culture. After taking the time to get to know the community, she again approached Mr. Hamed about her research project and invited him to critique her study and suggest ways she might amend her project to be more culturally sensitive to the Sudanese community. Mr. Hamed listened to her ideas and offered suggestions. He also helped Amira to approach potential participants for her study.

Guideline 5: Culturally Appropriate Counseling Skills

Because not all therapeutic dyads consist of White middle-class counselors treating White middle-class clients (APA, 2003), it is important also to consider scenarios in which psychologists should use culturally appropriate skills in dealing with clients from diverse social class backgrounds (as well as other culturally different backgrounds). In the following vignette, the counselor (an Asian American upper-middle-class female) is faced with the task of recognizing and confronting her own social class background and its intersection with her racial/ethnic heritage and gender as they pertain to her client (a White lower class male).

Recognition of Differences: The Case of Yun Jin

The first time Yun Jin met James, he was dressed in jeans and a T-shirt with
the sleeves cut out. James had been referred to Yun Jin for vocational counseling after his fourth consecutive layoff. James looked tired, disheveled,
and less than enthusiastic about the idea of meeting with a vocational
counselor. Yun Jin immediately recognized the potential barriers that were
forming between herself and her client. They were of different races, gen-
ders, and socioeconomic statuses, and additionally James seemed mistrust-
ing and defeated. Yun Jin's initial doubts were solidified after their first session. James was bitter and resentful toward authority figures, and saw Yun
Jin as yet another person who would not understand his situation. James's
highest level of education was 8th grade; he had married at 17, had four
children, and had not held a job for longer than 2 months over 5 years. He
was receiving welfare and supported his growing children with a sporadic
and unreliable income. He scoffed at Yun Jin's attempts to get at the root
of his inability to hold a job. Yun Jin offered to talk to James the following
week and gave him a list of businesses to contact in the meantime. She
asked him to bring in his resume and list of references. After his departure,
Yun Jin reflected on her perceptions of James, realizing uncomfortably that
she had made many assumptions about him (e.g., that he was poor, un-
dereducated, defensive, and unmotivated). She wondered whether he was
abusing substances, and if this could be the reason for his recent job history. Even though James said that he had never even used tobacco, Yun Jin
assumed he had lied.

     Yun Jin contrasted her impressions of James with her own socioethnic
background, realizing that education, economic success, and prestige
were highly valued, not only in her culture of origin, but also among her
immediate family members. Yun Jin wondered how her own status as an
educated, upper-middle-class Asian American female affected her perceptions of James and his situation. She knew that her tendency was to view
her client as lazy and unmotivated and to point to flaws in James as the root
of his current problem. She had not explored his values, experiences, or
worldview, or considered the larger, systemic issues that might have played
a role in his situation. During their next session, Yun Jin asked James to describe his experiences with prejudice and discrimination: "In what ways do
people make assumptions about you based upon your appearance and income?" James looked surprised at the question, but commented that people
thought that he was lazy. He went on to explain that his wife had been in
a car accident 6 years earlier and thus was unable to work full-time or do
much around the house. Consequently, James had assumed many household duties, making it difficult for him also to juggle full-time work. As he
described the physical and emotional stress of caring for four children and
his wife, and working odd jobs, Yun Jin listened intently, noting the stark

contrast between the James she was now becoming familiar with and the James she had first perceived in her office the previous week. She knew that in order to help James, she would have to be aware of the ways in which her values and worldview affected her ability to act as a multiculturally competent counselor.

Guideline 6: Agents of Organizational Change

Some have argued that the psychologist's role is more than that of a counselor and educator and includes acting as an agent of organizational change. It is imperative not only that we engage in interdisciplinary dialogues with ethicists and social movement scholars with the hopes of revealing avenues for further social intervention, but also that we challenge mainstream assumptions and values that serve only to propagate injustice and stifle change (Vera & Speight, 2003). In order to do so, we first must acknowledge the contribution of social class to issues concerning the mental health care profession (APA, 2003). In the following vignette, the contribution of one psychologist to the development of culture-centered organizations is described.

Integrating Solution to Counseling Needs: The Case of Martin

After working in Manhattan for 20 years, Martin decided to move his practice to the South Bronx. He wanted to begin addressing some of the issues affecting the youth of the poor, largely Hispanic neighborhood, such as drugs, gang violence, teen pregnancy, sexually transmitted diseases, and school dropouts. Martin rented a small office and posted many signs advertising his services. Yet, after a month, he still had received no phone calls and no drop-ins. Martin was dismayed—he could see the problems many of the neighborhood's youth faced, but still no one desired counseling. Martin soon realized that he was attacking the issues of social class and race/ethnicity as if they were two disparate pieces of a person's identity. The neighborhood's youth would not approach him, he realized, because mental health care was most likely not a family norm, nor was it a culturally accepted method of self-care for many of the poor, Hispanic families. In fact, Martin realized that seeking out mental health services might be seen as a sign of weakness and moral failing. In order to infiltrate the community while respecting the social class and cultural considerations unique to the neighborhood, Martin sought grant money to open a clinic inside a local high school, where he could work alongside a nurse to provide services to local adolescents. In this way, the youth easily could be referred to Martin for services when visiting the nurse for other reasons. Conceptualizing the problems of the neighborhood as functions of social class and race/ethnicity opened Martin's eyes to more integrative solutions. Martin's plan made mental health care services available to the neighborhood's teenagers with the same immediacy as other health care. In addition, working with other health care professionals helped break down some of the stigma associated with mental health care and instigated interdisciplinary dialogues about change in the community.

CONCLUSION

Unfortunately, the dearth of literature related to issues of social class leaves those psychologists who wish to incorporate social class considerations into their work with little to no guidance for how to do so. This chapter outlined the Multicultural Guidelines (APA, 2003) as a structural framework to provide useful and concrete ideas for psychologists to deal with the social class issues of their clients. These ideas range from increasing individuals' awareness of the impact of social class issues in counseling interactions to changing the policies and practices currently in use with specific social class groups. Recommendations also include integrating social class considerations into psychological education and research, an area where social class largely has been neglected as a cultural construct. Furthermore, the case vignettes illustrate the concept of social class with varied ethnic and cultural groups, and thus highlight the importance of considering intersections between social class and other cultural factors when conducting various types of psychological work.

Although the ideas and cases presented in this chapter are simply a first step in increasing individuals' awareness of social class issues within the practice of multicultural psychology, concrete knowledge of how to apply the Guidelines to issues of social class is likely to initiate a generation of further research and theory. Increasing awareness around social class issues and their incorporation into psychological education, research, practice, and advocacy are important steps in furthering the psychology profession's commitment to multicultural recognition and competence.

REFERENCES

American Psychological Association. (2003). Guidelines on multicultural education, training, research, practice, and organizational change for psychologists. *American Psychologist, 58*, 377–402.

Constantine, M. G. (2002). The intersection of race, ethnicity, gender, and social class in counseling: Examining selves in cultural contexts. *Journal of Multicultural Counseling and Development, 30*, 210–215.

Fox, D. R. (2003). Awareness is good, but action is better. *The Counseling Psychologist, 31,* 299–304.

Harley, D. A., Jolivette, K., McCormick, K., & Tice, K. (2002). Race, class, and gender: A constellation of positionalities with implications for counseling. *Journal of Multicultural Counseling and Development, 30,* 216–238.

Leathers, L. (2004, July). Education, social class, and feminist therapy. In S. R. Ali (Chair), *Feminist therapy and social class across disciplines.* Symposium conducted at the 112th annual meeting of the American Psychological Association, Honolulu, HI.

Liu, W. M. (2002). The social class-related experiences of men: Integrating theory and practice. *Professional Psychology: Research and Practice, 33,* 355–360.

Liu, W. M., Ali, S. R., Soleck, G., Hopps, J., Dunston, K., & Pickett, T., Jr. (2004). Using social class in counseling psychology research. *Journal of Counseling Psychology, 51,* 3–18.

Liu, W. M., Soleck, G., Hopps, J., Dunston, K, & Pickett, T., Jr. (2004). A new framework to understand social class in counseling: The social class worldview model and modern classism theory. *Journal of Multicultural Counseling and Development 32,* 95–122.

Vera, E. M., & Speight, S. L. (2003). Multicultural competence, social justice, and counseling psychology: Expanding our roles. *The Counseling Psychologist, 31,* 253–272.

13

Religious and Spiritual Issues

Mary A. Fukuyama,
Carlos Hernandez,
and Shari Robinson

"Truth is one; sages speak of it by many names."
(Vedic scriptures, cited in
Cousineau, 2003, p. xvi)

A keystone for multicultural work is to understand the nature of paradox, which is holding a position that might appear to be contradictory, but in fact is true and necessary to make the whole truth. For example, cultural diversity discussions invariably include exploring differences and identifying similarities. Nowhere is this principle more important than in the subject of religion and spirituality. Religious diversity means acknowledging that there are truths to be found in all religious worldviews. Huston Smith, Professor Emeritus on world religion, states, "Beware of the differences that blind us to the unity that binds us" (cited in Cousineau, 2003, p. 36). Whereas we will discuss differences in religious and spiritual expressions primarily through a racial/ethnic lens in this chapter, we also affirm that there is "unity in diversity," and we value this human connection in the search for meaning and purpose in life.

In this chapter we will (1) provide definitions of religion and spirituality applicable to psychotherapy with people of color, (2) address applications of the APA Multicultural Guidelines (APA, 2003) to this topic, (3) discuss two selected ethnic cultural groups and provide case vignettes, (4) list strategies for developing religious and spiritual competencies, and (5) highlight religious trends. Throughout the chapter we will provide several personal narratives (indicated by the author's initials) that share our personal and professional experiences.

DEFINITIONS OF RELIGION AND SPIRITUALITY

Religion is described as an organized system of faith, worship, cumulative traditions, and prescribed rituals (Worthington, 1989). Paul Tillich (1964), a 20th-century theologian, described religion as the depth dimension of human existence. He said, "Religion is the aspect of depth in the totality of human spirit. . . . Religious aspects point to that which is ultimate, infinite, unconscious in man's [sic] spiritual life. Religion, in the largest and most basic sense of the word, is ultimate concern" (p. 7). The terms *religion* and *spirituality* often are used interchangeably, each with its own nuance. *Spirituality* is defined as the human need for meaning and value in life and the desire for relationship with a transcendent power (Clinebell, 1995). Deriving from the Latin root *spiritus*, which means breath, spirituality refers to the essence of life or the life force. We like the metaphor that religion is like a cup, and spirituality is the essence held within (Artress, 1995). In cultural terms, religion is also a container that shapes social group identity and customs.

The United States is a religiously diverse nation, with perhaps over 2,000 identifiable expressions of religion and spiritual paths (Creedon, 1998). Demographic trends through immigration continue to influence the diversification of U.S. religious life (Hoge, 1996). Although culturally and religiously diverse, the "dominant paradigm" in the United States continues to be Judeo-Christian, with an emphasis on Christianity. For example, national holidays tend to include Christmas, and the weekly "day of rest" tends to be Sunday (whereas Fridays and Saturdays are predominately the days of worship in Islam and Judaism, respectively). Religious affiliation is an important component of cultural identity. The challenge for counselors is to be comfortable in their own cultural and religious identity and open to working with and understanding different cultural and religious worldviews (Frame, 2003; Fukuyama & Sevig, 1999; Miller, 2002).

APPLICATIONS OF THE APA MULTICULTURAL GUIDELINES

Guideline 1: Attitudes Toward Religious Beliefs and Values

We begin with attention to personal awareness. Most multicultural diversity training begins with the adage "counselor, know thyself." We have observed that many people are drawn to the mental health professions out of a desire to help others, a value also embraced by most religions. It is not unusual for mental health professionals to have religious backgrounds, whether or not they are currently religiously active. In some instances, mental health professionals may have "religious wounds" or disillusionment with organized religion. It is important for counselors or psychologists to be clear about their biases, both "for and against" religion. Just as counselors may have hidden prejudices related to race/ethnicity, they also may have unconscious negative attitudes toward various expressions of religion and spirituality. It is important that these attitudes be examined and negative stereotyping unlearned.

Zinnbauer and Pargament (2000) suggested that there are four world-views that counselors may hold toward religious beliefs and values. The *rejectionist position* is antagonistic toward religion, the *exclusivist* believes in absolute religious beliefs and values, the *constructivist* sees beliefs as socially constructed by the individual, and the *pluralist* recognizes a spiritual absolute with multiple interpretations. The most compatible orientations for effective work on religious or spiritual issues are the constructivist and pluralist orientations. The least compatible are rejectionist and exclusivist (i.e., the belief that there is only one right way).

Guideline 2: Connection Between Ethnicity and Religion

Professionals are asked to expand their knowledge of ethnic cultural groups. Likewise, the understanding of religious worldviews, historical contexts, and religious identity development are important dimensions for consideration. For example, theories of faith and spiritual development may parallel racial/ethnic identity development. Religious groups also suffer from persecution (e.g., anti-Semitism) and may align with the minority experience in the United States. Concurrently, churches may be protective against the forces of oppression, such as racism, particularly evident in the role of the African American church (Frame & Williams, 1996).

New immigrant groups may gravitate toward congregations of their own ethnicity and language, for example, Korean Baptist, Chinese Methodist, Spanish Catholic, Guatemalan Pentecostal, and Iraqi-Muslim. As social institutions, organized religions serve as an important source of social support and order during times of transition. Even second- or third-generation members of ethnic groups may prefer to worship in congregations of those ethnicities (Cimino & Lattin, 1998). Paraphrasing Dr. Martin Luther King, Jr., it has been said that Sunday worship may be one of the most segregated hours in American society. Ethnicity and religion are strongly intertwined (Fukuyama & Sevig, 2002).

Guideline 3: Examination of Religious and Spiritual Issues

Focusing on incorporating constructs of multiculturalism into psychological education, Guideline 3 recommends that psychologists receive training in multicultural counseling competencies to become skilled practitioners. Casas,

Ponterotto, and Guiterrez (1986) asserted that individuals who are not "trained or competent to work with culturally diverse clients should be regarded as unethical" (p. 347). The primary focus traditionally has been on the cognitive mode of teaching and learning, which usually does not include behavioral or spiritual aspects of promoting self-awareness. There tends to be little emphasis on how the personal lives of counselors, which includes religious and spiritual identity, influences their professional competence (Toporek & Reza, 2001). Recently, mental health professionals have begun to investigate the interface of spirituality with the helping professions. There appears to be a growing interest in spirituality intersecting with professional psychology, evidenced by an increase in publications and conferences on the topic (Powers, 2005).

Now the question is no longer "should spirituality and religion be included" in professional psychology, but rather "how to include it" using a multicultural competent model or framework (Pedersen, Draguns, Lonner, & Trimble, 2002). Spirituality has a natural home within multicultural counseling and psychology, and clinicians who aspire to be multiculturally responsible need to become familiar with spiritual and religious diversity (Pedersen et al., 2002).

However, traditional mental health educators have hesitated to examine religious and spiritual content, due partly to an emphasis on science and partly to specializations in higher education. Such compartmentalization unfortunately limits the scope of understanding of the intersections of religion, culture, race, and ethnicity. By incorporating discussions that are religious and spiritual in nature, a broader, more holistic view is presented. Different ways of "knowing" the truth also are accessed, including intuitive, philosophical, and existential perspectives (Fukuyama, Murphy, & Siahpoush, 2003). Recently, coursework has been developed to examine religious and spiritual issues in counseling (Fukuyama & Sevig, 1997; Ingersoll, 1997; O'Conner, 2004; Patterson, 2000). Examples of course topics have included spiritual worldviews and development, synergy of multiculturalism and spirituality, spirituality and health, science and religion, healthy and unhealthy expressions of spirituality, counseling issues, spiritual interventions, and ethical concerns (Fukuyama & Sevig, 1999).

The traditional rift between religion and science is being bridged by interdisciplinary initiatives that encourage dialogue and engagement. New discoveries in quantum physics have lent credibility to wisdom from mystical traditions (Capra, 1999). Academic centers for the study of spirituality and health have focused on the intersection of science, faith, and healing (Levin, 2001). Many of these resources are accessible through the Internet. Consider the following examples: The George Washington Institute for Spirituality and Health (http://www.gwish.org/) was established in May 2001 as a leading organization on educational and clinical issues related to spirituality and health. Similarly, the Center for Spirituality and Health at the University of Florida was established to promote meaningful dialogue on these issues (http://spiritualityandhealth.ufl.edu). Harold Koenig also has reviewed research in this area through the Center for Spirituality, Theology and Health at Duke University (http://www.dukespiritualityandhealth.org/scientists/hkoenig.html).

Guideline 4: Incorporation of Religious and Spiritual Domains in Research

As multiculturalism influences research, the topics of religion and spirituality may be incorporated into other sociopsychological dimensions of study. Research projects that include religious and spiritual domains are gaining recognition (Koenig, 1997; Koenig, McCullough, & Larson, 2001). Guideline 4 speaks to the importance, especially for practitioners, of conducting culture-centered psychological research, specifically outcome-based and process research (Borgen, 1992). The literature suggests more emphasis should be placed on collaborative efforts between leaders in the field of psychology, practitioners, and members of the community. For example, an innovative research project could be developed on how African American churches in the Black community offer therapeutic support for their congregations (McRae, Thompson, & Cooper, 1999; Queener & Martin, 2001). Having "hands-on" experience in the Black community and establishing relationships with religious leaders will provide access and credibility for practitioners to learn firsthand how spirituality and religion intersect with the therapeutic process (Burke, Chauvin, & Miranti, 2005).

A second area of research is assessment. A multitude of measurement instruments have been developed to examine spirituality and religiosity (Friedman & MacDonald, 2002; Hill & Hood, 1999). The professional disciplines of transpersonal psychology (Association of Transpersonal Psychology), the psychological study of religion (Division 36, APA), and spirituality and values in counseling (Association for Spiritual, Ethical, and Religious Values in Counseling, [ASERVIC]), provide excellent resources. However, this is still a relatively new area of inquiry, and the field lacks consistency. Additionally, we are somewhat cautious in endorsing research on spirituality per se. The nature of spirituality may defy an analytical approach. Consider the following quote from a Celtic spirituality theologian:

> The soul was never meant to be seen completely with the brightness or with too much clarity. The soul is always more at home in a light, which has a hospitality to shadow. . . . Now in modern life, we have a neon kind of consciousness and much of the spiritual world is now completely pervaded with the language of psychology, and too often the language of psychology has a neon kind of clarity to it that is not able to retrieve or open up the depth and density of the world of soul. (O'Donohue, 1996)

Guideline 5: Interventions Sensitive to Religious and Spiritual Dimensions

Developing culturally appropriate skills for working with ethnic/racial groups is essential for competent therapy. Developing interventions that are sensitive to religious and spiritual dimensions continues to be refined in the field. A task force for ASERVIC, a member association of the American Counseling Association, developed a list of counseling competencies for working with religious and spiritual issues. The guidelines for spiritual competencies ask counselors, in part, to be able to:

1. Describe religious and spiritual beliefs and practices in a cultural context
2. Engage in self-exploration
3. Demonstrate sensitivity to and acceptance of a variety of religious and/or spiritual expressions in the client's communication
4. Assess the degree to which clients' beliefs aid and/or hinder problem solving
5. Identify the limits of one's understanding of a client's spiritual expression (Cashwell & Young, 2005).

There may be both explicit and implicit dimensions of spirituality found in psychotherapy. Addressing spiritual concerns in therapy requires skills that attend to subtle and symbolic language, as well as listening to explicit stories (Griffith & Griffith, 2002). Engaging in dialogue about spiritual matters is a delicate process, sometimes facilitated by use of metaphors (Griffith & Griffith, 2002) and dreamwork (Taylor, 1993).

Guideline 6: Protection of the Sacred and Freedom of Religion

Guideline 6 asserts the need for psychologists to be key players in promoting and facilitating organizational change and policy development. As leaders in the field and in our community, we are in influential positions to effect change in education, research, and practice. An innovative step toward developing frameworks and models for multicultural organizational development is found in the research conducted by Toporek and Reza (2001), who expanded Sue and colleagues' (1982) original model of multicultural counseling standards and competencies. Asserting a need for integration of the individual (personal) and institutional levels in a model of multicultural competence, the Multicultural Counseling Competency Assessment and Planning model suggests that culture-centered change include three domains: affective, cognitive, and behavioral learning. One limitation of the model is that it overlooked the spiritual domain.

Some organizations and corporations have recognized spirituality and values in the workplace. Another area for exploration is building bridges between professional organizations to enhance collaboration. For example, I (M.F.) have had meaningful exchanges with hospital chaplains on themes of cultural diversity in health care (Anderson & Fukuyama, 2004). Interfaith initiatives also are needed. According to Cimino and Lattin (1998), "Rather than spark interfaith conflict, American religious pluralism can defuse tension. With so many faith groups interacting in the public square, tolerance—if not always interfaith understanding—makes more sense than religious warfare" (p. 188).

We offer two caveats when considering organizational change. First, it is important to retain separation of church and state. Current events suggest that religion has merged into the political mainstream, and this is of great concern to many U.S. citizens. Conservative politicians seem to push toward the evolvement of a theocracy, not the democracy envisioned by our founders. It is essential to protect freedom of religion as well as freedom of the individual. Second, approaching religion and spirituality through traditional academic endeavors runs the risk of diminishing the Sacred. As the Celtic spiritual tradition quoted above suggests, a "neon kind of consciousness" may be antithetical to understanding this depth dimension of humanity.

ETHNIC CULTURAL GROUPS AND CASE VIGNETTES

We will summarize briefly in this section some empirical and conceptual information that is relevant to the themes of religion, spirituality, and the mental health of people of color. Brief summaries from Latina/o and African American perspectives will be presented in preparation for a discussion of the clinical case vignettes that are included. (Names and details have been changed to protect the confidentiality of the clients.) We focus on examples from these specific ethnic groups as "populations of convenience" from our clinical experiences, recognizing that it is impossible to fairly represent all groups of color, given the limitations of a chapter.

Latina/o Perspectives

Most of the Hispanic/Latina/o population is Catholic, although Latina/os practice many world religions. Missionary efforts in Latin America have exposed Latina/os to many of the mainline Protestant denominations, Pentecostals, Jehovah's Witnesses, and various types of evangelical fundamentalist religious groups (Falicov, 1999). One also can find Latina/os who are of the Jewish faith or engage in indigenous spiritual practices. Religion traditionally has been an integral part of the Hispanic/Latina/o culture and way of life.

It is important for mental health professionals to be aware that most Hispanic/Latina/os have little or no experience in seeking help from therapists. They are more likely to seek assistance from a priest, a physician, or a family member (Burke et al., 2005).

According to a Latina/o handbook on health, illness is perceived as a result of the following:

> 1) psychological states, such as embarrassment, envy, fear/fright, excessive worry, turmoil in the family, improper behavior, or violations of moral or ethical codes; 2) environmental, natural conditions such as bad air, germs, dust, excess of cold or heat, bad food, or poverty; and 3) supernatural causes, such as malevolent spirits, bad luck, witchcraft, or living enemies (believed to cause harm out of vengeance or envy). (Centro San Bonifacio, 1997, p. i)

Spiritual beliefs are intertwined with physical symptoms, psychological problems, and healing. Some spiritual practices are considered part of secret societies, and Latina/o clients are not likely to talk to their therapists about rituals and beliefs that involve communing with spirits (Zea, Mason, & Murguia, 2000). At the same time, Latina women who have psychic abilities may be promoted in status, for example, within Cuban American communities in their work as mediums (Espin, 1997). Another example of a hybrid Latina/o religious system is found in *Santeria*, which literally means the "worship of saints." It is a mixture of Catholic and Yoruba beliefs, and is practiced in the Caribbean region, including some of the Latina/o populations in south Florida. It has been described as a magico-religious system that emerged from cultural contact and struggle of West African (Yoruba) enslaved persons and the Spanish-speaking Roman Catholic missionaries. The Africans transformed the forced worship of the Catholic saints into the veiled worship of their spirit ancestors (Gonzalez-Wippler, 1992). *Santeria* is largely an oral tradition, and one's initiation and its practices generally are kept secret from society. However, it is an earth-based religion. Nature is seen as a manifestation of God, and a pantheon of gods are worshiped, such as *Yemaya* (ocean, maternity), *Chango* (fire, passion, joy, victory), and *Oshun* (river water, love, marriage). People may fear curses or malevolent spirits.

Reactions to the practice of *Santeria* are mixed among Hispanics and Latina/os. One of the authors (C.H.) recalls his introduction to *Santeria*: As a young boy, I heard stories from my Cuban mother that *Santeria* was a mystical religious practice that was to be respected and feared. It was presented as a religious practice that was different from Catholicism and one that could be used to cast spells. I remember my mother being afraid of *Santeria,* and she would protect us from the spell casting practice of the *Santero*. For example, I was told to avoid eating or drinking at the home of someone thought to be practicing *Santeria,* to minimize the possibility of digesting any potion that may have been put in the food or drink. In addition, I was to avoid leaving any personal effects, such as hair or nail samples, or articles of clothing. The hair, nails, and clothing samples could be used to personalize the spell. The belief was that for the spell to work, it had to be either digested or come in contact with one's skin, such as through cologne or perfumes. It is important for health care providers to be aware of these beliefs and to avoid pathologizing the client until further clinical evaluations can be performed.

These previous examples from the Latina/o culture reflect diverse beliefs about the causes of illness and the necessary treatments, both physically and spiritually (see also Chapter 4, this volume). The process of assessing spiritual and religious beliefs may include beliefs in spirit possession, spirit guides, and rituals for healing. Mental health professionals may need to refer to and/ or collaborate with spiritual and religious leaders on such matters.

The Intersection Between Religion and Sexual Orientation: The Case of Hector. The following case study illustrates the intersection that can be found between religion and sexual orientation among the Hispanic/Latina/o population.

> Hector was a 19-year-old Cuban male sophomore majoring in engineering. With the encouragement of his resident assistant, Hector came to the university counseling center. During the intake, Hector revealed that he was losing his ability to concentrate in school and was performing below standard. Hector also disclosed that he was tired most of the time, his appetite and activity levels had declined, and he was missing classes. During the intake, Hector was guarded, but engaged. General exploration of Hector's psychosocial profile revealed that he was the only male child of four siblings, identified as Hispanic and Christian, and had been raised in the United States. The client reported limited dating experience and, upon further inquiry, revealed his confusion over his sexual orientation. He reported having feelings of attraction toward male friends throughout high school, but said that he "could not be gay" due to the fact that he wanted to get married and have kids. As the only male, he had an obligation to continue the family name. He reported that his family would disown him and that the Bible states that "homosexuality is a sin."

Hector's confusion and exploration of his sexuality are common in a college setting, a time that provides opportunities to individuate and to encounter different cultures, activities, and situations that may challenge previously held assumptions, beliefs, and values. He appeared to be dealing with issues of sexual orientation, homophobia, and conflicting cultural and religious beliefs and values that were affecting his academic performance. In working with Hector, it was important not to label his sexual attraction to men until further exploration and assessment into his same-sex attraction could be made. The helping professional needed to create a culturally sensitive environment from which Hector could explore and disclose feelings and thoughts that he might never have been able to share with another individual. In a label-free and nonjudgmental atmosphere, Hector was able to give meaning to his feelings. It was essential that Hector trust his therapist and know that he was supported through the self-exploration stage of the therapeutic process.

Over time, through psychoeducation, disputing negative stereotypes, and making friends in the LGBT community, Hector was able to integrate his sexual orientation with his cultural and religious views, which led him to feel more satisfied with himself and how he would navigate his world. It was important for the therapist to keep an open view toward his developing multiple identities, rather than try to assign him to a specific category (Fukuyama & Ferguson, 1999). For Hector, it was important to retain his ethnic identity while forming his sexual orientation. It was also helpful for him to realize that being a Christian was not antithetical to being gay (O'Neill & Ritter, 1992).

Many gay men and lesbians often search for spiritual and religious understanding and need a community of people who share and celebrate their faith. Unfortunately, many religious groups remain judgmental about homosexuality, with a few notable exceptions (Barret & Logan, 2002). For this reason, many gay men and lesbians reject pursuing a religious or spiritual life because of the negative comments and homophobia they feel from organized religion. On the other hand, support groups from diverse religious traditions are forming and can be accessed through the Internet (one website is http://www.iwgonline.org/links/).

According to APA's Multicultural Guidelines, mental health professionals need to recognize their own attitudes and beliefs regarding homosexuality, spirituality, and working with ethnic minorities. Before the therapeutic alliance can be achieved, the mental health professional must ensure that he or she is confident about the ability and willingness to work with diverse clients and a variety of presenting problems, and to avoid coming across as judgmental, biased, or discriminatory (see also Chapter 9, this volume). Barret and Logan (2002) have outlined several suggestions for practitioners who may encounter sexual orientation and religious issues in counseling:

1. Keep an open mind about religions and religious practices that are different from your own
2. Understand that LGBT individuals might be trying to heal from wounds left from religious oppression and rejections
3. Offer to meet with family members who may be struggling with similar issues

4. Find community resources such as supportive religious leaders to whom you can refer your clients
5. Recommend books, organizations, and religious activities that represent the diversity among religious and spiritual organizations that support LGBT individuals
6. Be an activist

African American Perspectives

African American worldviews include collectivistic and holistic values. This worldview redefines "self" as "extended-self," which includes family and community. It portrays community and elements of survival through collective strength. Nancy Boyd-Franklin (1989) has emphasized the importance of understanding the strengths in the African American extended family and support networks through Black churches. Black churches provide not only social support in the face of institutionalized oppression like racism, but also therapeutic responses through worship, prayer, catharsis, and validation of life experiences. Counselors may need to look to communities and shift definitions of clients from the individual to groups and families.

As discussed in Chapter 3, the counseling literature documents that a large percentage of African Americans affiliate with some kind of organized religion (Taylor, Chatters, Jayakody, & Levin, 1996) and ascribe to spiritual or religious beliefs. Because of this important emphasis on religion and spirituality, it is both ethical and sound clinical practice to acquire a deeper appreciation for African Americans' worldviews (Fuentes, Bartolomeo, & Nichols, 2001). According to Blaine and Crocker (1995), a primary coping mechanism for African Americans is their spirituality and religious affiliations. The role of the African American church has been identified as important to community, social justice, and family life. Other themes from African American spirituality concern issues of liberation and social justice (Frame & Williams, 1996; Morris & Robinson, 1996). These themes are reflected in music (gospel and rap) and in social movements, such as advocating for civil rights and elimination of racism. Frame and Williams (1996) suggested that counselors explore the role and importance of music as a form of personal expression, help clients to access community resources and extended family, and utilize culturally relevant metaphors and proverbs when appropriate.

Creation of a New Spiritual Identity: The Case of Angela. The following case study illustrates the intersection of the client's and counselor's religious faith systems, in working with a women presenting with a history of childhood abuse and religious wounding.

Angela was a 20-year-old African American single college sophomore. She had a prior history of self-injurious behavior, chronic depression, and disordered eating tendencies. She reported that she had low self-esteem, that her self-image was based on how others perceived her, and that she was a people-pleaser. She described being raised in an abusive home, where she and her older brother frequently witnessed their father physically and sexually abusing their mother, as well as physically abusing them. Angela's father was a Pentecostal pastor of a nondenominational church during the abusive years.

Although Angela considered herself a Christian, she believed she was not living up to her mother's or church's expectations. She felt conflicted about being a Christian and having normal college experiences that involved dating and going to parties. Angela felt an overwhelming guilt because she lost her virginity instead of waiting until marriage. Consequently, she believed she was no longer worthy to pray and ask for God's forgiveness. As a child, church was a place of refuge and comfort when her home life was so tumultuous. She reported that spirituality and religion had served as major sources of strength and had been one her primary coping mechanisms. Because she had not joined a local church and rarely attended services, she felt disconnected and spiritually empty. She said that she missed church and wished for a local ministry as a source of comfort, guidance, and support during a time that was filled with emotional and psychological pain. She continued to struggle with accepting forgiveness from herself and God, and consequently she continued to struggle with recurring depression.

For Angela not to have the church family as part of her coping mechanism created an emotional and spiritual disconnect that led to feelings of hopelessness and despair (McCullough, 1999). This contributed to serious clinical implications; there were multiple suicidal attempts that necessitated hospitalization. Angela was conflicted about preserving her spiritual identity from childhood and forsaking these same religious traditions and beliefs as a young person in college. Abuse by a parent with religious authority contributed to "religious wounding" (Judy, 1996).

Although Angela and I (S.R.) shared similar worldviews related to ethnicity and religious affiliations, it was important that Angela be seen as a "multicultural being." Counselor and client cultural heritage, racial identity development, gender socialization, and socioeconomic backgrounds become part of this "multicultural equation" involving all aspects of treatment from intake to termination (Arrendondo et al., 1996). Therefore, it was imperative to establish a working alliance that recognized and appreciated "within-group differences" and simultaneously affirmed her spiritual identity (Wolsko, Park, Judd, & Wittenbrink, 2000).

There were several concrete strategies employed with Angela to establish and build a working alliance (Teyber, 2000). The first strategy was to acknowledge the "resistance from within," that Angela had a healthy degree of cultural suspicion that created enough resistance that she felt uncomfortable with the therapeutic process and her discussion of personal and familial matters was inhibited (Boyd-Franklin, 1989). Therefore, it became important to demonstrate from the beginning that spirituality and religion were significant factors in the counseling process. It was acknowledged and processed how being in therapy went against her religious teachings. Angela needed to be empowered to create a healthy reframe that being in counseling did not convey a lack of faith or belief in God on her part and could be seen as accessing another resource and support base in times of crisis (Burke et al., 2005).

In our therapy sessions, we had many candid discussions that empowered Angela to begin creating her own spiritual identity based on her needs and values and not those of her parents. Another strategy in this area was to create a therapeutic relationship based on collaboration and mutuality, to demonstrate to Angela that she was not alone in this process, and that we were working collaboratively toward making positive and productive change. Although we shared the same racial and ethnic background, there were distinct differences in our life experiences (Neville & Mobley, 2001). The only way to address this "cultural misunderstanding and communication problem" was for me to intentionally gain a deeper understanding of her worldview, and not act as if I understood her because we both were African American women. In essence, this was the first strategy and perhaps most effective to alleviate the resistance and disconnect that initially were present in the therapeutic relationship. Angela was encouraged to share her perceptions of how it felt to be an African American student at a predominately White university and how she experienced acculturative stress as she attempted to integrate into the university culture. We talked about the importance of her finding a local church family, and the need for a spiritual "big brother or sister" for guidance and mentoring, especially in times of stress (Boyd-Franklin, 1989).

Several additional strategies were included: A focus of treatment was to facilitate healing from the psychological scars from the shame and guilt that originated in her family's religion (Burke et al., 2005). Second, a genogram was constructed to examine the role and dynamics of her church family back home (Boyd-Franklin, 1989). Third, Angela's mother was invited into two therapy sessions with the goal of acknowledging and respecting their intergenerational differences. Finally, the most important intervention was the acknowledgment and facilitation of her spiritual pain that was caused by unresolved guilt and her not having been raised in an idealized family. Angela was encouraged to participate in a mentoring relationship with a female professional who could provide her with career guidance and model a strong religious and spiritual background. It was also recommended that she join a

Black women's support group to provide opportunities to engage in racially sensitive dialogues, receive validation and strengthen her ethnic identity, and learn how to receive and give support on various topics that were pertinent to African American female students at her college.

STRATEGIES FOR
DEVELOPING RELIGIOUS AND SPIRITUAL COMPETENCIES

We recommend that counselors engage in both didactic and experiential learning. Students enrolled in a multicultural counseling course are encouraged to research topics related to religion and spirituality. We also offer the following activities that will expand awareness of religious and spiritual differences:

- Attend and observe religious or spiritual events that are different from your spiritual background or religious heritage. Examples include visiting a worship service at a church, mosque, or synagogue; attending an open 12-Step Program meeting.
- Participate in spiritually nurturing and/or developmental types of experiences (e.g., meditation, religious study, dream interpretation, or yoga or tai chi).
- Write a personal journal to develop personal awareness and insight into reactions.
- Attend relevant lectures, watch films, and read literature (e.g., James McBride, 1996).
- Take a class on comparative world religions and/or spirituality and health.
- Study indigenous healing practices (Moodley & West, 2005).

In addition, the following are intended to further clinical skills:

- Draw a genogram or community ecogram that incorporates spiritual/religious history and/or resources (Frame, 2003).
- Discuss with a supervisor possible clinical biases and/or countertransference issues.
- Consult with religious leaders (e.g., pastor, priest, rabbi, Imam, medicine man/woman).
- Practice use of metaphors (Griffith & Griffith, 2002) and/or do dreamwork (Taylor, 1993).
- Develop focusing skills (Gendlin, 1998).
- Adapt cognitive reframing for disputing dysfunctional religious beliefs (Propst, Ostrom, & Watkins, 1992).

Finally, we offer these selected websites that represent a mere sampling of the many resources on the topic of integrating spirituality and religion into therapy and health:

- Center for Mindfulness in Medicine, Health, and Society (http://www.umassmed.edu/cfm)
- Institute of Noetic Sciences (http://www.noetic.org)
- New Religious Movements (http://religiousmovements.lib.virginia.edu/home.htm)
- Ontario Consultants on Religious Tolerance (http://www.religioustolerance.org/)

RELIGIOUS TRENDS

A recent special report on religious trends in the United States published by *Newsweek* (Adler, 2005) highlighted the following phenomena: increased interest in direct communion with God, a steady decline in church attendance (45% of poll respondents said they attended church weekly), an increase in evangelical Protestantism, increasing culturally diverse expressions of religion as influenced by immigration patterns, and a shift toward more inclusiveness, that is, believing that there is more than one path to "salvation." Examples of diverse religious expressions included, Buddhism, Islam, Hindu, new religious sects, Paganism, and eco-theology.

Poll respondents were more likely to describe themselves as spiritual than as religious (79% vs. 64%). Consulting with religious experts and leaders, the reporters found that "spirituality, the impulse to seek communion with the Divine, is thriving" (p. 50). According to Alan Wolfe, director of the Boisi Center for Religion and American Public Life at Boston College, American faiths have been characterized by creativity and individualism; "rather than being about a god who commands you, it's about finding a religion that empowers you" (p. 52).

In addition, almost all aspects of society have been affected by technology, and religion is no exception. The Internet offers a variety of websites and listservs in which religion and spirituality can be explored. Information about the world's religions can be accessed easily. Satellite television and the cable industry have created another platform for TV ministries to reach around the world. Many followers choose to watch a church service or mass in the privacy of their homes. For the elderly, disabled, or infirm, this form of "religious ministering" provides an outlet for religious affiliation and practice, but may cause social isolation because personal contact is limited. Spanish broadcasting stations make religious programming accessible to Spanish-only or bilingual individuals. The impact of TV ministries on traditional places of worship is not fully known. What is known is that TV ministries are a visible and influential part of popular culture (Cimino & Lattin, 1998).

Another phenomenon of religious and spiritual worship is the Megachurch. Huge memberships, some of more than 3,000 people, characterize these churches. Often Megachurches use an array of media (Internet, radio, and cable) to project their religious messages. Cimino and Lattin (1998) suggested that "Megachurches embody the consumerism, eclecticism, and the conservatism shaping the religious future. They are the evangelical answer to Home Depot" (p. 56).

Helping professionals should be aware of these religious trends in their community so they can assist clients in deciding their preferences for forms of worship and levels of religious participation. For some, religious and spiritual affiliation can be a source of empowerment, healing, affirmation, and contentment that can aid the therapeutic process and the client's sense of well-being. It is also important to keep in mind that religious or spiritual participation in any form, or a lack of it, can be associated with psychological distress (e.g., depression, isolation, rejection, guilt, anxiety, stress).

CONCLUSION

Spiritual issues may be both explicit and implicit in counseling (Fukuyama & Sevig, 1999). It is important that counselors recognize the complexity of the individual and social context, which includes social, political, educational, spiritual, psychological, and physical health factors. If the therapist understands and explores how these factors affect the client's life, the therapeutic process ultimately can enhance the client's well-being and ability to cope with pressures and stressors (Kelly, 1995). Including spirituality in the counseling relationship can make the process more human and real for both the counselor and client. Embracing diversity culturally, religiously, and spiritually enhances a holistic approach to counseling persons of color and illuminates the road to finding "unity in diversity."

REFERENCES

Adler, J. (2005, September 5). In search of the spiritual—special report, *Newsweek*, pp. 46–64.

American Psychological Association. (2003). Guidelines on multicultural education, training, research, practice, and organizational change for psychologists. *American Psychologist, 58*, 377–402.

Anderson, R. G., & Fukuyama, M. A. (Eds). (2004). *Ministry in the spiritual and cultural diversity of health care: Increasing the competency of chaplains.* Binghamton, NY: Haworth Press.

Arrendondo, P., Toporek, R., Brown, S., Jones, J., Locke, D., Sanchez, J., & Stadler, H. (1996). Operationalization of multicultural counseling competencies. *Journal of Multicultural Counseling and Development, 24,* 42–48.

Artress, L. (1995). *Walking a sacred path: Rediscovering the labyrinth as a spiritual tool.* New York: Riverhead Books.

Barret, B., & Logan, C. (2002). *Counseling gay men and lesbians: A practice primer.* Pacific Grove, CA: Brooks/Cole.

Blaine, B., & Crocker, J. (1995). Religious, race, and psychological well-being: Exploring social psychological mediators. *Personality and Social Psychology Bulletin, 21,* 1031–1041.

Borgen, F. H. (1992). Expanding scientific paradigms. In S. D. Brown & R. W. Lent (Eds.), *Handbook of counseling psychology* (2nd ed., pp. 111–139). New York: Wiley.

Boyd-Franklin, N. (1989). *Black families in therapy: A multi-systems approach.* New York: Guilford Press.

Burke, M. T., Chauvin, J. C. & Miranti, J. G. (2005). *Religious and spiritual issues in counseling. Applications across diverse populations.* New York: Brunner-Routledge.

Capra, F. (1999). *The tao of physics.* Boston: Shambhala.

Casas, J. M., Ponterotto, J. G., & Guiterrez, J. M. (1986). An ethical indictment of counseling, research and training: The cross-cultural perspectives. *Journal of Counseling and Development, 64,* 347–349.

Cashwell, C. S., & Young, J. S. (2005). *Integrating spirituality and religion into counseling: A guide to competent practice.* Alexandria, VA: American Counseling Association.

Centro San Bonifacio, Erie Family Health Center. (1997). *Nuestra cultura, nuestra salud: A handbook on Latin American health beliefs and practices.* University of Illinois at Chicago.

Cimino, R., & Lattin, D. (1998). *Shopping for faith: American religion in the new millennium.* San Francisco: Jossey-Bass.

Clinebell, H. (1995). *Counseling for spiritually empowered wholeness: A hope-centered approach.* New York: Haworth Pastoral Press.

Cousineau, P. (2003). *The way things are: Conversations with Huston Smith on the spiritual life.* Berkeley: University of California Press.

Creedon, J. (1998, July–August). God with a million faces. *Utne Reader,* pp. 42–48.

Espin, O. M. (1997). *Latina realities: Essays on healing, migration, and sexuality.* Boulder, CO: Westview.

Falicov, C. J. (1999). Religion and spiritual folk traditions in immigrant families: Therapeutic resources with Latinos. In F. Walsh (Ed.), *Spiritual resources in family therapy* (pp.104–120). New York: Guilford Press.

Frame, M. W. (2003). *Integrating religion and spirituality into counseling: A comprehensive approach.* Pacific Grove, CA: Brooks/Cole.

Frame, M. W., & Williams, C. B. (1996). Counseling African Americans: Integrating spirituality in therapy. *Counseling and Values, 41,* 16–28.

Friedman, H. L., & MacDonald, D. A. (2002). *Approaches to transpersonal measurement and assessment.* San Francisco: Transpersonal Institute.

Fuentes, J. N., Bartolomeo, M., & Nichols, C. M. (2001). Future research directions in the study of counselor multicultural competency. *Journal of Multicultural Counseling and Development, 29,* 5–12.

Fukuyama, M. A., & Ferguson, A. D. (1999). Lesbian, gay, and bisexual people of color: Understanding cultural complexity and managing multiple oppressions. In R. M. Perez, K. A. DeBord, & K. J. Bieschke (Eds.), *Handbook of counseling and psychotherapy with lesbian, gay, and bisexual clients* (pp. 81–105). Washington, DC: American Psychological Association.

Fukuyama, M., Murphy, M., & Siahpoush, F. (2003). Weaving multicultural and humanistic perspectives into transpersonal education: Bridging the gaps. *The Humanistic Psychologist, 31,* 182–200.

Fukuyama, M. & Sevig, T. (1997). Spiritual issues in counseling: A new course. *Counselor Education and Supervision, 36,* 233–244.

Fukuyama, M. A. & Sevig, T. D. (1999). *Integrating spirituality into multicultural counseling.* Thousand Oaks, CA: Sage.

Fukuyama, M. A., & Sevig, T. D. (2002). Spirituality in counseling across cultures: Many rivers to the sea. In P. B. Pedersen, J. G. Draguns, W. J. Lonner, & J. E. Trimble (Eds.), *Counseling across cultures* (5th ed., pp. 273–295). Thousand Oaks, CA: Sage.

Gendlin, E. T. (1998). *Focusing-oriented psychotherapy: A manual of the experiential method.* New York: Guilford Press.

Gonzalez-Wippler, M. (1992). *The Santeria experience.* St. Paul, MN: Llewellyn.

Griffith, J. L., & Griffith, M. E. (2002). *Encountering the sacred in psychotherapy: How to talk with people about their spiritual lives.* New York: Guilford Press.

Hill, P. C., & Hood, R. W. (Eds.). (1999). *Measures of religiosity.* Birmingham, AL: Religious Education Press.

Hoge, D. (1996). Religion in America: The demographics of belief and affiliation. In E. P. Shafranske (Ed.), *Religion and the clinical practice of psychology* (pp. 21–41). Washington, DC: American Psychological Association.

Ingersoll, R. E. (1997). Teaching a course on counseling and spirituality. *Counselor Education and Supervision, 36,* 224–232.

Judy, D. H. (1996). Transpersonal psychotherapy with religious persons. In B. W. Scotton, A. B. Chinen, & J. R. Battista (Eds.), *Textbook of transpersonal psychiatry and psychology* (pp. 293–301). New York: Basic Books.

Kelly, E. W., Jr. (1995). *Spirituality and religion in counseling and psychotherapy: Diversity in theory and practice.* Alexandria, VA: American Counseling Association.

Koenig, H. G. (1997). *Is religion good for your health? The effects of religion on physical and mental health.* Binghamton, NY: Haworth Press.

Koenig, H. G., McCullough, M. E., & Larson, D. B. (2001). *Handbook of religion and health.* New York: Oxford University Press.

Levin, J. (2001). *God, faith, and health: Exploring the spirituality–healing connection.* New York: Wiley.

McBride, J. (1996). *The color of water: A Black man's tribute to his White mother.* New York: Riverhead Books.

McCullough, M. E. (1999). Research on religion-accommodative counseling: Review and meta-analysis. *Journal of Counseling Psychology, 46,* 92–98.

McRae, M. B., Thompson, D. A., & Cooper, S. (1999). Black churches as therapeutic groups. *Journal of Multicultural Counseling and Development, 27,* 207–220.

Miller, G. (2002). *Incorporating spirituality in counseling and psychotherapy: Theory and technique.* New York: Wiley.

Moodley, R., & West, W. (Eds.). (2005). *Integrating traditional healing practices into counseling and psychotherapy.* Thousand Oaks, CA: Sage.

Morris, J. R., & Robinson, D. T. (1996). Community and Christianity in the Black church. *Counseling and Values, 41,* 59–69.

Neville, H. A., & Mobley, M. (2001). Social identities in contexts: An ecological model of multicultural counseling psychology processes. *Counseling Psychologist, 29,* 471–486.

O'Conner, M. (2004). A course in spiritual dimensions of counseling: Continuing the discussion. *Counseling and Values, 48,* 224–240.

O'Donohue, J. (1996) *Anam cara: Wisdom from the Celtic world.* Tape 1, "Your solitude is luminous." Audiotapes produced by Sounds True Audio, 735 Walnut, Boulder CO 80302, ISBN 1-56455-376-0, Order F039 800-333-9185

O'Neill, C., & Ritter, K. (1992). *Coming out within: Stages of spiritual awakening for lesbians and gay men.* New York: HarperSanFrancisco.

Patterson, J. (2000). Spiritual issues in family therapy: A graduate-level course. *Journal of Marital and Family Therapy, 26,* 199–210.

Pedersen, P. B., Draguns, J. G., Lonner, W. J., & Trimble, J. E. (Eds.). (2002). *Counseling across cultures* (5th ed.). Thousands Oaks, CA: Sage.

Powers, R. (2005). Counseling and spirituality: A historical review. *Counseling and Values, 49,* 217–225.

Propst, L. R., Ostrom, R, & Watkins, P. (1992). Comparative efficacy of religious and nonreligious cognitive-behaviroal therapy for the treatment of clinical depression in religious individuals. *Journal of Consulting and Clinical Psychology, 60,* 94–103.

Queener, J. E., & Martin, J. K. (2001). Providing culturally relevant mental health services: Collaboration between psychology and the African American church. *Journal of Black Psychology, 27,* 112–122.

Sue, D. W., Bernier, J., Duran, A., Feinberg, L., Pedersen, P., Smith, E., & Vasquez-Nuttal, E. (1982). Position paper: Cross-cultural counseling competencies. *The Counseling Psychologist, 10,* 45–52.

Taylor, J. (1993). *Where people fly and water runs uphill: Using dreams to tap the wisdom of the unconscious.* New York: Warner Books.

Taylor, R. J., & Chatters, L. M., Jayakody, R., & Levin, J. S. (1996). Black and White differences in religious participation: A multi-sample comparison. *Journal for Scientific Study of Religion, 35,* 403–410.

Teyber, E. (2000). *Interpersonal process in psychotherapy: A relational approach.* Belmont, CA: Wadsworth.

Tillich, P. (1964). *Theology of culture.* New York: Oxford University Press.

Toporek, R. L., & Reza, J. V. (2001). Context as a critical dimension of multicultural counseling: Articulating personal, professional, and institutional competence. *Journal of Multicultural Counseling and Development, 29,* 13–30.

Wolsko, C., Park, B., Judd, C. M., & Wittenbrink, B. (2000). Framing interethnic ideology: Effects of multicultural and color–blind perspectives on judgments of groups and individuals. *Journal of Personality and Social Psychology, 78,* 635–654.

Worthington, E. L. (1989). Religious faith across the life span: Implications for counseling and research. *The Counseling Psychologist, 17,* 555–612.

Zea, M. C., Mason, M. A., & Murguia, A. (2000). Psychotherapy with members of Latino/ Latina religions and spiritual traditions. In P. S. Richards & A. E. Bergin (Eds.), *Handbook of psychotherapy and religious diversity* (pp. 397–419). Washington, DC: American Psychological Association.

Zinnbauer, B. J., & Pargament, K. I. (2000). Working with the sacred: Four approaches to religious and spiritual issues in counseling. *Journal of Counseling and Development, 78,* 162–171.

14

Social Justice Issues

Anika K. Warren and
Madonna G. Constantine

> In a society where the good is defined in terms of profit rather
> than in terms of human need, there must always be some group
> of people who, through systematized oppression, can be made
> to feel surplus, to occupy the place of the dehumanized infe-
> rior (e.g., people of color, working-class people, aging popula-
> tions, women, physically and mentally challenged individuals,
> immigrants, gaylesbi populations). (Lorde, 1984, p. 114)

In response to the growing numbers of people of color in the United States
and to emerging data on the diverse mental health needs of historically marginalized individuals and groups within U.S. society, the American Psychological Association published the "Guidelines on Multicultural Education,
Training, Research, Practice, and Organizational Change for Psychologists"
(APA, 2003). As pointed out in Chapter 1, the APA Multicultural Guidelines
were developed to encourage psychologists and other mental health professionals to engage in culturally competent practice with people of color
and other societally oppressed groups (Constantine & Sue, 2005). By calling
attention to the need for mental health professionals to address more effectively the issues of marginalized populations, the Guidelines are an act of
social justice—a call for mental health professionals to commit to social justice
action in their work with culturally diverse individuals (APA, 2003).

An exhaustive review of the mental health literature suggests that social
justice is multidimensional (Bell, 1997; Drew, Bishop, & Syme, 2002; Fondacaro & Weinberg, 2002; Fox, 1993; Ivey & Collins, 2003; Kiselica & Robinson, 2001; Prilleltensky, 2001; Vera & Speight, 2003). Specifically, social
justice is about:

- Allowing all groups in a society full and equal participation, bargaining power, need gratification, and resource distribution
- Creating a society in which all people feel physically and psychologically safe and secure
- Advocating for all individuals to have a sense of their own agency and social responsibility
- Facilitating the awareness that all people in a society should possess the power and ability to express their wishes and needs
- Exploring and dismantling micro (individual and family), meso (community and organization), and macro (ideological and policy) inequities across strata to promote fairness and equity on behalf of oppressed, marginalized, and disenfranchised groups
- Unifying with oppressed, marginalized, and disenfranchised groups in various social justice struggles
- Promoting social change and performing social action that advance psychological prevention, psychoeducation, and well-being
- Empowering oppressed people, resisting authority, and demobilizing the status quo through nonconformity

Although the Guidelines extensively delineate the relevance of cultural pluralism and inclusiveness in mental health education, training, research, practice, and organizational settings, less attention has been paid to identifying concrete examples and strategies for implementing the Guidelines into these professional contexts. The primary objectives of this chapter are to (1) discuss the importance of integrating social justice issues and perspectives into the educational, training, research, clinical, and organizational settings in which mental health professionals work; and (2) provide psychologists and other mental health professionals with practical strategies for integrating social justice issues into their various work contexts and roles.

INTEGRATING SOCIAL JUSTICE ISSUES INTO MENTAL HEALTH EDUCATION AND TRAINING

Over the past few decades, graduate-level mental health programs, particularly those in the field of counseling psychology, increasingly have integrated multicultural and social justice issues into their programs of study (Chambers, Lewis, & Kerezsi, 1995; Goodman et al., 2004; Johnson, 1987). In accordance with the Guidelines, this integration will require faculty and supervisors to facilitate students' movement from passive learners to active participants. Students must understand the extent to which they are responsible for their own learning, their classmates' education, and their clients' growth and learning. Moreover, graduate students should gain sensitivity to the injustice and innocent suffering in the world, know the conditions that cause and perpetuate human suffering, and learn skills that will allow them to intervene effectively and contribute to a vision of social justice (Vera & Speight, 2003). Programs at institutions such as Boston College, Teachers College of Columbia University, University of Wisconsin–Madison, California State University at Hayward, and Indiana University have used community collaboration, participatory research, consultation, service learning, experiential learning laboratories, outreach experiences, and other traditional and nontraditional course and practicum experiences to broaden graduate students' training in multicultural and social justice issues (Blustein, McWhirter, & Perry, 2005; Goodman et al., 2004; Kenny & Gallagher, 2000; Kiselica, 2004; Thompson & Shermis, 2004). Several educators have found that in vivo training and service-learning models and methodologies in this regard provide students with a foundational understanding of systemic issues as they pertain to racial and cultural phenomena, and transform their training experiences by preparing them for socially active and collaborative professional roles (Goodman et al., 2004; Kenny & Gallagher, 2000; Vera & Speight, 2003).

Over the past two decades, graduate students in the counseling psychology program at Teachers College of Columbia University have been required to complete a course currently titled Racial-Cultural Counseling Laboratory (RCCL), which was motivated by cross-cultural and multicultural movements in psychology. Based on the work of Paul Pedersen, Allen Ivey, and other cultural psychologists, Samuel D. Johnson (1987) designed a course concerned with addressing the dichotomy between "knowing that" and "knowing how" with regard to issues of cultural competence in counseling. Specifically, RCCL is a didactic and experiential skills-oriented course intended to provide advanced training in the integration of racial and cultural factors with general counseling skills and techniques, and to increase students' awareness of and sensitivity to racial/cultural factors in the context of mental health counseling (Carter, 2003; Johnson, 1987). Although RCCL is focused primarily on racial- and ethnic-group memberships that have long-standing historical roots in the United States (e.g., Native Americans, African Americans, Asian Americans, European Americans, and Latina/o/Hispanic Americans), many of the conceptual and experiential learnings can be applied to the experiences of other cultural groups (e.g., women, persons with disabilities, gay and lesbian individuals). In addition, service-learning models, such as those at Boston College, provide students with training experiences in real-world contexts outside of classrooms (Kenny & Gallagher, 2000). These models facilitate opportunities for students to develop and implement innovative social justice interventions and a practical understanding of meso and macro social inequalities (Goodman et al., 2004; Kenny & Gallagher, 2000).

SOCIAL JUSTICE CONSIDERATIONS IN CONDUCTING
RESEARCH WITH CULTURALLY DIVERSE POPULATIONS

Prior to Clark and Clark's (1940) study on racial self-perceptions of African American school-aged children, the constructs of race, ethnicity, and culture had not gained empirical recognition. Rather, most psychological research conducted before 1940 focused on White people as superior and normal, and people of color as inferior and abnormal. Thus, in many respects, Clark and Clark's study marked the beginning of both social justice and multicultural research in applied psychology. Although empirical investigations on U.S. populations of color and on the constructs of race, ethnicity, and culture have increased dramatically in recent decades (APA, 2003), many researchers in the field of applied psychology and in other mental health disciplines continue to (1) use deficit models when examining people of color and other marginalized groups; (2) assume White heterosexual people as normative; and (3) neglect to describe, address, examine, or discuss the racial and ethnic background of study participants (Goodman et al., 2004; Kiselica, 2004). As a result, empirically derived information about people of color remains underrepresented, potentially having an impact on many mental health professionals' and students' ability to work effectively with diverse cultural populations.

The Guidelines challenge psychologists and other mental health professionals to recognize that all human-based research inherently reflects the values, biases, assumptions, and beliefs of its researchers. Thus, when attempting to examine, explore, and explain the human behaviors of various populations, researchers have the power to define what is normal, natural, and healthy and what is not considered so. Such assumptions suggest that all research is political and, in many respects, that all research, either consciously or unconsciously, reflects aspects of researchers' attitudes or values concerning race, ethnicity, and culture. Thus, research tends either to perpetuate or to challenge the status quo (Denzin & Lincoln, 1994; Prilleltensky, 1994). In accordance with the Guidelines, all empirical investigations focused on mental health issues should be conducted with cultural sensitivity at each stage of research development and implementation.

For many mental health professionals, conducting multicultural research with a social justice focus will mean balancing the need to create research that is appropriate for tenure at some institutions (e.g., high production of scholarship that is "scientific" and quantitative) with developing research that empowers, engages, and integrates participants at each stage of development (e.g., production of scholarship that is qualitative and collaborative). Participatory action research (PAR) is one example of social justice-based multicultural research that aims to give participants power to voice and expand their knowledge and to confront the ways in which social, political, cultural, and economic contexts establish power over oppressed societies worldwide (Benmayor, 1991; Fals-Bora, 1988). The basic ideology of PAR is that marginalized people will use their awareness of self, others, and communities to become more critically conscious, while progressively transforming their environment through their own praxis (Rahman, 1988). PAR requires investigators to immerse themselves in the communities of the populations of interest and to fully collaborate with participants (as co-researchers) with regard to research design, assessment, and analysis, and even consciousness raising of the issues pertinent to the populations under study (see Lykes, 1997).

INTEGRATING SOCIAL JUSTICE ISSUES INTO CLINICAL PRACTICE

Just as some of the multicultural and feminist movements in the field of mental health were beginning, the U.S. Congress passed the landmark Community Mental Health Center Act (CMHCA) of 1963, which called for closing of large institutions and localizing the treatment of mentally ill persons within their communities (Sue et al., 1998). Over 40 years after the CMHCA, people of color and other marginalized populations continue to receive less access to appropriate treatment and lower qualities of care than do their White American counterparts (Fuertes, Mislowack, & Mintz, 2005). The 2001 Surgeon General's Report linked mental health care disparities among people of color with poverty, language and information barriers, stigma associated with mental illness, and institutional racism and discrimination, suggesting that psychologists and other mental health professionals have not addressed adequately the mental health needs of populations of color at the micro, meso, or macro levels (U.S. Department of Health and Human Services, 2001). Going forward, these professionals must attempt to intervene with clients of color by addressing simultaneously cultural and systemic issues that relate to these clients' presenting concerns. Otherwise, appropriate coping strategies may not be developed, healing may not occur, and presenting concerns may persist. In addition, a focus on the individual, couple, or family in therapeutic interventions, without examining social structures and norms of oppression, may result in "blaming the victim," which has been and will continue to be particularly damaging to the mental health of people of color and other marginalized individuals.

Following are practical strategies for mental health professionals to consider when working with U.S. populations of color in clinical settings. These strategies were adapted from the work of scholars who have identified ways in which mental health professionals might work more effectively with populations of color (e.g., Brabeck & Ting, 2000; Constantine, Hage, Kindaichi, & Bryant, in press; Sue et al., 1998).

1. Encourage clients of color to share their beliefs about the etiology of their concerns and what they perceive as appropriate for alleviating their problems or concerns.
2. Identify culturally based values (e.g., having a strong communal orientation) that might encourage clients of color to use multiple therapeutic resources (e.g., support groups, family therapy) to alleviate their problems or concerns.
3. Elicit the assistance of close friends and family members with treatment goals when possible or warranted (e.g., ask friends or family members to join support groups with clients).
4. Help clients to engage effectively with oppressive structures and achieve their goals without devaluing or losing their sense of self (e.g., teach them how, when, and to whom to write letters when they feel that their rights have been violated).
5. Be open to incorporating a variety of nontraditional healing interventions (e.g., art therapy, religious or spiritual practices, aromatherapy) that might help people of color and other marginalized clients alleviate their concerns or problems.
6. Assume that clients may not be the inherent sources of their problems and concerns. Rather, help clients to explore how their status as a marginalized person (e.g., loci of ethnic, racial, age, social class, gender, religious, linguistic status, sexual orientation, and other oppressions) might contribute to their presenting concerns.
7. Attend to the unique problems and concerns of clients of color without stereotyping their experiences or identities as consistent with their racial-, ethnic-, or cultural-group memberships.

ADDRESSING SOCIAL JUSTICE
ISSUES IN ORGANIZATIONAL SETTINGS

In a move to develop multiculturally competent organizations, the Guidelines encourage psychologists and other mental health professionals to increase their awareness about the importance of integrating multicultural and social justice considerations into educational curricula, governmental policy, mental health agencies, and for-profit hiring practices (APA, 2003; Fine, 2000). Because social and organizational change usually is met with varying levels of resistance, mental health professionals will need strategies for dealing with resistance to organizational culture, blocks to administrative and institutional change, and monocultural perspectives of people and organizations.

Sue (1995) identified the following strategies for developing multiculturally competent organizations and minimizing resistance to cultural change:

1. A thorough assessment of the institutional climate with respect to multiculturalism
2. An understanding of the interrelationships of interacting subsystems
3. A commitment from institutional leaders to exert strong leadership around building and maintaining an inclusive organizational environment
4. A well-designed plan for establishing organizational change prior to initiating changes
5. An understanding that people from *all* racial and ethnic populations are not immune from inheriting the racial biases, stereotypes, and prejudices of the larger organization and society

However, institutional analyses of social inequities in organizational settings rarely have been conducted in the field of mental health or in organizational settings (Darling-Hammond, 2000; Fine, 2000; Goodman et al., 2004).

A move toward institutional analyses of social inequities in organizational settings could prevent mental health professionals from colluding in camouflaging organizational structures that stratify people by race, ethnicity, gender, class, sexual orientation, abilities, age, or mental illness (Fine, 2000). This work is of particular importance because psychologists and other mental health professionals will treat clients with presenting concerns that reflect failures of organizations to design policies, practices, and procedures that protect people of color and other marginalized groups from structures of oppression. Moreover, engaging in social justice work within organizational settings might enable mental health professionals and students to develop knowledge of the services that various organizations provide, develop positive relationships with institutional leaders and powerbrokers, and create client advocacy opportunities at the meso and macro levels.

STRATEGIES FOR ADDRESSING SOCIAL JUSTICE ISSUES IN MENTAL HEALTH SETTINGS AND CONTEXTS

Psychologists and other mental health professionals who are committed to abiding by the Guidelines and becoming social justice workers must recognize the oppressions facing U.S. populations of color and enact alternatives that eliminate oppression through *praxis*—the integration of theory with action (Prilleltensky, 2001; Vera & Speight, 2003). Freire (2000) asserted that social justice (and multiculturalism) require learning, dialoguing, analyzing, and intervening across factors such as race, social class, gender, culture, language, and ethnicity. He further suggested that racism cannot be analyzed or eradicated without considering the interplay between racism and classism (social class and socioeconomic status). Thus, psychologists and other mental health professionals also should consider larger scale intervention and prevention efforts and aim to eradicate issues related to classism, sexism, heterosexism, ableism, ageism, and anti-Semitism (Kenny & Gallagher, 2000; Lee, 1997; Riger, 2000). By understanding the historical experiences of slavery, legal and de facto segregation, and the racial violence that continues to lock African Americans, Native Americans, Latina/o Americans, and Asian Americans out of positions of economic and social advancement, psychologists and other mental health professionals are taking a critical first step toward creating a just society (Bell, 1997).

The following strategies for aligning social justice with the Guidelines were adopted from the work of several multicultural researchers and social justice advocates (Brabeck & Ting, 2000; Constantine et al., in press; Goodman et al., 2004; Mulvey et al., 2000; Prilleltensky & Prilleltensky, 2003):

1. *Educate and promote*–teach self and others (i.e., clients, students, community members, educators, and powerbrokers) about existing social inequities that challenge people of color and other oppressed groups at the individual, cultural, and social levels, and about how such challenges might be experienced similarly or differently between and among various individuals, groups, organizations, and systems. Educate people of color about how to interact effectively with powerbrokers. Promote comprehensive and remedial mental health interventions and programs aimed at equalizing opportunities for people of color, clients, community members, educators, and powerbrokers. Promote cross-cultural understanding and trust, while minimizing perceived power differentials.

2. *Engage and evaluate*–engage in ongoing critical self-exploration (with emotional and mental depth and vulnerability) about how biases, beliefs, values, and worldviews concerning people of color and other oppressed groups might affect mental health professionals' work at the micro, meso, and macro levels and their perceptions of oppression, power, and privilege. Evaluate mental health research, practice, and training issues to ensure that culturally appropriate and culturally relevant considerations exist with regard to understanding the experiences of people of color. Through dialogues, determine how individual biases, beliefs, values, and worldviews might interfere with mental health professionals' work as researchers, educators, and practitioners.

3. *Advocate and empower*–work with and on behalf of clients of color and others who have been oppressed or marginalized. Advocate on behalf of populations of color through: (1) consciousness raising (enhance

understanding of historical, social, and political forces that affect
people and systems at multiple levels); (2) power sharing (between
and among people of color and powerbrokers); (3) strength building
(assume that people of color have knowledge, skills, and awareness
about themselves and social issues and that social justice workers
and powerbrokers are facilitators of power and not emancipators);
and (4) empowering oppressed people (give people of color the tools,
resources, and voice necessary to get their needs met). Stop
"pathologizing" certain segments of U.S. populations, such as people
of color and other oppressed groups (women, gay and lesbian
individuals, financially impoverished persons, elderly individuals),
and start advocating for equity and visibility of oppressed populations.

4. *Synergize and collaborate*—merge values (sensitivity, compassion,
caring, and awareness) and people (clients, community members,
educators, and powerbrokers) across cultures and mental health
disciplines to work together in the fight against social inequities.
Encourage collaboration among helping professions to synergize
ideas in the fight against injustice. Develop alliances with
professional, educational, and social organizations designed to
support people of color and other marginalized groups.

CONCLUSION

The Guidelines encourage psychologists and other mental health professionals to assist in promoting the well-being of *all* individuals, particularly those
who have been oppressed or marginalized. These Guidelines note that mental health professionals must do their part to confront social structures and
systems of oppression at micro, meso, and macro levels. However, because
people and systems tend to resist change, mental health professionals and
students who work in accordance with social justice aspects of the Guidelines
should be prepared to deal with challenges such as emotional burnout, backlash from colleagues and students, loneliness and hopelessness, harassment
from intolerant individuals, and little financial reward (e.g., research grants,
publications in tier-one journals, and tenure rewards) (Freire, 2000; Goodman et al., 2004; Kiselica & Robinson, 2001). Social justice workers (i.e., advocates and activists who are critical agents of social change working toward
social equity) should be prepared for the struggles of initiating transformative
actions by promoting mental health and social change in education, training,
research, practice, and organizations, while recognizing that doing so may be
antithetical to some ethical guidelines and to the status quo (Murphy, 1999;

Prilleltensky & Prilleltensky, 2003). Because social justice and multicultural challenges stimulate discussions of and concerns for morality and equity (Helms, 2003), mental health professionals and students may find solace by engaging in discussions and collaborating on projects with other social justice advocates and activists.

REFERENCES

American Psychological Association. (2003). Guidelines on multicultural education, training, research, practice, and organizational change for psychologists, *American Psychologist, 58*, 377–402.

Bell, L. A. (1997). Theoretical foundations for social justice education. In M. Adams, L. A. Bell, & P. Griffin (Eds.), *Teaching for diversity and social justice* (pp. 3–15). New York: Routledge.

Benmayor, R. (1991). Testimony, action research, and empowerment: Puerto Rican women and popular education. In S. Berger & D. Patai (Eds.), *In women's words: The feminist practice of oral history* (pp. 159–174). New York: Routledge.

Blustein, D. L., McWhirter, E. H., & Perry, J. C. (2005). An emancipatory communitarian approach to vocational development theory, research, and practice. *The Counseling Psychologist, 33*, 141–179.

Brabeck, M. M., & Ting, K. (2000). Feminist ethics: Lenses for examining ethical psychological practice. In M. M. Brabeck (Ed.), *Practicing feminist ethics in psychology* (pp. 17–35). Washington, DC: American Psychological Association.

Carter, R. T. (2003). Becoming racially and culturally competent: The racial-cultural counseling laboratory. *Journal of Multicultural Counseling and Development, 31*, 20–30.

Chambers, T., Lewis, J., & Kerezsi, P. (1995). African American faculty and White American students: Cross-cultural pedagogy in counselor preparation programs. *The Counseling Psychologist, 23*, 43–62.

Clark, K. B., & Clark, M. K. (1940). Skin color as a factor in racial identification of Negro preschool children. *Journal of Social Psychology, 11*, 159–169.

Constantine, M. G., Hage, S. M., Kindaichi, M. M., & Bryant, R. M. (in press). Social justice and multicultural issues: Implications for the practice and training of counselors and counseling psychologists. *Journal of Counseling and Development.*

Constantine, M. G., & Sue, D. W. (2005). The American Psychological Association's guidelines on multicultural education, training, research, practice, and organizational psychology: Initial development and summary. In M. G. Constantine & D. W. Sue (Eds.), *Strategies for building multicultural competence in mental health and educational settings* (pp. 3–18). Hoboken, NJ: Wiley.

Darling-Hammond, L. (2000). School contexts and learning: Organizational influences on the achievement of students of color. In R. T. Carter (Ed.), *Addressing cultural issues in organizations: Beyond the corporate context.* (pp. 69–88). Thousand Oaks, CA: Sage.

Denzin, N. K., & Lincoln, Y. S. (1994). *Handbook of qualitative research.* Thousand Oaks, CA: Sage.

Drew, N. M., Bishop, B. J., & Syme, G. (2002). Justice and local community change: Towards a substantive theory of justice. *Journal of Community Psychology, 30*, 623–634.

Fals-Bora, O. (1988). Some basic ingredients. In O. Fals-Bora & M. A. Rahman (Eds.), *Action and knowledge: Breaking the monopoly with participatory action-research* (pp. 3–12). New York: Apex Press.

Fine, M. (2000). "Whiting out" social justice. In R. T. Carter (Ed.), *Addressing cultural issues in organizations: Beyond the corporate context* (pp. 35–50). Thousand Oaks, CA: Sage.

Fondacaro, M. R., & Weinberg, D. (2002). Concepts of social justice in community psychology: Toward a social ecological epistemology. *American Journal of Community Psychology, 30,* 473–492.

Fox, D. R. (1993). Psychological jurisprudence and radical social change. *American Psychologist, 48,* 234–241.

Freire, P. (2000). *Pedagogy of the oppressed: 30th anniversary edition.* New York: Continuum.

Fuertes, J. N., Mislowack, A., & Mintz, S. (2005). Multicultural competencies in clinical and hospital settings. In M. G. Constantine & D. W. Sue (Eds.), *Strategies for building multicultural competence in mental health and educational settings* (pp. 145–159). Hoboken, NJ: Wiley.

Goodman, L. A., Liang, B., Helms, J. E., Latta, R. E., Sparks, E., & Weintraub, S. R. (2004). Training counseling psychologists as social justice agents: Feminist and multicultural principles in action. *The Counseling Psychologist, 32,* 793–837.

Helms, J. E. (2003). A pragmatic view of social justice. *The Counseling Psychologist, 30,* 305–313.

Ivey, A. E., & Collins, N. M. (2003). Social justice: A long-term challenge for counseling psychology. *The Counseling Psychologist, 31,* 290–298.

Johnson, S. D. (1987). Knowing that versus knowing how: Toward achievement expertise through multicultural training for counseling. *The Counseling Psychologist, 15,* 320–331.

Kenny, M., & Gallagher, L. A. (2000). Service-learning as a vehicle in training psychologists for revised professional roles. In F. T. Sherman & W. R. Tolbert (Eds.), *Transforming social inquiry, transforming social action: New paradigms for crossing the theory/practice divide in universities and communities* (pp. 189–205). Boston: Kluwer Academic.

Kiselica, M. S. (2004). When duty calls: The implications of social justice work for policy, education, and practice in the mental health professions. *The Counseling Psychologist, 32,* 838–854.

Kiselica, M. S., & Robinson, M. (2001). Bringing advocacy counseling to life: The history, issues, and human dramas of social justice work in counseling. *Journal of Counseling and Development, 79,* 387–397.

Lee, C. C. (1997). The global future of professional counseling: Collaboration for international social change. *International Journal of Intercultural Relations, 21,* 279–285.

Lorde, A. (1984). Age, race, class, and sex: Women redefining difference. In A. Lorde (Ed.), *Sister outsider: Essays and speeches* (pp. 114–133). Freedom, CA: Crossing Press.

Lykes, M. B. (1997). Activist participatory research among the Maya of Guatemala: Constructing meanings for situated knowledge. *Journal of Social Issues, 53,* 725–746.

Murphy, B. K. (1999). *Transforming ourselves, transforming the world: An open conspiracy for social change.* New York: Zed.

Mulvey, A., Terenzio, M., Hill, J., Bond, M. A., Huygens, I., Hamerton, H. R., & Cahill, S. (2000). Stories of relative privilege: Power and social change in feminist community psychology. *American Journal of Community Psychology, 28,* 883–911.

Prilleltensky, I. (1994). *The morals and politics of psychology: Psychological discourse and the status quo.* Albany: State University of New York Press.

Prilleltensky, I. (2001). Value-based praxis in community psychology: Moving toward social justice and social action. *American Journal of Community Psychology, 29,* 747–778.

Prilleltensky, I., & Prilleltensky, O. (2003). Synergies for wellness and liberation in counseling psychology. *The Counseling Psychologist, 31,* 273–281.

Rahman, M. A. (1988). The theoretical standpoint of PAR. In O. Fals-Bora & M. A. Rahman (Eds.), *Action and knowledge: Breaking the monopoly with participatory action-research* (pp. 13–23). New York: Apex Press.

Riger, S. (2000). *Transforming psychology: Gender in theory and practice.* London: Oxford University Press.

Sue, D. W. (1995). Multicultural organizational development: Implications for the counseling profession. In J. G. Ponterotto, J. M. Casas, L. A. Suzuki, & C. M. Alexander (Eds.), *Handbook of multicultural counseling* (pp. 474–492). Thousand Oaks, CA: Sage.

Sue, D. W., Carter, R. T., Casas, J. M., Fouad, N. A., Ivey, A. E., Jensen, M., LaFromboise, T., Manese, J. E., Ponterotto, J. G., & Vasquez-Nuttall, E. (1998). *Multicultural counseling competencies: Individual and organizational development.* Thousand Oaks, CA: Sage.

Thompson, C. E., & Shermis, S. S. (2004). Tapping the talents within: A reaction to Goodman, Liang, Helms, Latta, Sparks, and Weintraub. *The Counseling Psychologist, 32,* 866–878.

U.S. Department of Health and Human Services. (2001). *Mental health: Culture, race, and ethnicity–A supplement to Mental Health: A report of the Surgeon General.* Rockville, MD: U.S. Department of Health and Human Services, Public Health Office, Office of the Surgeon General.

Vera, E. M., & Speight, S. L. (2003). Multicultural competence, social justice, and counseling psychology: Expanding our roles. *The Counseling Psychologist, 31,* 253–272.

About the Editor
and the Contributors

Madonna G. Constantine, Ph.D., is a Professor of Psychology and Education in the Department of Counseling and Clinical Psychology at Teachers College, Columbia University. She received her doctorate in Counseling Psychology from the University of Memphis and completed bachelor's and master's degrees from Xavier University of New Orleans. Dr. Constantine is a highly esteemed researcher in the areas of Black psychology and multicultural counseling. The scope of her work includes exploring the psychological, educational, and vocational issues of African Americans; developing models of cross-cultural competence in counseling, training, and supervision; and examining the intersections of variables such as race and ethnicity in relation to mental health and educational processes and outcomes. Dr. Constantine is currently involved on several editorial boards in her field, and she serves in various leadership capacities in counseling and psychological associations across the country.

Saba Rasheed Ali, Ph.D., is an Assistant Professor in the Department of Counseling Psychology at the University of Iowa. She earned her doctoral degree in Counseling Psychology from the University of Oregon in 2001. Her main research interests include the career development of rural high school students of lower socioeconomic status. She was recently awarded a grant from the Roy J. Carver Charitable trust to implement career education programs in high schools with large populations of immigrant students whose parents are migrant workers. Dr. Ali also has co-authored publications examining the career development of adolescents of lower socioeconomic status, as well as articles examining the use of social class variables in counseling psychology research.

Fred Bemak, Ed.D., is a Professor in the Counseling and Development Program and Director of the Diversity Research and Action Center at George Mason University. He received his doctoral degree in Counseling from the University of Massachusetts at Amherst. Dr. Bemak is a former Fulbright Scholar, a Kellogg International Fellow, and a recipient of the World Rehabilitation Fund International Exchange of Experts and Research Fellowship. He was selected by the American Psychological Association as a Visiting Psychologist and is a past recipient of the American Counseling Association Counselor for Social Justice O'Hana Award. Dr. Bemak is a former director of an Upward Bound program, the Massachusetts Department of Mental Health Region I Adolescent Treatment Program, and a NIMH-funded consortium that provided national consultation and training to community-based mental health programs. He has published numerous professional journal articles, book chapters, and four books that address cross-cultural counseling, equity, and social justice.

Christina M. Capodilupo, Ed.M., is an advanced doctoral student in the Counseling Psychology program at Teachers College, Columbia University. She received her B.A. from the College of the Holy Cross, and her Ed.M. from Harvard University. Her research explores the intersections of race, gender, and body image. More specifically, she is interested in how body image is formed and affected by sociocultural influences and experiences of oppression. In 2006, she was named a Junior Investigator Travel Award Fellow by the Academy for Eating Disorders.

Rita Chi-Ying Chung, Ph.D., received her doctorate in Psychology from Victoria University of Wellington, New Zealand. She is a Professor in the Counseling and Development Program at George Mason University. Her research focuses on the psychosocial adjustment of refugees and immigrants, interethnic group relations and racial stereotypes, trafficking of Asian girls, coping strategies in dealing with racism and its impact of psychological well-being, and cross-cultural and multicultural issues in mental health. She has served as the Chair of the American Counseling Association Human Rights Committee and the American Counseling Association International Committee and is currently on the Executive Council of the International Association for Counseling. With Dr. Fred Bemak, Dr. Chung has co-authored a book on the psychosocial adjustment of refugees and is currently co-authoring a book on social justice and multiculturalism. She received an American Counseling Association Counselor for Social Justice O'Hana Award for her work in social justice.

Y. Barry Chung, Ph.D., is an Associate Professor of Counseling Psychology at Georgia State University. He received his M.A. and Ph.D. degrees in Counseling Psychology from the University of Illinois at Urbana-Champaign. His research interests include multicultural counseling, career development, and lesbian, gay, and bisexual issues. He has served on five journal editorial boards, including the *Journal of Multicultural Counseling and Development* and *Journal of GLBT Issues in Counseling.*

Cynthia de las Fuentes, Ph.D., is an Associate Professor at Our Lady of the Lake University. She received both her doctoral and master's degrees from the University of Texas at Austin. Dr. de las Fuentes' research focuses on multicultural, Latina/o, and feminist psychologies, in addition to bilingual training for psychologists, ethics, and education and training. She is the recipient of several awards for contributions to the professional development of ethnic and racial minorities in psychology, education, and scholarship. Dr. de las Fuentes also chaired the first Latino Psychology conference, now a biannual event sponsored by the National Latino Psychological Association, on which she serves as an executive committee member. She is currently president of the Society for the Psychology of Women.

Kristen English, M.S., is a doctoral candidate in the Clinical Psychology program at Chestnut Hill College in Philadelphia, PA. She holds an M.S. in Counseling Psychology from Chestnut Hill College and earned a B.A. in Psychology from Swarthmore College. She is currently working on her dissertation examining the experiences of siblings of lesbian women and is a regular contributor to *The Family Journal.*

Alice Fridman, B.A., is a third-year doctoral student in the Counseling Psychology program at the University of Iowa. She obtained a B.A. at Carleton College in 2003 and spent one year working as a counselor at an adolescent behavior treatment facility prior to beginning her doctoral program. Ms. Fridman received the Presidential Fellowship and Special Graduate Assistantship at the University of Iowa. She also has co-authored a chapter titled, "Social Class in School Counseling" for the upcoming *Handbook of School Counseling.* Her main research interests include social class and multicultural issues.

Mary A. Fukuyama, Ph.D., received her doctorate from Washington State University and has worked at the University of Florida's Counseling Center for the past 24 years as a counseling psychologist, supervisor, and trainer. She is a clinical professor and teaches courses on spirituality and multicultural counseling for the Department of Counselor Education and the Counseling Psychology Program. She is an active member of the University of Florida's Center for Spirituality and Health and her research interests include "multicultural expressions" of spirituality. With Todd Sevig, she co-authored a book titled

Integrating Spirituality into Multicultural Counseling and was recently recognized as a Fellow by Division 17 of the American Psychological Association.

Angela R. Gillem, Ph.D., a Professor of Psychology at Arcadia University, received her doctorate in Clinical/Community Psychology from Boston University and served three years as Assistant Dean of Multicultural Affairs at Haverford College. Her clinical experience includes work in a variety of mental health settings including the Aradia Feminist Counseling Center for Women in Boston, and student counseling centers at Harvard Law School, University of Pennsylvania, and Swarthmore College. Her honors and awards include the 2001 American Psychological Association (APA) Division 44 Distinguished Racial/Ethnic Diversity Contribution Award, the 2004 AWP Christine Ladd-Franklin Award for Distinguished Contributions to Feminist Psychology, the 2005 APA Presidential Citation in Recognition of Visionary, Creative, and Courageous Leadership, and the 2006 Arcadia University Cultural Ally Award. Her current research areas are racial identity development of biracial people and multicultural counseling/psychotherapy competency.

Alberta M. Gloria, Ph.D., is the Director of Training for the Department of Counseling Psychology doctoral program, as well as an affiliate faculty member of the Chicana/o Studies Program at the University of Wisconsin-Madison. She received her doctorate in Counseling Psychology from Arizona State University. Her primary research interests include psychosociocultural factors for Chicana/os and other racial and ethnic minority students in higher education. Dr. Gloria recently served as an Associate Editor for the *Journal of Multicultural Counseling and Development* and is currently on the editorial board for *The Counseling Psychologist.* She is presently Chair of the Section on Ethnic and Racial Diversity for Division 17, Secretary for the National Latina/o Psychological Association, and Member-at-Large for Division 45. She was awarded the Emerging Professional Award from Division 45 of the American Psychological Association in 2002 and the Kenneth and Mamie Clark Award for her contributions to the professional development of ethnic minority graduate students in 2003.

Thomasin Hall, B.A., is a doctoral student in the Counseling Psychology program at the University of Iowa. She has assisted in a project examining social class issues among the homeless population and is currently serving on a research team providing career education to Latino students in rural high schools in Iowa.

Carlos Hernandez, Ph.D., is a Clinical Assistant Professor in the Counseling Center at the University of Florida. He received his doctorate and specialist degrees in Mental Health Counseling from the Department of Counselor Education at the University of Florida, specializing in multicultural counseling. His clinical and research interests include multiculturalism, sexual orientation, and vocational issues. He also is involved in the training and supervision of practicum and specialist interns and provides seminars on counseling sexual minorities. Dr. Hernandez co-created and co-taught the first-ever graduate course in the Department of Counselor Education entitled, "Counseling the Lesbian, Gay, Bisexual, and Transgender Client." He provides individual, group, and couples counseling to students with a variety of clinical, vocational, and interpersonal issues and concerns.

Nneka Jones, M.A., is a doctoral candidate in the Virginia Consortium Program in Clinical Psychology. In 2003 she received her MA degree in Clinical Psychology from East Carolina University in Greenville, North Carolina. She is a member of the Phi Kappa Phi Honor Society at Old Dominion University, and was awarded a psychology internship position with Cermak Health Services (Cook County Jail) in Chicago, Illinois. Her research and clinical interests include gender and race issues, relapse prevention with sexual offenders, cognitive-behavioral therapy, and correctional mental health.

Bryan S. K. Kim, Ph.D., is an Associate Professor in the Department of Psychology at the University of Hawai'i at Hilo. Dr. Kim received his M.Ed. in School Counseling from the University of Hawai'i at Manoa in 1995 and his Ph.D. from the UCSB in 2000. Dr. Kim's research focuses on multicultural counseling process and outcome, the measurement of cultural constructs, and counselor education and supervision. Dr. Kim currently serves on the editorial boards of the *Journal of Counseling Psychology; Cultural Diversity and Ethnic Minority Psychology; Psychotherapy: Theory, Research, Practice, and Training;* and *Measurement and Evaluation in Counseling and Development.* In 2005, he received the ACA Research Award from the American Counseling Association and the *Measurement and Evaluation in Counseling and Development* (MECD) Journal Editor's Award from the Association for Assessment in Counseling and Education. In 2006, Dr. Kim received the Fritz and Linn Kuder Early Career Scientist/Practitioner Award from the Society of Counseling Psychology of the American Psychological Association.

Mai M. Kindaichi, M.A., M.Ed., is an advanced doctoral student in the Counseling Psychology program at Teachers College, Columbia University. She received her B.A. from Georgetown University and her master's degrees from Teachers College. In addition to working with Dr. Madonna G. Constantine as a former coordinator of the Teachers College Winter Roundtable on Cultural Psychology and Education and as a research assistant, Ms.

Kindaichi has counseled diverse adolescents in a community setting and adults with cancer in a hospital setting. Her interests include the psychological experiences of multiracial and transracial adoptive individuals and families, intersections of cultural identity, multicultural counseling competence and training, psychosocial oncology, and group counseling with culturally diverse adolescents.

Leslie Leathers, B.S., is a fourth-year doctoral student in the Counseling Psychology program at the University of Iowa. She received a B.S. in Psychology from Xavier University of Louisiana. Her research interests include multicultural, women's, and social justice issues. She is particularly interested in conducting research on and working with African American populations.

Sean Kathleen Lincoln, Ph.D., is an Adjunct Professor in the graduate psychology programs at Widener and Arcadia Universities and Chestnut Hill College. She holds a doctoral degree in Clinical Psychology from Boston University and is in private practice in the Philadelphia area. Her clinical and teaching interests include women and trauma, biracial individuals, and cultural competency. Dr. Lincoln also provides organizational assessment and development, diversity assessments and training, and executive coaching for senior managers. She has been the administrator in charge of outpatient mental health, substance abuse and social services in community-based organizations in Boston and Philadelphia, and has designed and implemented staff diversity and work/life balance initiatives for The Children's Hospital of Philadelphia. She is a member of American Psychological Association and the Greater Philadelphia Society for Clinical Hypnosis.

Juanita K. Martin, Ph.D., is a psychologist and the Director of the Counseling, Testing and Career Center at The University of Akron. She also has taught graduate classes on multicultural counseling and provided training and consultation on diversity issues to various agencies. She earned her bachelor's degree in Psychology from Brown University, a master's in Urban Multicultural Education from the University of Hartford, and a doctorate in Clinical Psychology from Kent State University. She is a member of Division 45 of the American Psychological Association, the Association of University and College Counseling Center Directors, the Ohio Psychological Association, and the Association of Black Psychologists. Her research and professional interests include African American mental health, identity development, stress management, and multicultural counseling. Dr. Martin received the Donfred F. Gardner Student Affairs Professional Award in recognition for her service to students at The University of Akron.

Sylvia C. Nassar-McMillan, Ph.D., is an Associate Professor of Counselor Education at North Carolina State University. She earned a master's degree in Counseling from Eastern Michigan University in 1986 and her doctoral degree from the University of North Carolina at Greensboro in 1994. Her special interests include gender and ethnicity, and her recent focus is on post-9/11 acculturation and ethnic identity issues among Arab Americans. She received an American Counseling Association Faculty–Best Practices Award in 2003. In 2006, she received both the UNC Greensboro Department of Counseling and Educational Development Alumni Excellence Award and the North Carolina Counseling Association Research and Professional Writing Award for her seminal work on counseling Arab Americans.

Rhoda Olkin, Ph.D., is a Distinguished Professor in the Clinical program and Faculty Advisor to Students with Disabilities at the California School of Professional Psychology at Alliant International University. She received a B.A. degree from Stanford University and her Master's and Doctoral degrees from the University of California, Santa Barbara. Dr. Olkin has written extensively on disability issues in psychology and was the principle investigator on a study of parents with disabilities. She is on the staff of Through the Looking Glass, an agency in Berkeley, California, that serves families with disabilities. Her book on disability and her training film on working with clients with disabilities have been well-received. In 2001 she received the American Psychological Association's Carolyn Attneave Award, as well as an award from the National Multicultural Conference and Summit. In 2003 she received the Alliant University President's Award for Faculty Excellence. Dr. Olkin also is on the editorial board for Rehabilitation Psychology.

John J. Peregoy, Ph.D., is the current president of the Society of Indian Psychologists. He received a doctorate from Syracuse University where he studied under Paul B. Pedersen. He maintains a consulting service in the area of diversity and is in private practice. His areas of research interest include American Indian and Alaskan Native mental health issues and education. He serves on several editorial boards, including the *Journal for Counseling and Development*.

Shari Robinson, Ph.D., is a Clinical Assistant Professor at the University of Florida's Counseling Center. She received a doctoral degree in Counseling Psychology from West Virginia University. She is coordinator of the ASPIRE program and Diversity Lunch Series at the University of Florida, programs that provide dynamic and provocative programming on various diversity topics, issues, and concerns. Dr. Robinson's research interests include a qualitative study on the Black and multicultural Greek-lettered organizations, consultations examining academic success, and retention concerns with targeted minority populations and first-generation college students.

Janis Sanchez-Hucles, Ph.D., is Professor and Chair of the Department of Psychology at Old Dominion University. She also is a faculty member at the Virginia Consortium for Clinical Psychology and the Eastern Virginia Medical School. She holds degrees from Swarthmore College and Purdue University and completed her doctoral work in Clinical Psychology at the University of North Carolina–Chapel Hill. Dr. Sanchez-Hucles's work has focused on clinical training, women of color, multiculturalism and diversity, feminism, and trauma. She is a fellow of the American Psychological Association (APA) in the Division for the Psychology of Women and is past chair of APA's Committee on Urban Initiatives. Dr. Sanchez-Hucles has served on an APA Presidential Task Force on Violence and the Family, the APA Council of Representatives, and the Board of Educational Affairs. She is the author of numerous publications and is co-editor of a forthcoming volume, *Women and Leadership: Transforming Visions and Diverse Voices.*

Anika K. Warren, Ph.D., is the Director of Advisory Services at Catalyst Inc., where she advises and partners with businesses and the professions to create and implement inclusive workplace strategies and organizational development solutions. She received a B.B.A. in Finance from Howard University, earned her M.A. and M.Ed. in Psychological Counseling at Teachers College, Columbia University, and completed a Ph.D. in Counseling Psychology at Boston College. Prior to joining Catalyst, Dr. Warren was a full-time lecturer at Teachers College, Columbia University in the Counseling Psychology program and worked for over 4 years as a financial analyst at The Gap and Charles Schwab. Dr. Warren is a specialist in the areas of multicultural counseling competence, work–family issues, career counseling and development, racial and gender identity development, and counseling diverse populations.

Index